IN PU

MW01132525

GIANT
BASS

BY BILL MURPHY

CO-WRITTEN BY PAUL PROROK

IN PURSUIT OF
GIANT BASS

Written By Bill Murphy
Co-written By Paul Prorok
Illustrations By The Author

First Printing -1992
2nd Printing - 1995
3rd Printing - 1999

© COPYRIGHT 1992, BILL MURPHY

ALL RIGHTS RESERVED. No part of this book may be reproduced, in part or in whole, by any means, except for brief quotations embodied in articles and reviews.

Cover Photo By
Steve McKay

Photo Credits:
Back Cover- Chuck Garrison

Text Photos- Carole Murphy
Paul Prorok
Bill Murphy

Assisting in photo sequences-
Ken Marshall
Carole Murphy

Photo of Bill Wade- Jim Putney

Lead Photo- Harlon Bartlett

Nordlund Photo- Donald Hatosy

ISBN 0-9633120-0-6
Printed In The United States Of America

For Additional Copies write to:

GIANT BASS PUBLISHING
P.O. BOX 1025 • EL CAJON, CA • 92022
Third Printing

Table of Contents

In the early years, the successful big bass fisherman depended on his practiced skills, a certain amount of natural intuition, and a lot of hard work. Today, even with all the latest modern equipment, very little has changed.

FOREWARD

Several years ago I was traveling through southern California and I met a man who would forever change my outlook on bass fishing. I was going to write an article about lunker bass fishing in San Diego County, and when I inquired at a local tackle shop about who was the areas top big bass fisherman, I was handed a paper with a phone number and the name Bill Murphy.

I met Murphy the following day at his home in Santee, and was greeted with a blacksmith-like handshake and a warm smile through a thick red beard. After the introductions, we sat in Murphy's family room where it quickly became evident why Murphy was so highly acclaimed. On wood-paneled walls surrounding a fireplace hung 20 of the biggest bass I had ever seen! Murphy pointed to each and told its story: there was a 17 lb. 1 oz. largemouth-his biggest landed; a 16 lb. 2 oz. bass - his biggest taken on a live crayfish; his three biggest caught trolling were 16 lbs. 15 oz., 15 lbs. 14 oz., and 14 lbs 12 oz. respectively; and a 15 lb.10 oz. specimen was his largest caught on a plastic worm, a fish which held the record for several years as the largest bass ever caught in a fishing tournament.

With some reluctance, Murphy finally showed me his fishing album crammed 10-inches thick with hundreds of articles, newspaper clippings, and big bass photos. From the San Diego Union, there were articles by George Herrick, Harlon Bartlett, and Rolla Williams. From Western Outdoor News there were stories by Chuck Garrison, George Kramer and Harvey Naslund. And there were dozens of articles from Outdoor Life, Bassmaster, Field and Stream, Fishing Facts, In Fisherman, and Sports Afield. Murphy is not bragging; he loves bass fishing and he loves to talk about it.

It's easy to see why Murphy has attracted so much attention. To date he has officially weighed and registered 39 largemouths weighing from 13-pounds to 17-pounds apiece. And that doesn't include another 20 or so unrecorded giant bass which he released on the water and figures were "teen fish". He has also caught hundreds in the 8 to

Huge lunker bass like the one the author is holding represents the force that drives all big bass fishermen.

12-pound class, and untold numbers over 5-pounds! From the early days before catch and release was popular, I saw one picture of a two-man limit which weighed 87 lbs., including three bass over 10-pounds and several 8 and 9-pounders.

What I found most refreshing about Murphy was his attitude toward the sport. Most fishermen are influenced to some degree by popularity, public opinion, and self-imposed restrictions. Murphy has none of that. Everything he does is guided by the fish themselves. Long ago he traded in his bass boat for a 15 ft. aluminum boat powered by a 25 h.p. motor because he needed a rig better suited for accurate trolling and precise anchoring. Why? Because there were times when he could catch more bass by trolling, or anchoring on a spot, than simply fishing with a trolling motor. His anchors are made from flat steel plates because they hold on all bottom compositions better than conventional anchors. He uses long 7-1/2 ft. spinning rods and light saltwater spinning reels because he has found them to be a more versatile combination for giant bass. He has spinnerbaits tied with monkey hair and jigs made with large turkey maribou feathers because he has found situations where big bass want that type of bait. He custom-paints his plugs because he has discovered there are times when they outproduce factory colors. Everything Murphy uses is a result of decades of trial-and-error fishing. Each time he lost a big bass as a result of some type of equipment failure or limitation, he looked for a way to make it better and more efficient. His whole philosophy is a combination of hundreds of tiny details.

His attention to the smallest detail is the one quality which separates Murphy from every other expert bass angler I've met. Most good fishermen believe that depth and speed control are the most important elements in bass fishing, but Murphy showed me that the smallest detail from the hook size to the color of the line can have a dramatic impact when you're fishing for big bass in pressured lakes. I learned how selective bass could be as I watched Murphy fish one spot on Lake Morena for three consecutive days. The first day he caught five 4-pound bass on live crayfish. The second day he caught nine bass, but they would only strike a jig and pig. On the third day, Murphy caught a five-bass limit weighing 37-pounds, and every fish was taken on a plastic worm. Murphy fished a variety of worms but

Freelance outdoor writer and accomplished bass angler Paul Prorok from Chicago, hoists a 14-pound trophy largemouth, his best to date from Lake Morena in California.

the fish would only hit one color. And why they wouldn't bite a live crayfish when they jumped all over a jig and pig is anyone's guess? That episode taught me that you could fish a spot with the right speed at the right depth, but if you weren't using what the fish wanted, you could easily draw a blank.

The importance of detail didn't sink home until I tried Murphy's stitching technique on my home waters in southern Wisconsin. By using Murphy's system anchoring method and following his advice on color and presentation, I caught 223 bass (some of which were trophy fish), by stitching plastic worms during a two-month period-an unheard-of feat in that area. Detail made all the difference! Detail in how I set up the spot, my casting angle, the lure size and color, and how I worked it through the spot. I not only caught more bass than with conventional approaches when they were active, but I also caught limits right after severe cold fronts. I only lost one bass using Murphy's skin-hooking technique; that's about as efficient as you can get.

I consider **In Pursuit of Giant Bass** the best information available for catching trophy bass from pressured lakes. Murphy has spent his entire life trying to perfect every aspect in the art of catching giant bass, and his relentless search for angling truth has given him insights into the sport few will ever achieve. You might not grasp the importance of all his detail until you make it work for yourself, but when the pieces begin coming together I know you'll catch bigger bass more efficiently than you ever thought possible. From my vantage point of having traveled coast to coast fishing with the best local anglers, guides, and tournament pro's in the country, I believe Bill Murphy is the finest pure structure technician and the most versatile deep water angler in the country today. He is a philosopher and a true Ambassador to the sport of big bass angling. Quite an accomplishment for a weekend angler.

Paul Prorok

AUTHOR'S NOTE:

I wish to sincerely thank my friend and colleague Paul Prorok for his masterful effort on this project despite experiencing great personal pain and tragedy.

I also wish to thank my partner and the executive producer of this project Carole Murphy for her tireless effort and dedication.

Big bass fishermen spend many hours off the water experimenting with methods that will unlock the big bass "Enigma".

INTRODUCTION

The Enigma

The word enigma is described in the dictionary as anything that puzzles or baffles as something perplexing or confounding. There couldn't be another single word that describes with such accuracy, the mystery that has surrounded the trophy largemouth bass for all these years. Except for spawning season, few anglers catch trophy bass consistently enough to formulate usable parallels or patterns. But if you learn their habits and develop skills to catch them, trophy bass can be patterned, regardless of how obscure that pattern may be, just like their smaller counterparts.

To consistently catch big bass, you must change the focus of your fishing. It's interesting to note, first off, that few seasoned big bass

Large trophy bass such as this monster remain completely isolated from most anglers.

anglers catch large numbers of big bass. Being consistent can mean catching as few as six trophy fish in one season and that could be a great year. The one thing however, that separates all successful big bass anglers is the focus of their fishing; they have changed the focus from small bass patterns to big bass patterns. These two patterns are totally different, and except for spawning season, small fish patterns and big fish patterns rarely mix.

For every pound a bass gains in weight from 4-pounds to 20-pounds, there is an obstacle that must be taken into consideration. For every pound a bass gains in weight, it becomes a more complex creature. A 10-pound bass is generally more difficult to fool than a 5-pound bass, and a 15-pound bass is more difficult to catch than a 10-pounder. It's hard to think of the overall picture of bass fishing and then realize that big bass are actually isolated from the bass population as a whole with characteristics all their own, but this is a fact. There are obstacles between catching small bass and big bass, but the obstacle is within you! Successful big bass angling starts in your own mind, by focusing on the things that appeal to a bass of a different size.

I believe the single most important element in making consistent catches of big bass from heavily-fished waters is **ATTENTION TO DETAIL.** Each year bass fishing gets more popular and the bass get more complex. Fishing pressure takes the edge off a spot. In other words, when a spot is fresh and hasn't been worn down, the bass are more congenial and will hit a wide variety of lures. But when a spot gets fished hard, bass become more sensitive and temperamental, and you have to fish with greater detail; this is the way bass are starting to act on most of our popular waters. In many cases, however, big bass populations in older lakes are just as good as, and sometimes even better than, the glory days of the past. But the biggest bass may be harder to catch because they have different patterns of behavior and they have moved to spots away from the mainstream of angling pressure. If you want to catch big bass in pressured lakes, you'll have to be more in-tune than the rest of the fishermen. You'll have to become more detailed about the habits of big bass: where they live, how they feed, and how they react to changing conditions and fishing pressure. You'll have to be more detailed in your presentation; finding the right depth, the right speed, the right color, and you'll have to learn how to create a natural atmosphere when fishing. As conditions become tougher, detail becomes even more important. When two people fish together and one angler catches all the fish, I can assure you it isn't luck. The successful angler figured out how the fish layed in the spot, discovered what color they wanted, and used a retrieve that caused the fish to react positively. **DETAIL IS THE KEY!** Attention to detail is the missing link that transforms a good bass fisherman into a good big bass fisherman.

As you read this material, keep in mind that you may not realize exactly what I've written until you find the **KEY** to the particular lake or reservoir you're fishing. Every lake has a key-key spot, key presentation, key color, etc. Finding the keys to every situation is something traveling tournament fishermen understand well. Anglers who travel extensively and fish a variety of waters have to find the key unique characteristic of each water. Even in southern California, every lake is unique to its neighbor lake. I can't tell you exactly what the key is in your lake because I don't know what those keys are. But whether the structures you fish vary from the types I describe doesn't matter because while there are things that make one lake unique from another, there are also key elements that stay the same. Lakes may all be different, but bass remain the same. This book will give you the tools necessary to find those key spots and the key techniques. Big bass fishing is a mind game; the best big bass fishermen are the ones that think the best. Finding key spots and figuring out the key presentation is 95% of the game. From that point on, the mechanical skills necessary to catch big bass are negligible. The thought process behind making those catches is what big bass fishing is all about.

The focus of this book is how to catch giant bass from heavily fished waters where bass fishing is considered tough. I won't be covering basics like how to fish visible cover or what temperatures bass spawn at, etc; these basics have been written about hundreds of times. Rather, I would ask you to consider this book an advanced course to help break through conventional thinking and unlock the enigma of big bass fishing for yourself.

ADULT CHARACTERISTICS

An Affinity for Deep Water

Bass begin life in shallow water feeding on zooplankton, tiny insects, and larvae, and hiding from predators in weedbeds, rock outcroppings and brush thickets. During the first years of life the majority of bass travel in small groups or schools, and they rarely leave the security of the shallows except when pursuing prey.

When bass reach a size of about 4-pounds, they normally undergo a change in personality - they begin to lose the habits of smaller bass and take on the characteristics of adults. Their larger size makes them too big to be preyed upon by birds and most other predators, and they begin to display the attitude and arrogance of adulthood.

One of the most obvious changes upon reaching adulthood is a shift in location from shallow habitats to outer edge areas close to deep water. Small bass live longer by taking shelter and hiding from predators, but big bass tend to move out and dominate. Years of trial-and-error experiences while growing up in their environment teaches adults which areas are best suited to their needs, and they instinctively set up in locations with ideal conditions.

One reason why big bass gravitate toward deeper areas is the size of prey. As prey species grow larger, they also tend to move from shallow zones into deeper areas. Large shiners orient to deeper ledges near isolated pieces of cover. Big bluegill frequent outer rock piles and irregular hard-bottom features where smaller life forms live and hide. Large crappie school in deeper water too, although their habit of roaming makes them a less consistent big bass prey in most lakes. But it's important to understand that as everything gets bigger it tends to move from shallow to deeper water-both bass and their prey. A big largemouth bass has perhaps the strongest jaws of any freshwater gamefish and can crush even the largest shad, shiner, or panfish. An adult body allows bass to exploit an ecological niche with larger prey that can't be exploited by smaller bass. A big bass doesn't want to chase tiny bluegill, it wants bluegill 1/2-pound or bigger, so when bass outgrow their food sources in the shallows, they move out into deeper zones utilizing larger prey that match their body size. In lakes where bass feed on bluegill, you'll normally find small bass feeding on small bluegill in the shallows, and bigger bass feeding on big bluegill in deeper zones. But this preference that big bass have for deep water is not a random thing. A big bass knows where the best feeding opportunities are at all times. They learn by repetition that baitfish always come by certain areas, or live in certain places, and that's the reason why big bass are there; they know that it happens time after time because as adults they've spent a long time in these spots. Big bass establish prime feeding areas; roaming helter-skelter throughout a lake looking for a meal is more a small bass pattern. Prey is an important part of everything a big bass does. Some biologists portray bass as poor predators that have a hard time feeding, especially in winter, but in a healthy, well-balanced lake, big bass are exceptional predators that feed all the time! But they just don't all feed at the same time! Like hawks, eagles, and other higher forms of predatory animals, big bass are pure hunters and **VERY** proficient killers. Except for a once-a-year urge to procreate, once bass reach a size where predation from birds and other fish isn't a factor, **EATING** is their sole purpose on earth. Severe cold snaps may temporarily halt feeding but big bass **NEVER** remain dormant for long. Big bass are fat, healthy and beautiful all winter long. Even up north, largemouths are frequently caught through the ice and these fish are big and green with beautiful color. There's nothing dormant about a big bass. It's true that active feeding cycles may become fewer in number and of shorter duration during the hottest and coldest months of the year, but feeding never takes a back seat to anything in the life of a healthy big bass. Catching bass with empty stomachs only reflects that the best time to catch them is when they're hungry and actively seeking food; an empty stomach doesn't mean they haven't been eating. When people speculate that big females feed more heavily in early spring to replenish fat reserves exhausted from a long and relatively foodless winter, I would counter that it only

Trophy bass like this seventeen pounder reflect a perfect adaptation to their environment.

seems that way because spring is a time when more big fish come into shallow zones where a majority of people fish and where these fish are more prone to hit methods and lures most people use. How often do you see a big bass in early spring that is skinny? Females are fatter in early spring because they've been feeding all winter. Bass may feed less often in winter but they eat all winter long. People only assume big bass are dormant in winter because they are difficult to catch. I thought they were dormant too until I discovered where they were and how to make them bite.

When you talk about feeding activity, you have to distinguish between large and small bass. Like kids growing up, small bass have to feed all the time to support a growing body rather than simply maintaining an adult form. The growth cycle of bass slows down as bass get bigger-the bigger they are and the slower they grow, the less their need for greater amounts of food. Big bass don't expend energy chasing after prey like small bass because they don't have to support as high a body metabolism. Big bass are more selective and feed less often than small bass, but they consume more at each feeding.

Another distinction between large and small bass is how they feed. A big largemouth may appear fat and lazy, but it can capture the fastest prey in open water. At the Bull Shoals Boat Dock in Lakeview, Arkansas, there are a few dozen largemouth ranging from 4-to-7-pounds apiece that live near the dock waiting for handouts as dock operators encourage people to buy bait and feed the bass. In the clear water it's a great opportunity to watch how big bass feed. Most of the time the bass just fin in one position and wait. But when a shiner or shad is tossed in, they make lightning-like movements and savagely strike the bait the instant it hits the surface. Some bait escapes the initial surge and flees for its life, but no matter how big or fast the bait, once a big bass spots it, the bass explodes on the bait and overtakes it in the blink of an eye, even at sizable distances. Small bass often have more success by chasing and flushing prey because they are still learning the habits of bait schools and other prey. But big bass rarely pursue bait for long distances; they overtake baitfish with short bursts of very fast speed. If a baitfish manages to evade the initial rush, a trophy-size bass generally breaks off the chase and returns to its original holding area. Big bass don't need to chase. They put themselves in locations where they know food is likely to pass by. When a big bass works a deep water structure, it instinctively knows what direction prey normally moves through the area, and the bass will hold just off an area where bait will be the most vulnerable and wait. They instinctively know that if they wait long enough, baitfish will come by because experience has taught them that's what baitfish do. Big bass position on outside edges of points and drop-offs and use these places to ambush prey because when a school of bait travels along a ledge, any projection or turn in the contour of that ledge causes a temporary disorientation of the school, and as soon as the bait is in a vulnerable position a large bass darts out and grabs a quick meal; the baitfish really doesn't have a chance. Holding tight to certain outside structural features is characteristic lunker bass behavior in structured lakes. These spots attract larger prey which big bass like, and they make perfect ambush points. Occasionally, a lunker bass will aimlessly search after prey and become an opportunistic feeder, but roaming and searching for food is generally a trait of smaller bass. Big bass typically congregate in a prime feeding area and wait for prey to come to them. They may chase after prey but usually the chase is confined to their preferred hunting area.

Besides providing excellent feeding opportunities, deep open water is a place where the biggest bass find security. Shallow cover is the most secure habitat for yearling bass, but a large and fast adult bass can use the vast expanses of open water to disappear at the first hint of danger. The connection between deeper open water and security is so strong, the biggest bass generally will not use a spot unless deep water is so close it can move into the depths with just one swish of its tail. Every time you hook a big bass on an outer edge spot, it instinctively swims toward deep open water. Because of their affinity for deep water, large bass are often reluctant to move shallow even during spawning season. For this reason, the largest bass typically spawn deeper than the bass population as a whole, and they select spawning locations which have a quick access to deeper open water. Caution and security govern everything they do. The characteristics of big bass in many ways parallel the habits of the biggest buck deer. The biggest bucks live in the best part of the forest. They need to be secure and secluded, and they need the right kind of feeding pattern; all these ingredients are essential to where a big buck makes its home. Big bass also select parts of a lake that offer good feeding opportunities and security. Many of the early pioneers of bass fishing knew what they were talking about when they stated that the secret to catching bigger bass is to fish a little deeper than you normally would. Fishing deeper proved effective because fishing deep water meant working the outer edge area where big bass spend most of their time. Generally speaking, outer edges close to deeper water is the whole secret to catching lunker bass consistently.

When I say that big bass are deep-water oriented, I don't want to imply that all big bass are always near deep water. Adult fish are individuals, and there are always some big bass that live up on shallow flats and along shallow shorelines where small bass live. But this is a book about how to catch trophy bass in structured lakes, especially in lakes where big bass are hard to catch. By structured

Success like this is a matter of being in the right place at the right time.

lakes, I mean a water that has deep basins and deep creek channels with structural features like underwater bars, humps, rock piles, reefs, and drop-offs. I'm not talking about fishing sloughs, rivers, or eutrophic, bowl-shaped lakes with mud bottoms and silted-in basins where the only usable habitat is shallow cover. If a water has deeper zones with adequate bottom structure and food sources, it has been my experience that the biggest bass in those lakes will most likely be found around the outside edges of structural features near deep water. And even in shallow lakes that are almost entirely silted in, the few remaining hard-bottom structures can be big bass magnets at certain times of the year. In many shallow lakes in Florida and the upper Midwest, big bass populations relating to deeper structures go virtually undetected and unexploited because most fishermen have been conditioned to fish shallow in shallow lakes.

The preference of big bass for outer edge areas is the main reason why more trophy bass aren't caught other than during spring. Pinpointing the best deep structures takes time and presenting a lure or live bait properly to deep fish is more detailed than fishing shallow. However, I find that lunker bass are more plentiful in deeper zones, and they are often easier to catch because deep bass are more relaxed and are therefore more susceptible to your presentation. But finding the right spot is **ALWAYS** the key! How good you become at locating the prime outer edge areas ultimately determines how good a big bass fisherman you will be.

Survival Instincts

The ability of big bass to avoid getting caught as easily as smaller bass is a product of having acquired greater survival instincts. As bass grow in size they become more cautious and they are able to recognize things that seem out of place. A small bass might strike out of curiosity, but the same stimulus might trigger an opposite or negative reaction from a cautious adult. Big bass have greater survival instincts because they have lived in their environment longer and are more in-tune with it. Small bass have yet to find their place and to establish themselves; they lack a cautious nature because they are still learning.

To truly understand big bass behavior, you have to perceive them in the world in which they live. It's a very simple world down there; it's very quiet and all sounds are dramatically amplified. A crayfish scratching its shell, or a split shot scraping over a rock, is audible from great distances. Big bass become familiar with the natural sounds they live with, and no matter how quietly you move through their area, the unnatural movements and sounds of your boat are an intrusion on the natural atmosphere of that spot. Big bass know how quiet it is when you're not there, and they certainly can tell when new sounds are present. I don't think bass comprehend what a fisherman is, or even care, but I do know that bass can be upset or put off their feed by an unnatural intrusion into their world. When you're at home watching TV and relaxing in your favorite easy chair, a car loudly backfiring can startle you. Even after you get up and investigate the disturbance, your heart is still beating fast and your nerves are tight for some time. That's how I suspect a cautious and sensitive lunker bass reacts when you bang down a trolling motor, drop an anchor too close, or repeatedly move overhead and meter its home, and it may take the fish some time to calm down and feel as secure as before the intrusion. Bass aren't smart enough to figure out that they might get caught, but big bass have greater survival instincts which cause them to stop feeding when something is not right. Line size can have the same effect. Bass have brilliant eyesight, and if a line is too thick or the wrong color, where it looks out of place, the line may cause a cautious bass to shy away. It's not that the fish realize they're about to get hooked, it's just an instinctive reaction that turns them off their feed and normal pattern of behavior. I suspect that bass learn things over time by association. They learn not to hit a certain lure, and they learn to react negatively to unnatural sounds and sloppy presenta-tions. Each bass you lose or release makes it harder to catch again.

All creatures have built-in survival instincts-it's nature's way of protecting her own. When a dog feels sick, it instinctively eats grass to regurgitate the problem. When you walk close to an earthworm stretched out on a lawn, it instinctively withdraws back into its hole. Beaver may swim right up to your canoe during closed season, but as soon as some are trapped the others begin slapping their tails on the water in alarm at the first sight of a canoe. Bass have survival instincts too, and the older they get, and the more experiences they have, the more cautious they become.

Many people believe that you can fish a lake out, but in reality you only remove the biters. Big bass aren't rare in most healthy lakes, they just seem rare because some bass are easy to catch and some aren't. There is always a certain percentage of "catchable" bass in any lake; these fish are "players" that are more apt to bite. On the other hand, there are bass that are "hard to catch" that rarely bite anything anglers offer. The hard-to-catch characteristics begin taking hold when bass reach maturity at about 4-pounds. When you eliminate most of the bass that are easy to catch, obviously what you have left are the bigger bass that are hard to catch. The hard-to-catch fish survive to spawn which produces a new batch of bass with hard-to-catch traits. After several generations you have a body of water with a population of predominantly hard-to-catch bass. When a bass population reaches this point, the easy fishing is over and people get the idea that the lake is fished out. Smaller bass will always be easier to catch, but if they make it to adulthood (about 4-pounds), their survival instincts take on more significance and they become harder to catch. They become more aware of lures, line, boat noise, and sloppy presentations.

Habitat is another reason often credited for boom and bust cycles in reservoir productivity. Young reservoirs with newly-flooded vegetation typically offer exceptional fishing. Young reservoirs generally have lots of brush or weeds along shorelines, and bass characteristically congregate around this cover. But as lakes age, fishing pressure along shorelines and reduced habitat make shallow zones less desirable for bass. The players are eliminated, and the larger and more cautious fish settle into deeper zones relating to off-shore structures, or suspending over open water, far from the mainstream of angling pressure. Most anglers and biologists blame the poor fishing on reduced habitat and low bass populations. However, in lakes with adequate spawning areas and healthy prey resources, bass populations thrive even though cover is sparse. What happens is that the habits and patterns of fish are not in-tune with what most fishermen are doing; in older reservoirs you need a different approach and a more detailed presentation to catch them.

All fish seem to react the same to fishing pressure. Even though bluegill are lower on the food chain, they react like bass to certain stimuli. When you first start fishing a school of bluegill, you sometimes can catch one on almost every cast. Even when the worm isn't hooked properly, they continue to eagerly bite. But after a while the school thins out and the fish that are left do not bite as eagerly unless the worm is hooked so that the hook is not exposed. The more the

Big bass have greater survival instincts. With each pound they become more difficult to fool.

school is fished down the harder it is to catch them, and the more every detail has to be just right. This explains how fishing gets tough. The fish that are left become more cautious, and you have to fish with greater detail if you hope to continue to catch fish in pressured situations.

Changing tactics has always been the answer for poor fishing in a healthy lake. I remember years ago, when black plastic worms first hit the market. They were so deadly you could hardly fish them without getting a bite. But at one point the bass stopped biting them. Fortunately, purple worms came out shortly after, and in places where I couldn't get a single bite on black worms I could limit out quickly with purple. When bass stop responding to standard techniques a switch in tactics is what's needed. There's always a certain amount of bass that are catchable with a new idea, and there's also a certain amount of fish that quit biting a particular presentation through negative association.

Changing environmental conditions can also cause big bass to stop biting a particular lure. Sometimes a certain technique works for about five years and then the fish quit responding to it. Instead of this reaction being caused by negative association, it's very possible that the five-year boom period was a result of a certain lake cycle or weather pattern. Buzzbaits can be hot when the fish are shallow due to high water or abundant new weed growth. But when these conditions change, the fish may move out. Buzzbaits stop working because the majority of big fish move deeper. The lake isn't fished out, and the fish haven't stopped biting buzzbaits because of association, the bass have simply changed patterns and you have to change accordingly. Change is a natural event. Times change and so does bass fishing. If it were not so, you would always catch them the same way every time out.

Personally, I believe changing reactions and negative associations stem from numbers of fish. When numbers are low due to fishing pressures or natural causes, big bass instinctively know that something is wrong. And as soon as an animal or big bass senses that something is wrong, it instinctively goes into neutral and can't be easily caught. This is nature's system of protecting its own.

The feeling that something is wrong can be triggered in many different ways. Too few fish, or too many fish, can trigger the something-wrong response, but it all works in the same response mechanism. Over a period of time a lake may become fished down to a point where the surviving fish feel that something is wrong. That "read" can be very intense to the fish even though it may not be apparent to us. But you have to understand that fish live in a world that is very simple and void of detail. Consequently, things that may not seem important to us can be very important to a cautious fish. A big bass might take the most insignificant thing as a **GLARING** warning sign. Nature maintains a perfect balance of all its life forms and won't allow a successful natural balance to become out of balance. When you put crayfish or minnows into a container, their numbers will die down to the number that size container can support.

Even though adequate oxygen is present, that's how nature works. Nature will not allow a species to overpopulate, or to become extinct, if not interfered with. Bait schools periodically die off during cold winters or other severe conditions, and bass populations follow suit by culling down to a certain point because of the reduction in bait. Lack of bait also affects the spawn. Surviving bass may lay fewer eggs, and there won't be as strong a spawn as during years with abundant bait. Stress affects appetite, sex, and a host of other things in all creatures. During dry years with limited food sources, deer produce fewer fawns and fewer sets of twins, and the survival rate of fawns is low. Nobody can accurately explain why creatures have fewer offspring, but this is how nature establishes a balance when there isn't enough food or when conditions aren't suitable. Nature ensures survival through a proper balance of predators and prey.

Every living creature except man has to be satisfied with the conditions dealt to them. Man is the only creature that has a high degree of control over environment. Bass don't have many options as they are trapped, more or less, in their environment. Over the years, bass learn to cope with different conditions and that's where survival instincts come from. Every creature, including man, has to learn to adjust to change. There are certain people that would starve or freeze to death in the wilds while others would survive. Bass do the same-some cope, others perish. That's why I believe it's not important to explain bass fishing in strict scientific reasoning. People have tried to correlate aspects of bass fishing with scientific data, but so much of bass behavior can't be explained that way. Nature is perfect and the balance is perfect, and each species has evolved into its most perfect form. Bass fishing is only a slice of the natural order of all things. When fishing pressure reduces a bass population to the point of becoming seriously low and out of balance, nature takes over by causing the remaining fish to instinctively become much more difficult to catch.

A superior survival instinct and genetic longevity is the reason why I believe in releasing lunker bass. It's better to remove small bass because they get replenished faster. But an old bass is hard to replace-it has a proven history of withstanding all the obstacles, and it has a superior gene pool. An old bass is like a prize bull that has

Even though this fourteen pound female was blind in one eye, she still was able to survive by strong survival instincts. She was released after picture was taken.

the genetic makeup to produce the very biggest of its species. When a trophy bass spawns, there's a good chance that its offspring will be very adaptable to their environment because there's a certain amount of heredity, survival instincts, and longevity passed on to the young. That particular year class might be a great year class of bass, especially if their parents had withstood years of poor conditions. Big, healthy trophy bass should be released, and the sick skinny ones removed-not the other way around. You might assume that any 3-pound bass has the capability of growing to 10-pounds, but you can't be sure. If big bass are, indeed, a special phenomenon, then special consideration should be directed toward releasing them and replenishing the stock.

Individual Behavior

Buck Perry was one of the first bass fishing pioneers to popularize deep structure fishing. Before depth finders were invented, Perry used a series of lures called Spoonplugs to fish the lake bottom and uncover previously hidden big bass spots. His method was to find bass by trolling, and then to anchor and cast the productive area. Perry was catching bass from deep water structures, and from the results he was getting he formulated a theory that lunker bass were school fish that moved as a group from deep to shallow water during periods of activity he called "migrations." To his credit, Perry was able to find big bass locations without the aid of even the most basic electronic depth finder, but future studies were to prove that bass are more complex in their movements than Perry envisioned.

In 1974, DFG biologist Mike Lembeck conducted a monumental bass tracking study on San Diego County reservoirs observing over 200 bass during a 3-year period. Bass implanted with transmitters ranged from 1-1/4 to 14-pounds. Included were one 14-pounder, one 12, four 11's, and several 8-to10-pound fish. In his 3-year study, Lembeck made over 800 observations, and he shared much of this information with me as it became available.

Lembeck's observations conclusively showed that bass in San Diego County lakes were very individualistic. For example, although most bass traveled more often in summer and early fall, there were also some bass that moved more often in the dead of winter when most other fish were slowing down.

Lembeck discovered that weather seemed to have little influence over position, movement, or depth. Windy conditions did not force even the shallowest bass to move, even on windy shorelines. Bright, direct sunlight also had little bearing on depth or position, even in the clearest water. Bass did not appear to favor the shady side of structural elements or cover, nor did they tend to drop deeper to avoid bright sunlight. Cloud-cover, wind, or rain caused no significant change in their position.

The spots where bass held were found to be of two different types: 1. Structures where bass would hold for some time, and 2. structures where transient bass would stay for a day or less. Even though some spots appeared to hold transient or moving fish most of the time, there were still some bass that would hold longer than others.

When bass were located on spots where they would hold for a while, they were usually there in big numbers. One rocky reef in San Vicente Lake held as many as 7 monitored bass at one time. Some bass which had been moving rather extensively came to this spot and seldom left. It's amazing how many big bass this spot held. While Lembeck monitored his fish, I fished this reef for four consecutive days and caught a 5-bass limit each day ranging from 28-to-38 pounds each, and I culled dozens of other bass. Surprisingly, only one monitored fish was caught. All bass were released.

When describing bass habits, Lembeck doesn't like the term "school of bass" because he believes it denotes too rigid a form of bass behavior. From his research, it was clear to him that bass, at times, hang out in groups but those were not solid groups or schools. It's the old saloon theory: You have a local saloon you always go to; there's always a bunch of people there, and once in a while the same people are there at the same time. When individual fish leave popular holding areas, they go in separate directions, while others remain. On many occasions, Lembeck would find two bass together, but the same fish would be widely separated by the next check. Lembeck was never able to identify groups of bass moving together for extended periods of time. In no instance, in any reservoir, did his monitored bass keep together for any length of time.

Giant bass always dominate the key areas in every situation.

When Buck Perry theorized that big bass migrated from deep to shallow water in schools, he was describing his experiences. He knew the spots where big bass would show up when active, and by the results of his catches he assumed that bass moved as a school. But what many of the early pioneers failed to realize before the full value of tracking studies came to light was that there are many individual bass personalities.

Big bass are individuals and they don't all do the same things at the same time. Some individual big bass spend most of their time traveling, some spend their time suspended out over open water, some big fish live mostly near shallow cover, while other fish make deep water structure their home. You can't think of big bass as a school fish because their habits are not that cut and dried. They have different personalities just like people. I think you sell these fish short when you try to categorize them into a certain type of program because big bass don't program well. They are individuals, especially after reaching 4-pounds and bigger.

The unique thing about big bass is that the bigger they become and the longer they live in their environment, the more unique and individualistic they are. They gain these individual characteristics through experience and time; they learn what works for them and they stick with it. Do you remember what a challenge it was to catch your first 6-pounder? There is so much change in catching a 6-pounder compared to a 3-pounder it's almost amazing. And the body of a 6-pounder is totally different-the jaw plates have more body and size, the tail gets fatter, the shoulders are wider, and the whole look of the fish is different. When you go from a 6-pounder to a 7-pounder there's a difference, and from a 7-pounder to an 8-pounder there's a difference too. All these changes are a result of **SURVIVAL**; the fish has survived another pound and hasn't been caught, but a lot of their sisters have dropped off along the way. So when a bass reaches a certain age or size, they become more solitary because they are so few in number. When a bass reaches a point where they are a trophy, or world-class fish, then they are really rare and extremely solitary; their habits change and they don't deal in the same manner as bass of lesser size.

Bass also break away from being a quote, "classic school fish" at about 4-pounds (both physically and behaviorally). They don't need the protection or benefit from group hunting anymore, and they change from a schooling fish to a dominating fish. They don't necessarily have to have their own territory, their territory becomes wherever they happen to be. When they move into an area to forage, they like to have that area to themselves. That's why you normally don't catch a lot of giant bass in the same spot, and why trophy bass generally move into a spot when smaller fish aren't present. Lunker bass may travel together in small groups of maybe two or three, but that would be considered a big group of big bass. If you find an area that has five or even ten big bass in one place, it will be a big area, and the only reason for all those big fish to be there is because it's a prime feeding area that attracts a lot of different individuals. When bass reach trophy size they like the same kind of hunting areas, and the fish will compete for these spots in lakes with limited prime areas. Big bass only come together at certain times when they vie for these special spots. I've seen whole schools of 8-to-10- pound bass swim through the shallows in spring, but the spawning season is the only time when lunker bass tend to have stronger schooling tendencies. Big bass are more apt to be grouped together in lakes with little or no fishing pressure. When Perry found so many schools of big bass, he was exploiting big bass populations that, in many cases, had never been tampered with. Fishing pressure like we have today on most lakes tends to disperse groups and create individuals.

Individual bass require an individual type of understanding; that's why trophy bass are becoming so hard to catch. There's a point in their life where they don't follow the rule book anymore. As an adult they don't need to follow, they only react to their own gyroscope. Big bass are masters of their world, and being masters they can choose to do whatever they like. This fact makes them somewhat unpredictable, but knowing this unpredictability can help in the long run. Smaller bass do the same things most of the time, but knowing big bass are individual creatures can motivate you toward a different direction. When you're after giant bass, you don't have the "set pattern" luxury that you do with the programmable bass in the 1- to 3-pound class. Sometimes no pattern can become a pattern in itself.

THE BIG B.
ANGLEk

Introduction

It was opening day on San Vicente Reservoir, a fair-sized impoundment located north of San Diego, California. The first spot that I had picked to go to failed to produce after about two hours so I decided to move. I left that spot and motored toward the dam area with no particular intention in mind. But as I got closer to the dam, I noticed that the buoy line which keeps boats away from the dam had been moved in about twenty-five feet. I knew there was an underwater reef in the area that couldn't be fished well when the buoys were in their normal position. So I lined up on the structure, dropped my anchors, tied to the buoy line, and cinched myself in. I cast out a large red crayfish and hooked a nice bass on the first cast. Over the next seven hours I went through 4 dozen crayfish, and caught and released over 30 largemouths all between 5-lbs. and 9-lbs. apiece! It was unbelievable!

I relate this story only to impress upon you what can happen when everything comes together. Many anglers don't pursue big bass because they mistakenly believe that lunker fish are too hard to catch, or if you fish for lunker bass you're really only fishing for one or two bites a day. True, lunker bass fishing can be like that, but then there are days like my experience at San Vicente. I can recall numerous catches like this where I just happened to hit large, big fish concentrations, and all were from San Diego County lakes, which because of their small size and close proximity to San Diego and Los Angeles are some of the most heavily fished waters in the country. But to make great catches from pressured lakes, you have to know what is necessary to catch them. Fishing pressure causes big bass to change their behavior and habits, and big bass anglers must change with them. Big bass are there and in big numbers in most waters, but in many cases

Trophy bass come to anglers who change their focus from small bass to big bass.

we need to be pointed in a different direction to catch them. Successful big bass fishing is nothing more than being in the right place at the right time and fishing in the right manner. Once all the pieces fit together, you will begin catching more and larger bass than you ever thought possible.

Tournament Influences

When tournament fishing became popular in the 70's, people were hungry for bass fishing to become a competitive sport and they were hungry for recognition. The younger generation generally embraced tournament fishing but many of the early pioneers did not. While reputable organizations like **B.A.S.S.** have had a positive influence on the sport of bass fishing, instigating the developments and refinements of safer and more efficient products, and helping educate the public in the art of catching bass, tournament angling is, by and large, a small-fish game. In a three-day tournament, successive limits of smaller bass will almost always win over a lesser number of larger fish. To place well, you must get bites, no matter how tough the conditions or how bad the weather. Experienced tournament anglers generally fish shallow water patterns because bass relating to visible cover are often easier to find in a limited amount of time on unfamiliar lakes, and shallow water is often the home of smaller bass which tend to bite more consistently. But few tournaments rarely produce healthy numbers of big bass. In most tournaments, a 4-pound bass is a big fish, and bass over 6-pounds are few and far between even with hundreds of people fishing.

In the old days, bass fishermen were simply called bass fishermen. Today, however, there are tournament style fishermen and big bass fishermen. Back in the old days there weren't any little bass fishermen. A bass fisherman made his reputation by how big his fish were and how many he caught when fishing was tough. If you were a good bass fisherman and another guy was considered an expert, the difference between you and the expert was that on the days that were really tough, he would always come in with something, and on the days that were good, he would come in with bigger bass than yours. But there was no such thing as a bass fisherman who went out primarily to catch small bass. Small bass were thrown back, and everyone was out to catch the biggest string of the biggest bass possible.

Tournament style fishing and big bass fishing are, in truth, light years apart. It's like a home run vs. a singles hitter-both take great skill and effort but the outcome is different. Fast-paced tournament fishing has no resemblance to the stalking, precise, detail-oriented, deep water approach necessary to consistently catch giant bass from structured lakes. If you make a few dozen casts or vertical drifts across a main-lake point, and then move down the lake, you can't assume that just because you didn't get a bite in ten minutes that the spot was void of bass. This approach does not extract the fullest potential from a spot.

Many modern anglers treat the accomplishments of the early bass fishing pioneers as if their contributions have been exceeded, and somehow disproved, by modern thinking and technology. Because of this belief, three of the most effective big bass techniques - anchoring, trolling and using live bait - are not widely practiced today, and few anglers grasp the significance of these excellent fishing systems. These techniques weren't discovered overnight; some anglers spent their whole lives working them out and died a little for this information. When the early pioneers talked about bigger bass being found on outside edges of offshore structures, these statements were a result of years, or even tens of years, of trial-and-error experimentation. You can't write this information off just because some angler wins $100,000 by catching limits of small bass in the shallows. When the early pioneers said trolling is a good way to catch big bass, they didn't mean you could get the same results by casting, they meant trolling is an important method and will sometimes produce exceptional catches of big bass when **NOTHING ELSE WILL!** When the early pioneers said anchoring is a great way to fish a spot, they didn't mean you can get the same results by holding over the fish with a trolling motor or vertically jigging. Instead of ignoring the contributions of the early bass fishermen, we should honor their sacrifice and sharing, and use what they learned to build upon. It's hard for the beginning anglers of today to be totally open to all angling possibilities in a sport that is so influenced by tournament style angling.

In the old days, there was a saying that 10% of the fishermen catch 90% of the bass, but modern anglers boast that today 30% to 50% catch 90% of the fish. However, in the old days they were only talking about big bass, not the smaller 1-and 2-pounders that are factored in today. Modern anglers probably catch more bass than their counterparts of yesteryear because they have more knowledge, efficient electronics, and better equipment, but the way I see it, it's all relative to the fishing pressure. Ten percent of 800 anglers means more people are currently catching more good bass; its more success than 20 years ago when 10% of 200 anglers caught the big fish, but it's still 10%. I don't see more people catching big fish. At the end of any given day the handful of good anglers come in when everyone else has gone home, and they have the best catches and the two or three biggest bass of the day. So, it's still in perspective.

The fish that were caught in the old days, however, are not the same fish we have today. Bass responded in certain ways in the old days, but now present conditions have them responding in different ways. Bass are heredity-oriented; they learn from experience and transmit some of that knowledge to their offspring. Tournament fishermen are releasing a whole crop of small bass that will be hard-to-catch when they become adults. The average angler of today is sophisticated enough to catch the cream off most spots, but as soon as the easy fish are extracted, all their noise and presentation flaws take their toll, and when the fish become harder to catch the average angler gets frustrated and searches for greener pastures. But a good big bass angler can often go back into these same areas and be very successful at catching these hard-to-catch bass by using a better presentation and the right technique. I use many of the same systems as the early pioneers did, only I've added greater detail to make them appeal to this new breed of bass. All I did was refine these early techniques and make them more effective in waters where fishing pressure has changed the nature of the bass, especially the big bass. Fine tuning techniques will be even more important in the future because bass fishing is only going to get harder.

Big bass fishing is not meant to rival or challenge tournament fishing, it is a bonus in the sport-something else to pursue. Big bass fishing is simply a different aspect of bass fishing, and it certainly is one of the most fun parts of the sport.

Versatility

As a bass fisherman, you have the freedom to do whatever you want in this sport. You can cast plugs, become a plastic worm technician, use live bait or whatever else that helps you catch bass and enjoy the sport. You can become versatile or focus on only one type of presentation and become an expert at it. How you fish is up to you, but if you don't practice true angling versatility throughout the entire year, you will never become an expert big bass fisherman.

Most good bass anglers have the ability to catch lots of fish, but they normally only catch big bass in certain situations. If you want to reverse this pattern and catch more big fish more often, you have to consider changing your approach. If you've been fishing hard all day with plastic worms and caught only small bass, while another guy who was using live crayfish comes in with five big bass, only an

Part of being versatile is having a boat that can do it all. The author has found that smaller aluminum boats are more ideally suited for all presentations.

angler who isn't serious about the sport would go out the next time without crayfish. If I were fishing for walleye, and I couldn't get a nibble on a jig or a plastic grub when everyone was catching walleye on nightcrawlers, hey, I'd try to find some crawlers! If you want to be successful, you can't be too proud to change tactics. It doesn't matter how you like to fish, the whole idea behind why you're out there in the first place is to catch bass, not to go through the motions. The fish keep acquiring greater survival skills and you have to keep changing with them. Jason Lucas was a purist, but he didn't catch bass like we do today even though he fished at a time when most lakes had little fishing pressure. Lucas basically only used plugs and various other hard lures; he wouldn't even consider anything else. He detested the use of live bait and condemned those who used it. I think this was a mistake.

If you want to catch big bass with any consistency you have to study them all year long. But how can you study them if they only respond favorably to the presentation you like to use four days out of every month? I've tried that approach-it doesn't work. In the dead of winter when bass aren't biting artificial lures, how well can you study the habits of big bass if you stay with artificials? If you go out week after week throwing a jig and pig, or using a jigging spoon, when the bass are biting live crayfish, you've just missed six weeks of the best fishing of the entire season! If you had been using live crayfish and catching big bass throughout this period, you could have been studying their movement patterns and monitoring their routine. Instead, you go home thinking that big bass don't bite in winter because you couldn't catch them. You don't have to use bait if you don't want to, but you're limiting yourself to a point where you'll never understand the total picture if you do. I used to be an artificial-only purist, and I hated the concept of using live bait because I didn't understand it and I had been conditioned against it. I'm still not crazy about the practice, but I allowed myself to learn how to use bait because I wanted to study all the variables. If bass bite live bait when they don't respond to artificials, then I'll use bait to get a better idea of what the fish are doing.

Nature is totally dynamic and bass are constantly changing. Their preference for lures change, and their preference for lure colors change. Their preference for bait can change too. These changes can be gradual, seasonal type changes, or they can happen overnight. But however the fish change, the student of big bass angling has to keep an open mind to the possibility of change and be prepared to change tactics. Purists will never grasp the total picture because through their stubbornness, ignorance and criticism they turn their backs on many of the very best lunker bass techniques. Perhaps the In-Fisherman founder Al Lindner summed it up best upon returning from a bass tournament in Florida; "It's frustrating when you can't get a bite on a plastic worm when the locals are catching 7-and-8-pound bass all around you with wild shiners." If you're not using trolling, anchoring or live bait techniques because they aren't fashionable, if you're worried about having the most expensive boat, and using the latest tackle and the most popular lures, if your image is more important than catching fish, then you will vastly limit your true potential in this sport.

Intuition

Have you ever had the feeling that a certain spot was loaded with bass and it was? Have you ever woke up one morning and just knew the fish were active and biting, and they were? Call it a sixth sense, believing in yourself, or the power of positive thinking, but however you explain this phenomenon, mental beliefs have an uncanny way of becoming physical reality. It's not important to understand the scientific explanations behind these forces-they may never be fully understood-it's more important to simply believe that it works. Modern man has lost this connection with nature because he lives in cities and separates himself from nature's force, but the ability to become closer to the forces which govern nature is a key to better big bass angling.

Many of my best catches were a result of intuitive thinking. Some inner voice directed me to a certain spot at a certain time. Nothing scientific about it, just a voice in my brain telling me that I had to fish a particular spot, and I had to fish it right then! You can't learn this type of intuitive behavior from reading books, it comes from experience and time on the water. Experience makes you conditioned to the elements like a certain way the wind blows and the air feels when the fish are biting. The more success you have, the more in-tune you become to the weaker signals that influence big bass behavior. As you begin to understand the fish better, your mind is stimulated to a higher level of understanding which, in turn, produces intuitive thinking. Your mind is the best computer. It compiles the information of all past experiences and promotes inclinations that instruct you to go to a certain spot at a certain time, or when to change tactics. If you love the sport, you never forget a spot, a technique or a person you've fished with. And once you have a good backlog of angling knowledge, your intuition begins to take over. All the best bass fishermen I've known said there's a certain amount of intuition in successful big bass fishing. Intuition is something an angler just feels because he's close to nature and intimate with the waters he fishes.

Believing that something will work or won't work has great power. When you believe in what you're doing, you fish more confidently, are more aware, concentrate better, become more open to the feelings and signals from nature, and in the end you become a better angler. You might not always catch the fish you believe you will, but if one does happen to bite you'll be ready. Now contrast this state of mind with a time when you lose confidence, become consumed with problems, fish in a haphazard manner, and are just going through the motions. Your fishing success generally reflects your frame of mind.

I like to wake up with a lake. I like to feel it and see how it's operating. I like to feel the momentum building as the light brightens from behind the mountains and see how the light falls on the water. I like to see which way the night wind was blowing and if it changes during the day. When I wake up with a lake, I feel more in-tune with nature and I approach that day accordingly. Based on the prevailing conditions, I let my backlog of experience and intuitive thinking be my guide for that day.

Successful big bass fishing is a mind experience, and you just have to trust your inner voices. Don't worry about water temperature or sky conditions, just go out and fish. If you think there's a fish at 45-ft., hey, give it a shot! I've been pleasantly surprised many times just because I had a hunch. That's the beautiful thing about bass fishing, science can't always explain the normal, sensitive relationship that bass and humans have with their environment. A good intuition is one of the greatest aids a big bass angler can have.

Attitude

Most people today lead hectic lives. They live in cities and have problems at home and work. But then they go fishing and expect everything to work out fine. Big bass fishing isn't a jock sport, there's little strength involved. Big bass fishing is an attitude sport. If your life is in turmoil, so is your bass fishing. If you've got your life together, your bass fishing picks up. You can divorce yourself from your life, and bass fishing can be your way out, but people that are the very best big bass fishermen seem to have the rest of their life in

13-pounds of perseverance. Author waited all day in the rain for a brief period when the big bass would bite.

pretty good order too. You don't do justice to the sport if something else is on your mind, you have to have the right attitude. You can't hit the lake like the 5 o'clock traffic. You don't necessarily have to slow down, but you have to change from the hustle-bustle approach of everyday life to a more relaxed attitude in order to approach these fish right. If you're too keyed up your whole approach will be wrong; you'll fish too fast, bang the trolling motor, be sloppy about dropping the anchor, and make noise in the boat. Impatience tends to throw off your continuity, and it will negatively influence the way you fish. Bass pick up on your presentation flaws, especially the big bass-they don't like it. They'll leave and come back later after you're gone.

To be an effective big bass angler you have to start controlling your emotions when you go out on a lake because the world bass live in is a serene, secluded type of atmosphere all the time. It's like you start out with 100 points, and every time you bang the trolling motor or do something wrong, you subtract a point. Every time you make a noise, or some type of sloppy presentation, you subtract another point. And when you finally settle into a spot and begin fishing, the amount of points left will determine the chances you have at catching a trophy bass.

When you see people launching their boat, you can just about tell how good a day they're going to have. You see this quiet old guy patiently waiting his turn in line. He doesn't yell at anyone, or get upset because someone hung their boat on the trailer or made a mistake. These things don't bother him because he's only got one thing on his mind-catching a giant bass. And that's the way he'll treat his whole day. He won't get upset if it's too hot or too cold, or if it's raining or snowing. He knows from experience that when you have a more forgiving attitude and go the extra mile, that's the mental state of mind that catches lunkers. Nothing gets in the way of a good fisherman's bass fishing.

Once I was fishing Lake Otay on a cold, rainy day. I sat out there most of the day without a bite. I was almost ready to quit, but it looked like a good period for big bass so I decided to try one more spot. The structure looked perfect. It was an outer edge spot that broke off into deep water in three directions, and they formed a high spot with a little tree on the edge. Instinctively, I knew there had to be a bass there. I anchored the spot in late afternoon and about an hour later the wind and rain calmed a little, and it suddenly got quiet and a bit warmer. Bingo! I got a bite and landed a 13-pounder. Needless to say, that one bite made my day. During the worst part of the storm, I was thinking how lousy I felt and maybe I should go home. But then I changed my mind because bass fishing was the reason why I was out there. And it paid off. I lasted the fish out and stayed with it until the fish were ready to bite.

Many people don't catch big fish because they don't take their fishing seriously. People who take fishing in stride generally don't do well. Fishing is fun, but the real fun is the end result. It's like an artist who truly enjoys his work; once the painting is done, he can stand back and look at what a beautiful thing he accomplished. He may call the whole event fun, but during the time when he's painting he's intent, he's thinking and he's working hard. That's how big bass fishing is. You work hard and you fail a lot. And when you fail, you pick yourself up and try again until you get it right. You fail, but then you get better because of your failures. Successful bass fishing is hard work, thought, intensity, creativity, ability, intuition, and all the human elements, but it is really too busy for most people to call fun. If you took the casual angler and demanded everything out of him that you demand from yourself, then you would ruin his fun because you'd take away his ability to relax. The enjoyment you get is the end product, recalling every moment that you battled a giant bass and that special feeling when it was finally in your hands. Nothing in the world is like that moment, and it was well worth all the pain and suffering to achieve.

I'm not a patient person by nature, but I make myself patient on the water because I have enough backlog to see where patience pays off. However, patience should not be without apprehension. I question a spots' integrity until it shows me different. I question my anchoring position. I question my efficiency in a spot. Is my retrieve path right? Is the lure coming over the spot in just the way the bass want? Is my lure in the proper zone? Does it look right to them? Why aren't they biting? These are questions that constantly go through the mind of a big bass angler-they have to be. A complacent angler is a loser. Daydreaming isn't going to make it. Every moment you should be thinking: Holy smoke, I've got to find these fish! What's wrong?! Why isn't this working? You have to constantly question yourself and focus on the problem at hand. You can't be satisfied to say that the fish aren't biting; I don't believe that. I think you can catch big bass on any day, during any moon phase, and during any weather condition, if you find what they want and present it in a manner they like. When a house cat is tired and sleepy, you can bounce a ball on a string in front of it, and eventually it will pounce. You can do the same thing with a bass, even a big bass. The fact that bass can be made, or goaded into hitting, is the beauty of big bass fishing.

Successful fishing ultimately boils down to desire. You can do anything or make anything happen if you have the desire and commitment. If you really want to succeed, you'll find a way. All you have to do is want it bad enough. And the feeling you get when you hold one of these giant bass in your hands is worth the sacrifice. It's like reaching a mountain peak and standing where you never thought possible. It's your fish. You fooled it. You caught it. You can be very proud because you did the things that made that moment happen. That feeling of accomplishment is what big bass fishing is all about.

Science vs. Nature

People need to change their opinion about making bass fishing so exact. It seems like to be acknowledged as an expert you have to give a solution for everything, but there may not be a logical solution. If bass always held in one spot or always reacted in the same way to a certain set of conditions, then it would be easy to give solutions. But you're dealing with a wild creature that is free to do whatever it wants to, or will do, in order to survive; you're not trying to describe how an automobile performs in different climates.

From a pure angling perspective, the only way to evaluate what bass do is by hook and line. You can't study them in an aquarium because a captive animal doesn't have the same attitude as it does in the wild. You can't examine them underwater because as soon as they see you, your presence influences their habits. Did you ever try to catch a tame bass that lives by a boat dock? Every time you try to feed it a nightcrawler, the bass moves up and sucks it down. But when you insert the tiniest hook on 4-pound line, the bass totally ignores the bait. Yet if you fished for that same bass when it was away from the dock and unaware of your presence, you might catch it on 12-pound line. When you put a transmitter into fish, who's to say it doesn't influence their normal behavior? They might be edgy and upset by the constant irritation and energy emitting from their body.

Catching bass is the only true form of learning **EXACTLY** what they do, and it's the only thing that will really teach you how to put more big fish in the boat. To be successful you need to think in a way that catches fish whether that thought process has any scientific basis or not. For example, I know trophy bass are individuals because that's how you catch them.Most scientific data is just data. Most researchers who correlate data don't know anything about catching bass, all they think about is the scientific connections. When Buck Perry formulated his theories about migration routes and fish behavior, science didn't enter into his mental process because all his theories were based on **RESULTS**! Perry analyzed his results and determined what the fish were doing. Perry discovered a successful system and he used it to catch big bass all across the country. A lot of good fishermen can't explain all the answers, they just do it. I know many of my statements are abstract but that's the way a person gains fishing knowledge. You look at the surface of a lake all day and try to picture what an invisible world looks like and what's going on down there. And your mind envisions a lot of things that may not be exactly correct, but that vision can work for you. Once you learn how fish live in their world, your intuition will begin to direct you in a successful way. In the sport of big bass fishing you just have to trust that some things are true; you can't prove it, so you just have to believe. But if you believe in something and it works-who cares if it's correct! We're trying to catch bass, not prove scientific fact. We don't care if it's true or not; if something works and you're in the frame of mind to make it work, then that's all that really matters.

All animals are not perfect, and they don't always calculate right. I once watched a cow give birth on the shore of El Capitan reservoir, and she dropped her calf half in and half out of the water and walked away. Later, the newborn calf dried off and stumbled over to its mother. But the mother paid no attention to the calf's predicament. If the mother had dropped the calf a few feet in the other direction, the calf would have drowned. Bass aren't the kind of creature where their instincts are always right either. A bass might spawn too deep and the whole spawn could be lost just because the fish was intimidated by all the action in the shallows. Science rarely considers the unusual, but examining fish that vary from the norm is what big bass fishing is all about.

All the modern studies have discounted the logic of the past, and now these new people are the experts. But to portray the early pioneers as somehow being less credible because they lived at a time without modern equipment is shortsighted. An old-timer might have said that he liked to fish when the air smelled like alfalfa. But what has alfalfa got to do with bass fishing? When the air smelled of alfalfa, the barometric pressure dropped causing a dew which stimulated an aroma of alfalfa, but it was the falling barometric pressure that actually stimulated the fish to become active. There doesn't have to be a scientific reason for a theory to work, the only thing that's important is the mental process that helps put you in the right place at the right time. Scientific fishermen are not necessarily the best fishermen.

Bass fishing should be freedom-freedom to experiment and fish whatever your instincts tell you no matter what everyone says. You don't have to use pork rind instead of plastic when the water is cold because pork is more pliable; all this is nonsense. Bass fishing is freedom and enjoyment. It's being able to go fishing and to catch bass because you have a good solid system that works, and it doesn't have to have any scientific value. You don't have to fish a certain zone because the water is a certain temperature. You've got to be free. You've got to have a lot of imagination to make this freedom work for you. Because the bass don't know! They don't know they're supposed to be at a certain place or in a certain cycle because that's what science determined. They just don't have any idea, and that's how you have to approach these fish.

THE STRUCTURE CONNECTION

When I began seriously bass fishing back in the mid 1950's, the tackle was crude and most everyone fished from rental boats. Arbogast Hula Poppers and Hawaiian Wigglers, and Creek Chub Injured Minnows were the popular bass lures of the day along with a few other assorted plugs and spoons.

The majority of bass fishermen in those days cast shorelines with surface lures and crankbaits, and occasionally with live bait. They'd typically fish early morning, leave during midday, and return late afternoon. Most anglers never fished anything deeper than from the bank out to about 10 ft. deep, so it was natural for them to have more success early and late. That's how fishing was back in the 50's and probably for decades before. Nobody had a clue that offshore structures held untold numbers of big bass.

In the early 1960's, however, a handful of anglers were discovering the benefits of fishing offshore spots, and they began focusing on deep water structures like underwater bars and high spots. Spots that could be found by hit and miss, trial and error searching. In southern California, and particularly here in San Diego, a few more creative anglers were making outdoor news headlines with their catches of big northern bass, using methods that were being developed for the very first time. One of these anglers was Mike Brown, a San Diego bass fisherman that gained notority by posting large limits of bass consistantly, using a new soft lure called a plastic worm. In the meantime, Bill Wade, (a master carpenter from Lakeside, California), was perfecting the art of catching big bass with various live bait presentations, and many of his accomplishments have become ledgendary. Henry "Red" DeZeeuw, (a mattress manufacturer in San Diego), was probably the best bass angler in

Bill Wade - Pioneer of many modern live bait methods.

my area, and he influenced just about everyone with his expertise. DeZeeuw visioned that bigger bass were on deeper offshore structures, and he would troll deep-diving plugs to find these hidden spots. Topographical maps of lake areas before they were flooded were available (although not as easily obtained as they are today) and resourceful anglers could have used them to help locate these offshore spots. DeZeeuw, however, took pride in finding these spots without the aid of maps.

When he found a place where he consistently caught bass, DeZeeuw would anchor his boat and work the area with Bombers or custom lead head jigs of his own design and patent. I was fortunate to have known these early pioneers of bass fishing and will always remember their contribution to the sport.

Because so little was known about the bass fishing here in Southern California, most of the fishing standards were set in the eastern part of the United States. We were too far west to be considered as a good fishing area, so Florida, the southern states, the midwest, and Texas, got most of the early media attention. It was hard

Henry "Red" DeZeeuw - One of the early pioneers of western structure fishing.

to find magazine articles that applied to our waters, and it wasn't until the Florida transplant program started producing giant bass in the 1970's that the rest of the country finally began looking west.

While California remained effectively cut off from the angling world, the mid 1960's was a renaissance of angling education and sharing in some areas. Terry O'Mally (an exceptional angler from Chicago, Illinois) was traveling the country conducting Buck Perry seminars and fishing schools with the emphasis on structure fishing, trolling, and anchoring techniques, and it was this atmosphere of openmindedness and sharing that inspired Fishing Facts Magazine - the first of the current how-to type magazines. But California was pretty isolated as far as the transfer of knowledge was concerned. The attitude out here was secrecy, and the people "in the know" wanted to guard what they had.

You can't really blame the old timers for being so secretive. Before locators, it took many years of trial and error fishing to find the better spots. Most of the old guys weren't interested in publicity, and didn't want the notoriety; they simply enjoyed the sport for the pure pleasure of catching bass.

One of the most important bits of knowledge I learned from my association with the early bass experts in my area was "finding the right spot." Every successful big bass angler I have ever met admitted that their success was not entirely due to a particular technique or special lure, rather their success was a result of **FINDING THE RIGHT SPOT!** Finding the right spot is the foundation behind every successful big bass system. The lure, color, retrieve speed, depth and everything associated with presentation is secondary to finding the place where lunker bass live and feed.

For the angler who fishes structured lake environments, **THE OUTSIDE EDGES OF BOTTOM STRUCTURES BORDERING DEEP WATER WILL BE THE FUNDAMENTAL BIG FISH PATTERN.**

The word "Structure" has been so misused by both anglers and media alike, few modern anglers use the term in its correct connotation or understand its true significance. Structure is not a tree, a bush, or a weedbed-as these elements are commonly referred to today-**STRUCTURE IS THE BOTTOM OF THE LAKE.** If you turned over a smooth aluminum bowl and beat it with a heavy object, the resulting bumps and depressions on the inside of the bowl would be comparable to the high spots, ridges, and depressions found on the bottom of structured lakes. Weeds, stumps, fallen logs, and anything that has

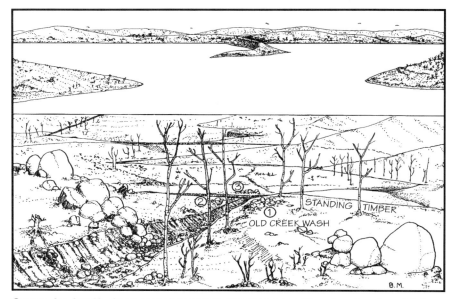

Cover, by itself, does not determine big bass location in structured lakes. Standing timber, stumps, rocks, weeds, or whatever types of cover are indigenous to the lake will not attract lunker bass unless associated with prime structural features. The main structural feature in this lake section is an old creek wash, but the prime structural area is where the creek wash junctures with another channel. Although the prominent rock slide and standing timber which line the old wash look promising, it is the subtle, subliminal rock humps (1, 2 & 3) at the creek channel junction that is the best big bass area. Intersecting channels form structures which break in two and three different directions, and these spots are always more attractive to big bass than a straight channel drop. You might catch lots of bass off the rocks and trees bordering the straight channel, but they'll likely be smaller than those found at the channel juncture.

settled onto the bottom, but is not actually the bottom itself, is not true structure; these features are **COVER ELEMENTS**, which, depending on their association with prime bottom structure, may or may not be attractive elements to big bass.

If a tree by itself is structure, then every tree in a cove filled with hundreds of flooded trees would be potential fish-holding structure, but every tree doesn't have that potential. When Buck Perry introduced the term structure, he specifically recognized only the bottom because he understood that bottom features, and not cover elements, were the key to finding prime big bass spots. If we examine a timber-filled cove from a bottom structure viewpoint, the trees in themselves become insignificant.

Examining a contour map of the cove reveals that the bottom is flat and featureless with the exception of one meandering creek channel. From a bottom structure viewpoint, the creek channel is the deepest water in the area, and the structures associated with the channel would be the first place to check for lunker bass. The most important places to look for bass would be the deeper edges of the channel which separate the shallow flats from deeper basins and holes.

To structurally break the cove down even further, an isolated high spot on the edge of a channel turn is **THE** primary structural feature in the entire cove. After fishing the high spot, you learn that a single tree on the edge of a fast-breaking drop-off is **THE** key big bass spot on that structure. But the tree by itself is not important. The tree only becomes important due to its **POSITION ON THE PRIME STRUCTURE**. All other trees not associated with the prime structure may never get visited by trophy bass; bass roaming through standing timber, or over flats, is more of a small bass trait. With the possible exception of spawning season, the primary structure would likely attract most of the trophy bass population throughout much of the entire year. The biggest bass always dominate the most ideal areas, and by using bottom structure, and not cover, as a guideline, you can learn to quickly eliminate unproductive water and focus on key spots.

Structural configurations may vary widely from lake to lake, but no matter where you fish, most of the underwater bars, ridges, high spots, and ledges **WON'T** attract lunker bass. Giant bass appear elusive because, in reality, only a few spots attract them. True lunker bass only gravitate to structural elements with certain ingredients. In smaller lakes, or smaller sections of larger lakes, there may be only one or two spots in the entire area that consistently attracts lunker fish. For example, if a creek arm has ten channel bends, the structural features associated with six of these bends may hold small-to-medium size bass, but only one or two bends hold lunkers. The bends that attract lunkers will be the most consistent spots in the entire creek arm. On days when activity is high, these super spots could produce

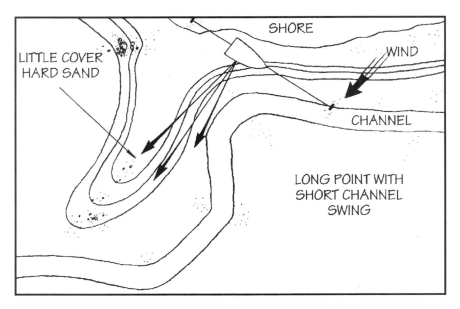

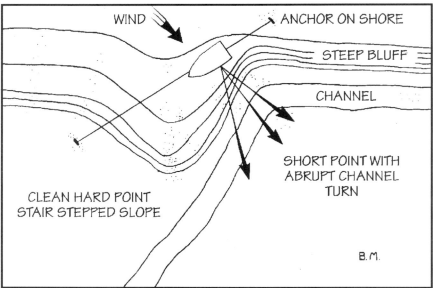

These structures are two examples of spots which are often looked upon as not being ideal big bass areas. Most anglers focus on the points, but the points are on the flat side and don't have a close access to deep water. The inside turns are the key spots. The turns have deeper channels creating an ideal entry and exit spot for big bass. Inside turns like these get little fishing pressure. Position the boat close to the shoreline, and cast out over and parallel to the breaks.

Isolated rock points often attract big bass because they are the dominant feature. The rest of the structure is more-or- less smooth and featureless. Rocks and broken down timber lead all the way from the shallow into deep water.

limits of big fish. And even when activity is low, these spots may yield a few nice bass when all other channel bends are empty. Once you become familiar with the key elements that make a structure a **PRIME BIG BASS STRUCTURE**, you can use this backlog of knowledge to locate potential trophy areas wherever you fish.

Deep Water Access

The best-looking structures will not attract trophy bass unless they have access into deep water. For the spot to appeal to giant bass it must have an abrupt depth change in the form of a drop-off, ledge, creek channel, ditch, or some other type of depression or the spot will only attract smaller bass. When analyzing the potential of a structure, always remember that the security of structure and cover is the only thing an old adult bass will give up deep water for, and **THE BIGGER THE BASS THE LESS LIKELY THEY'LL GIVE UP DEEP WATER**. Of course, deep water is relative; sometimes only a foot or two in depth change can be extremely important, but the deep water relationship

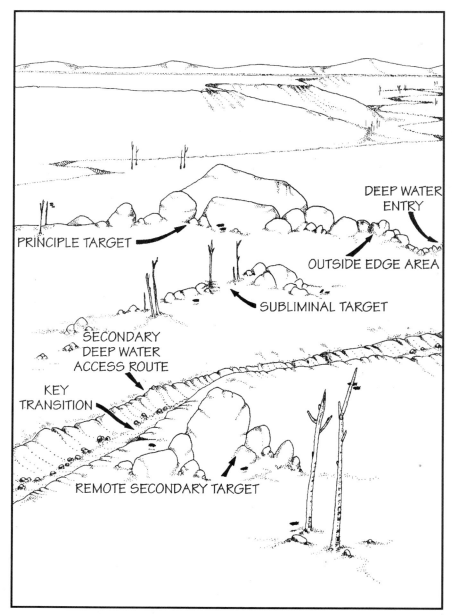

This diagram is an overview of principal and secondary targets. The large rock pile is the primary structural feature, but the smaller rocks on the outside edge forming a deep water entry is the key feature for big bass under most conditions. A strong active period may bring them shallower, but the outer edge near deep water is the area the biggest bass feel the most secure.

remains the same. Bigger bass are so deep water oriented, even during spring, shallow spawning flats must have some type of quick access into deeper water or the largest females won't use them. Trophy bass are so in-tune with their environment they'll establish themselves in areas where they're never far from deep water.

Big bass move around in their underwater world much like a crafty old buck moves through a forest. A buck doesn't travel out in the open on top of a ridge, it approaches feeding areas by using low spots for concealment. Big bass don't move along the crest of an underwater ridge, they come into contact with a particular structure via some type of deeper depression or draw. Everyone talks about how good certain structures are, but nobody talks about the deep water areas associated with those spots. Deep water connections, or access points, are the secret as to why lunker bass use a particular structure or not. You might locate a beautiful-looking point, but if the point has a gradual slope on all sides it won't attract trophy bass. A point by itself is no pathway-a point puts bass out in the open. There has to be quick access to deeper water for the biggest bass to feel secure. A big fish might look a point over from a flat side, but if it decides to move in on the point it will contact the structure via a deep water access point. Deep water contact points are the spots big bass move on and off structures. Without these access routes a structure will not attract trophy bass no matter how good they otherwise look.

Big bass are exceptional daylight feeders and when they hunt during daylight hours their strategy is to sneak using structure and cover elements for concealment. It's not that the fish are worried about fishermen or even know what fishermen are, sneaking is just a good hunting tactic when conditions are bright. A good hunter doesn't walk across a clearing, a good hunter moves along a low spot or hides. Lunker bass don't need the extra security, but sneaking and ambushing is an effective hunting strategy. At times, even a tiny rock or small stick is enough to make a bass feel secure and provide a spot to ambush prey. I've seen giant bass hold ostrich-like with only a small part of their head behind a stick with the rest of their body completely in the open. To a bass even the most innocent piece of cover or subtle drop in depth seems to offer security.

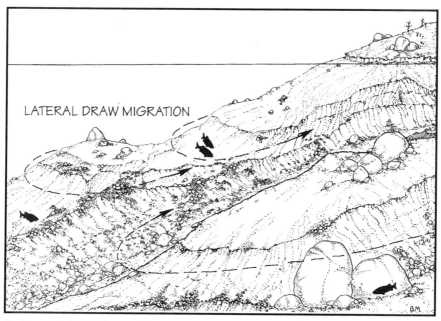

LATERAL DRAW MIGRATION

A channel, ditch, depression, or some type of draw is a natural migration route for bass. and it seems like the best big bass structures usually have some type of draw. Draws are like an off ramp on a highway. In other words, when bass cruise around a point, instead of just crossing over a draw, they instinctively move up and come back down it. Draws attract baitfish and crayfish, and for a hunting creature like bass they offer a perfect ambush point should bait appear. All cautious creatures use low areas for concealment—giant bass do too.

The only time giant bass will leave the security of deep water is for the security of cover, but deeper water is always their first security. The largest bass are so deep water oriented, just having a drop-off into deeper water often isn't enough. Trophy fish like structures near a main channel or main basin that contains the **DEEPEST WATER IN THE AREA**. These structures don't have to have direct access into the deepest water, but they have to be relatively close. In other words, it may not be enough if a structure drops off from 8 ft. to a maximum depth of 25 ft; a better spot might drop to 25 ft., flatten out for another 20 ft., and then drop off again to a maximum depth of 75 ft. The fish may not even use these extreme depths, but they seem to favor structures with the deepest water close by.

Maximum depths vary from lake to lake, but locating the deepest water in the areas is a good starting point when searching for structures that attract giant bass.

Another peculiarity about trophy bass is that the best spots are often located in open, wind-swept parts of a lake. Very seldom will you find good big bass structures tucked away in a corner of a small cove. Some spots are secluded, but most of the very best big bass structures tend to be in open areas exposed to the wind and waves and all the elements.

Outer Edge Spots

The key big bass areas on most prime structural elements are the outer perimeters close to deeper water, and the key feature on the outer perimeter is the edge of a sharp drop-off separating deep water from the shallows. Deeper edges offer security and the larger bass feel more relaxed. At times bass may suspend far off a structure over open water or move up to the shallowest cover, but the outer edges are the pivot points of big bass activity, and you'll normally intercept active, feeding bass either just off an outer edge or slightly shallower.

The more defined and pronounced an edge, the more it will attract. If a structure has only one significant edge, it would concentrate more bass than a structure with a series of stair-stepped edges extending from the top of a drop-off all the way into a basin. Structures with lots of options loose their drawing power because the bass have too many options and they tend to spread out.

An ideal big bass spot is an outer edge that breaks off in two or three different directions. A drop-off that runs straight without irregularities isn't attractive; big bass rarely use straight breaklines unless straight breaklines are the only option or unless overcrowding on more desirable features causes some fish to use secondary spots. Rounded structures with undercut ledges can harbor trophy bass, but rarely in concentrations like edges that drop in two or three different directions.

Look for combination edge spots wherever deep water areas come together: a channel contacts a main-lake basin, a stream cut or eroded draw intersects a basin or channel, or where two channels

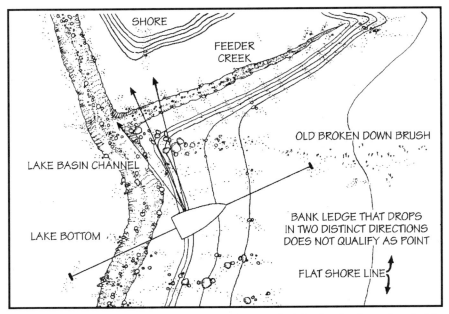

A feeder creek bisecting a main channel, or main lake basin, is a classic big bass structure found in reservoirs throughout the country. Anytime you have a feeder creek, or some type of depression, connecting with a main drop-off, it could be a great spot for giant bass, especially if there are no other prime features in the area. The more isolated these structures are the better they produce. The key spot breaks in two distinct directions. Even if it doesn't have cover, it would be definitely worth fishing.

meet; where deep features come together always has big fish potential. An erosion cut crossing a flat forms a two-sided edge where the cut meets the deep side of the flat. Spots that break in two directions can produce, but structures that break in three directions are best.

In natural lakes the best big bass spots are rarely as pronounced as in reservoirs. Edge spots which break in two or three different directions are still the key, but these edges tend to be more subtle and harder to locate in many natural lakes. But whether the lake you fish is a reservoir with standing timber along the edge of the drop-off or a natural lake with weedbeds bordering the drop, the same points, inside turns, cuts, and high spots on the outer edges close to deep water will be the key big bass spots in all cases.

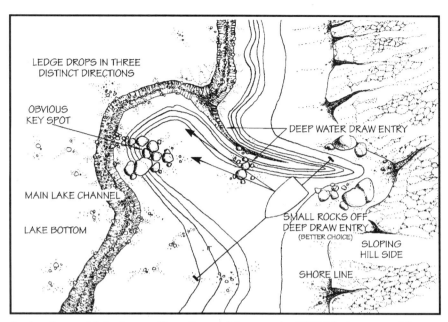

A structure which drops off on three sides can be THE big bass spot in any lake or section of a reservoir. The three-sided structure in this diagram is formed by a main lake channel and a small draw, but a similar feature on the edge of a natural lake basin would have the same big bass appeal.The large rock pile on the left corner is an obvious key spot, but sometimes when key areas get heavy fishing pressure, bass move to subliminal features nobody fishes.

Bottom Composition

When I analyze a spot for trophy bass potential, I analyze it from the ground up. I examine the bottom content and composition, how clean or silt covered the structure is, and even the composition of the bottom surrounding the structure-all are important considerations.

Successful fishermen know bottom composition is an important key. Big bass like hard or firm bottom conditions, and the key spot on any structure almost always has a foundation of clay, marl, rock, crusty soil, loamy sand, shell beds, or any other type of hard or firm bottom indigenous to the area. Decomposed granite rock is often a preferred trophy bass bottom composition in southern California.

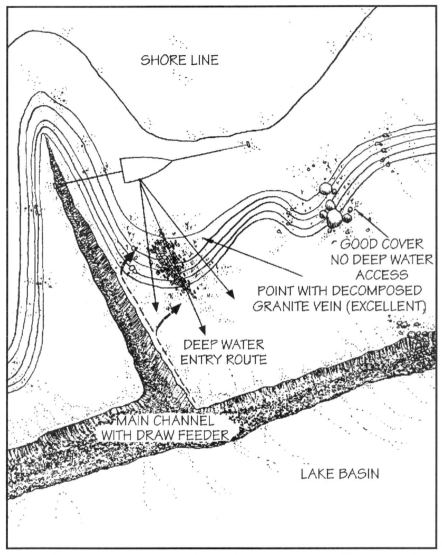

SHORE LINE

GOOD COVER
NO DEEP WATER
ACCESS
POINT WITH DECOMPOSED
GRANITE VEIN (EXCELLENT)

DEEP WATER
ENTRY ROUTE

MAIN CHANNEL
WITH DRAW FEEDER

LAKE BASIN

A vein of hard bottom in conjunction with a prime structural feature can be a big bass magnet. But because they lack cover, veins of hard bottom tend to be one-or-two-bass spots, and the bass can be spooky. Over the years, I've learned that the best way to fish these spots is to come all the way around far off the deep side, and sneak around from the back so the fish don't know that you're there. The rock pile to the right gets all the fishing pressure, but because it doesn't have the access to deep water it won't attract giant bass.

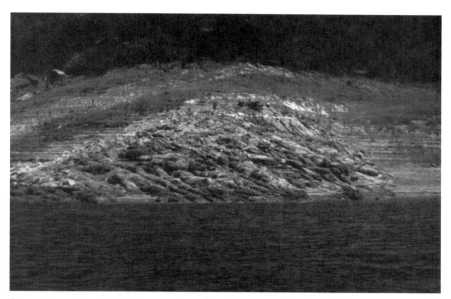

Sometimes the best deep water structures can be found by observing the shoreline. Whenever you find a vein of hard material surrounded by soft material up on a shoreline, it's a good bet that the vein also extends out into deeper water.

The worth of a spot starts with the smallest bottom particle and the tiniest microorganisms that live there. There is a direct correlation between the most minute form of life a structure supports and the size of bass that gravitate to that area. By catching my own crayfish for many years from streams and creeks, I've learned which bottom conditions are most productive. Pools that are clean and fertile, where leaves and vegetation have become a mulch, support great numbers of crayfish and minnows. But pools where muck and decaying vegetation cover the bottom rarely hold any crayfish or sustain few life forms. The same things happen on the bottom of a lake-some spots are healthy and full of life, while others are stagnant and dead. Bass and their prey, such as crayfish and other bottom dwellers, like a clean, crisp bottom composition. Trophy bass not only favor bottom areas that are hard or firm, they also require a bottom that is clean and free of muck and decaying vegetation.

Bottom Content Transitions—A resistant vein of rock and cobblestone stands out from a flat shoreline of decomposed granite, sand, and shells. Bottom composition transitions are key spots when associated with deep water.

Operated at normal power, fine bottom features may not show up well on a graph or flasher type locator, however, most units can be fine tuned to show subtle hard bottom areas remarkably well. Adjust the gain knob and increase the sensitivity until a second echo appears when traveling over a confirmed hard bottom area. Soft bottom will absorb this second reading. With a little practice you can locate hard or soft bottom by simply looking for a second echo. But you need a proper adjustment; too much gain produces a second echo all the time.

You can further examine bottom conditions by the way a lure feels scraping along the bottom. If the bottom is crisp and clean, the feeling of a jig or split shot resonates through the line and into your hands. You'll also get a sharp, crisp feeling when diving crankbaits skip and bounce across hard clean bottom. A lure sliding and burrowing through muck or mud feels heavy and dull. You'll see evidence of bottom composition on your line and hooks.

Two similar appearing but distinctly different depression entries;
Top photo: Ideal bottom composition and lead-in rocks (to right at water line).
Bottom photo: Soft bottom composition and no lead-in objects makes this a
poor big bass draw migration path.

The bottom composition surrounding a structure is also important. A rock pile on the end of a long underwater bar composed of
mud has about 1/3 the big bass potential of a rock pile on a similar
structure composed of hard material. A brush pile at the right depth
won't attract lunkers unless the brush is situated on a spot with the
right bottom type. Weedbeds growing over hard bottom have 100%
more attraction than weedbeds growing on soft bottom. Even in lakes
where natural conditions or heavy fishing pressure forces bass into
shallow weeds or brush, if you closely examine the bottom conditions
where big fish are caught, the productive area will inevitably have
firm or hard composition. Over the years big bass have learned where
all the best elements are, and they always relate to the prime spots no
matter if the fish are shallow or deep.

It's been my experience to catch more big fish from areas with
sparse or scattered cover than areas with solid mats and thickets.
Thick weedbeds or masses of heavy cover look promising, but solid
growth usually indicates that the entire bottom is composed of softer
material which lunker bass don't like. Scattered growth with numerous holes and pockets indicates that the bottom is alternately
composed of soft and hard material causing the vegetation to grow
in patches and giving the area a pockmarked appearance. These areas
are particularly appealing; cover offers security and a place to hide,
and hard areas provide openings to hunt and places to move about
freely.

Too much hard bottom can sometimes be a bad thing. Areas
where no vegetation grows, such as solid rock or slab rock, attract
few big bass. Only slime or moss grow on solid rock, and both
conditions are bad for lunkers.

Bottom condition has a lot to do with why structures suddenly
begin to produce or become barren. Some structures produce year
after year, but other productive spots can change and loose their
appeal. A productive spot may become algae infested or silt covered
to a point where big fish stop using it. Once a spot becomes sterile of
smaller life forms, it also becomes void of larger predators.

One condition which causes structures to change is a lowering
water level. As water levels recede, bass are forced to move deeper.
In many cases they relocate on deeper structures associated with deep

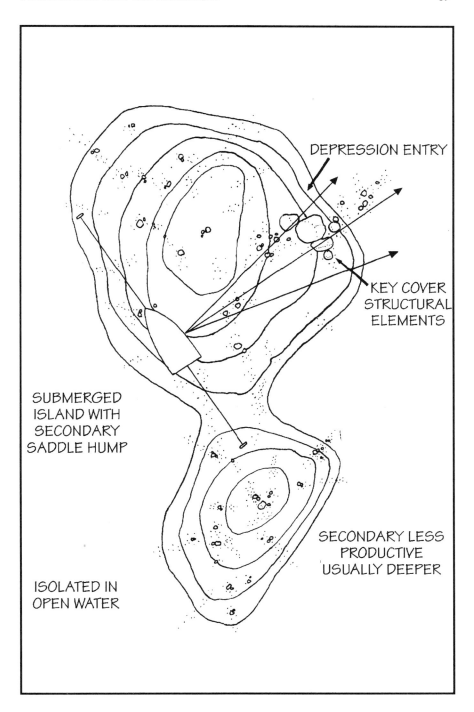

DEPRESSION ENTRY

KEY COVER
STRUCTURAL
ELEMENTS

SUBMERGED
ISLAND WITH
SECONDARY
SADDLE HUMP

SECONDARY LESS
PRODUCTIVE
USUALLY DEEPER

ISOLATED IN
OPEN WATER

basins and channels. In highland reservoirs these deeper structures are normally hard and clean and bass relocate without difficulty. But in some flatland reservoirs, moving deeper may not be feasible. In shallow reservoirs deep basins may be completely silted in or covered in mud, and when fish are forced to go deeper, structures with adequate bottom conditions aren't available. Even shallow structures that are normally clean can become covered with silt as falling water levels expose more basin, and wind and wave action stirs up the bottom. When suitable bottom conditions aren't available, bass respond by suspending which is a difficult time to catch trophies.

Fortunately, nature always has a way of correcting imbalances. During low-water periods, areas covered by silt and muck dry up and blow away as they become exposed to air and sunshine. Unsuitable material dries up and flakes off leaving a clean, desirable bottom surface. When water levels come back up to normal pool, bass gravitate toward these clean structures, and they once again become great spots for big bass.

Super Subliminal Spots

Once you find a structural element with the right configuration, access to deep water, and favorable bottom content-what next?

When confronted with a new structure, the first thing most anglers do is meter or graph the spot looking for areas on the structure where cover is most dense. However, it's been my experience that the largest bass are most often caught from the not-so-obvious areas adjacent to the better-looking features. For lack of a better word, I call these spots "Subliminal" because to the human eye there isn't much to relate to, and they don't graph or meter impressively. Subliminal spots are generally clear and open with only a scattering of cover. The best spots might have only a few small rocks or one tiny bush. But even though they lack impressive features, subliminal spots are often the key to catching the largest bass in many lakes, and discovering their location is like finding a pot of gold!

Fishermen who normally only fish the obvious or dense parts of structure may find it hard to comprehend that a flat, nothing-looking area on the edge of a drop-off may be the most consistent spot on a

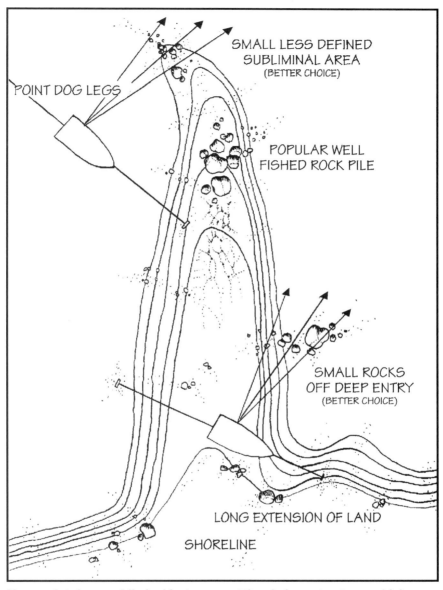

SMALL LESS DEFINED SUBLIMINAL AREA (BETTER CHOICE)

POINT DOG LEGS

POPULAR WELL FISHED ROCK PILE

SMALL ROCKS OFF DEEP ENTRY (BETTER CHOICE)

LONG EXTENSION OF LAND

SHORELINE

Many points have subliminal features past the obvious structures which seem to be the hot spots for giant bass in many lakes. People who fish the obvious top of the bar from the deep side of the point, often sit right over the key spot and never know it.Other key subliminal areas on long points can often be found on the sides of the points. These spots rarely get fished as they are a little too far from shore for the shallow fishermen, and a little too close for the outside fishermen.

structure. Thick brushpiles, heavy weed growth, and tangles of stump roots do produce bass, but in many cases fishing the heaviest cover on a structural element is more efficient for numbers of bass rather than true trophy class bass. Giant bass do relate to heavy cover, especially when waiting out neutral periods or harsh frontal conditions, but when they are active and feeding, open areas adjacent to deep water or next to heavy cover become the preferred hunting areas of truly large bass.

Why open areas? A big bass is like an old Cadillac; it's big and fast, and the more room it has to operate the better it performs. A baitfish near a brushpile has an even chance of escaping from a big bass, but out in the open even the fastest baitfish doesn't have a chance. Lunker bass prefer to hunt in open areas where they use their superior speed to overtake prey. What would be the sense for a lunker to sit around a brushpile waiting for a minnow to come out when the minnow could dart back in causing only frustration and loss of interest.

THE WHOLE SECRET TO CATCHING TROPHY BASS CONSISTENTLY IS FINDING THE RIGHT SPOT AND BEING THERE WHEN THEY ARE ACTIVE AND FEEDING. Interesting enough, bass have spots where they hold when not feeding and spots where they go to intercept prey. Bass may use various elements throughout an entire structure, but generally there are only a few places on any structural piece where bass actually hunt prey. Bass feed in certain areas because that's where they have the most success. Bait frequently move through these areas, and certain bottom contours and cover objects cause the bait schools to change rhythm and temporarily become disoriented and vulnerable. Big bass try to overtake prey with short bursts of speed, and when they miss, they'll often go right back into their original holding or feeding position. When you see a big bass blow up on the surface chasing baitfish, there's a good chance to catch that fish if you work its ambush point or hunting area. The feeding area is a spot bass use when they hunt, and it's the process of how you work that spot that makes it produce. Every time you fish that spot during an active feeding period you get a bite, and you're disappointed when you don't.

Subliminal hunting areas are great to find because you'll usually have them all to yourself. Spots that don't look good or graph well get less fishing pressure, and the lack of pressure alone can make subliminal features prime trophy bass areas. It's not in the nature of the biggest bass to relate to the obvious places where numerous smaller bass gather or where the majority of the fishing pressure is directed. Trophy bass are normally low-keyed and low-profile. Other anglers may see you catching bass from a particular spot, but when they investigate the structure after you leave, your fishing hole doesn't compute into anything that looks good, and they can't figure out how you fished it and made it produce. Usually they'll give up the spot thinking your success was due to some magic lure or special live bait.

All flats and featureless areas on structure do not attract big bass. Trophy bass gravitate to certain subliminal features due to a combination of certain components. Subliminal spots only produce when other criteria are met such as: firm bottom content, access to deep water, the right depth, and a consistent presence of prey. Electronically speaking, the best subliminal areas appear void of life, but when you acquire the ability to recognize these spots the way fish see them and deliberately fish subliminal areas simply because of their relationship with other structural elements, you'll have uncovered a hidden insight into the sport of trophy bass fishing and be light years ahead of the competition.

Observing the bank where you intend to fish is one of the easiest ways to find subliminal features. Whenever I fish a new structure, I always first analyze the area above the waterline. Generally, I look for areas that are sparse and clean up on the bank. If the bank is full of brush or timber, I try to find areas with less cover. It's not enough to find a clean area where the original cover decomposed over time, I want to find hard bottom areas where the trees and brush had a hard time growing **BEFORE THE LAKE WAS FLOODED.**

On a new lake it's sometimes a good idea to beach the boat and walk along the bank. Examine the ground to see what material it's made of and if there are shell beds or scattered rock or bushes; all these features generally carry out into the water. If you find firm bottom with some staggered boulders, chances are good there will

Two Kinds of Underwater Islands—The island at the top is a massive structure covered with large boulders and brush. The island at the bottom is small with only a few isolated rocks and stumps. The large island looks ideal, but the small island with the subliminal rocks is actually the best spot for giant bass. Big bass in pressured lakes often seek out features most fishermen ignore.

Sometimes getting out of the boat and walking the bank and feeling various bottom contents is the best way to find key transition areas. This spot was the only area on over a mile of shoreline with rocks, and it pointed the way to finding a key big bass area offshore.

also be that type of bottom offshore. Demarcation areas where different soils or rock types intersect is another key feature. A bank might turn from mud-to-clay, or shale-to-sand, but demarcations are good places to begin searching for bass out deeper. If you find a small outcropping of rocks or an isolated patch of timber, you can bet they'll be more of the same out from shore.

Having the ability to find subliminal features is one reason why good trophy anglers can often go to an unfamiliar lake and out fish the locals. Flat, nothing-looking shorelines often get bypassed by visual-oriented fishermen, and these subtle, subliminal type spots rarely get fished. But if you work them out far enough, at the right depth, you may discover a little secondary spot that holds monster bass.

The Significance of Changing Water Level

Have you ever found a great looking structure that appears to have all the elements but it fails to produce? It could be a productive spot, but about 90% of the time you fish it, the spot is either too shallow or too deep. **WATER LEVEL IS THE SINGLE MOST IMPORTANT CONSIDERATION WHETHER A STRUCTURE WILL ATTRACT BIG BASS OR NOT.** The bigger bass are so depth oriented and depth sensitive, the right depth is what makes a good big bass spot under every condition. A prime structure may consistently produce at a certain water level, but when the water level changes, if the structure doesn't have spots suitable for the new level, big bass will abandon the structure and relocate in more appropriate areas.

Natural lakes rarely experience extreme water level fluctuations, but reservoirs, especially drinking water and irrigation reservoirs, can go up and down dramatically in only a matter of days. When water is released from a reservoir, surface and middle layers are most affected, consequently, water with the highest oxygen content is removed which can have a dramatic influence on fishing, especially in summer when oxygenation is lowest. Changing water levels affect the whole environment and are important considerations in determining which structural features come into play.

When water levels are high, structures at the shallow end of a reservoir are generally productive. High water periods may stimulate off-colored water in the shallows which attracts baitfish and bass. This combination of bait and dark water can trigger a "peak" time in shallow sections. When water levels begin to recede, however, bass may abandon shallow spots, and structures in the deeper end of the lake now come into play. When the water level is lowered, secondary structures that never get fished, because they were too deep, now become productive. Local factors like weather, wind direction, current, and baitfish patterns ultimately determine daily bass activity, but water level has a dramatic influence on when structures produce at certain times of the year. A spot may be too deep or too shallow for the time of year you're fishing, but a water fluctuation can change the importance of an individual structure in a hurry.

WATER LEVEL FLUCTUATION

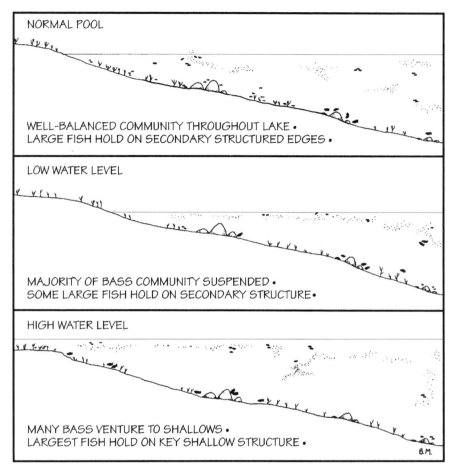

Changing water levels and heavy fishing pressure may move bass from primary areas to subliminal secondary targets. Subliminal targets don't graph well, consequently they rarely get fished, but this is exactly why trophy bass seek them out. Various structural elements must be linked closely together or big bass won't use them.

I like to fish a spot that is just coming into prime, rather than a spot that has been prime for a long time and is currently going out of prime. Very seldom does a productive spot just quit all of a sudden; it's usually a gradual process and if you fish often and monitor the bass, you'll notice indications that a spot is going bad. When you notice a spot beginning to wane, it's better to start looking to see if the majority of fish have moved to another location rather than to sit on the spot and work a tired horse to death. The water level could be changing and the bait shifting, or the fish could move simply because they aren't nailed down to any particular behavior. It's like grazing cattle; one week they're all at one side of the pasture and the next week they're all at the other side. Maybe just one moved and all the other followed. We don't have to get too scientific about water level; just be aware that a slight change can move bass. If the water level is slowly falling, you could begin searching for deeper edge spots on structures that are currently producing. If you keep fishing these deeper elements, eventually you'll connect when the water level is just right for the bass to be there. I know many spots where I can watch the water level and when the level gets just right the fish will be on them. I have one spot I check every week in late spring when water levels start dropping. On most trips I'll never get a bite, but then one day I might stop by and get a bite from a really big bass! When the water level reaches the optimum depth for a particular spot, bass fishing can change from nothing to unbelievable! A big secret to catching bass during changing water levels is to move away from structures that are going out of prime and focusing on spots that are just coming into prime.

Anglers who succeed during water fluctuations fish often and stay abreast of changing patterns. It's a lot easier to fish a lake often and stay with the bass rather than fishing only on occasion and trying to establish the current big fish pattern in only a day or two. Tournament anglers often choose to establish small fish patterns because big bass patterns can be difficult to figure out in a short practice period. But sport fishermen don't have that limitation. If you want to catch big bass consistently you'll have to fish often and monitor the fish. Just metering potential spots isn't enough; you're going to have to work hard and fish them too.

Few anglers fish undercut banks because they don't look like big fish spots. Yet the small ledges of harder, more resistant bottom content make ideal places for big bass to ambush prey.

Year-round Structures

The toughest time of the year to catch big bass is in conjunction with changing seasonal patterns. Changes in water level, caused by unstable weather conditions, water clarity, erratic bait movements, etc., can cause difficult tracking as bass change locations and the total number of reliable spots decline-the number of summer spots rapidly decline as fish begin shifting into fall locations, and winter patterns begin breaking down with the onset of early spring. But although the total number of productive structures decline, one or two of the very best spots normally continue to produce right through a seasonal transition lull.

The biggest bass don't like to make long locational movements when water levels fluctuate or conditions change. Big fish may roam from spot to spot, but moving around constantly is more a small-fish pattern. The biggest bass select areas where they can live for a long time during all changing conditions; they set up residency in places they can use spring, summer, fall and winter without having to move too far. That's the reason why you catch them in certain areas year after year.

The spots that produce best through all seasonal changes are the prime big bass structures I classify as year-round structures. These spots have a long history of big bass usage because they have ideal bottom composition, ideal structural mass, abundant food sources, and perfection in depth considerations. Year-round structures also have multiple breaks and other substructures at different break levels that lead all the way from the shallows into the deepest basins. These prime levels have edges and drop-offs at all depths so bass can relocate to adequate elements regardless if the water level is rising or falling, or if any other change should occur. Year-round structures also have shell beds, rock piles, or some other type of firm or hard bottom at all levels which attracts the entire food chain from the smallest parasites to the largest predators.

If a structure has a number of breaks and other fish-holding features connecting the shallows to the deepest water, chances are good that big fish will use that spot all year long. The deeper breaks may be too deep for the fish to use most of the year, but they come into play when water levels are low or during deep water movements such as a deep winter movement. But the deeper structures are the key that make the shallow spots produce on a particular structure. Without deeper connecting elements the best-looking shallow spots would be marginal or seasonal big bass producers at best. If a structure lacks any important elements either on the shallow or deeper end, the structure will have less year-round potential. Consistent fishing is a matter of optimum structure at the right depth, and year-round structures have prime elements at all depths. Finding year-round structures is the backbone of trophy bass fishing.

POSITION AND ACTIVITY DURING LUNAR PHASES

Active Periods

The likelihood of catching a record bass or making a spectacular catch of lunkers increases dramatically when fishing periods of heightened fish activity. Timing your fishing trips to coincide with peak activity can be so important to overall success, a skilled angler might fish for years and never contact a true lunker-size bass if he or she fails to be in the right spot during an active period, and this fact goes double on heavily fished waters. You have to make every effort to be on the water when the big fish are most active and catchable.

When I talk about active and inactive periods I'm referring to position, aggressive tendencies and willingness to bite. Inactive or neutral bass generally won't move far and they often hold tight to cover or suspend in more-or-less fixed positions in open water, consequently, inactive bass rarely chase prey; they may feed if an opportunity presents itself, but they rarely move far to pursue it. When you manage to tempt an inactive fish into biting, they often strike with less authority making them harder to hook and land. An active bass, on the other hand, is a completely different animal. Instead of being stationary, an active bass is more likely to roam an area in a feeding mood, and when it contacts prey, an active fish will often overtake the prey with a sudden burst of speed. Active bass are aggressive biters which translates into more solid hookups and more bass in the boat. Active bass also tend to be less cautious about angling pressure and less sensitive to sloppy presentations. From a pure angling point of view, it's always easier to fool lunker bass that are in a high state of activity rather than neutral or inactive fish.

One reason why trophy bass are seldom caught is because the feeding patterns of large bass vary significantly from feeding patterns of smaller fish. Big bass use a strategy of eating a lot at one time, taking what they need all at once, then settling down and conserving energy. A typical feeding pattern for large bass in the course of a 24 hour period would be a flurry of activity of fairly short duration followed by long periods of inactivity. Over the course of a week, you might encounter strong feeding activity for 3 days in a row followed by 4 days of relative inactivity. Two weeks of a particular month might have peak activity while the other two weeks are rather dead. Extended time between feeding periods is a frustration trophy bass hunters have to live with.

If you were fishing a primary big bass structure on a day with peak activity, you normally would have a chance at contacting a lunker bass for only a brief part of that day. Instead of a lingering all-day feeding spree, big bass bites are characteristically short, usually lasting less than an hour and in some cases only minutes. If a spot was attracting bass of all sizes, different groups of medium size bass would likely travel to the structure at various times throughout the day, but the biggest bass would only appear at one time during a peak daily active period. For example, you might catch four 2-to-3-pound bass, wait a few hours, then catch two 2-pounders and a 4-pounder. Action like this might continue throughout the day as different fish react to minor active periods. At 3 p.m., however, a peak active period stimulates the lunker fish to move, and you catch three 5-pounders and a 9-pounder in only twenty minutes. The big fish movement might consist of a small group or just one fish, but in either case the short time the fish actually visit the structure makes it extra important to be in the right spot when the feeding period takes place.

Whenever we go fishing, big bass will be neutral or inactive about 90% of the time. Instead of relating to primary feeding areas on structural features, inactive bass generally move into individual holding areas in the near vicinity of the structure. Some inactive fish disperse into open water while others move to isolated cover objects like an undercut rock ledge on the side of a drop-off or a tangled root system of a large stump. Most of these inactive holding areas harbor only one big bass, and the resident fish drive off outsiders that come too close. The bigger fish spend most of their lives in and around these natural holding areas bushwacking prey as feeding opportunities present themselves.

From an angling standpoint, these one-bass locations are difficult to recognize and almost impossible to fish. While it's relatively easy to probe for inactive bass hidden in visible shallow water cover, such as a fallen tree or thick weedbed, the same can't be said about deep water fish. A giant bass might be holding under a little ledge at 25 ft. along the side of a steep bluff that drops straight down into 60 ft. The fish is impossible to graph, and even if you knew it was there you can't effectively fish for it. All you could do was hope the fish would come out and intercept your offering as it fell off the ledge, but your chances are slim. With everything against you, it would be hard to persevere long enough until the fish became an aggressive feeder.

Instead of dealing with one-fish holding areas, most deep water anglers find it easier to focus on more recognizable features such as a long bar with brush or weeds; these spots graph better and have more appeal. But the fact is that most good-looking structures only attract small or medium size bass most of the time. In the old days big bass spent more time on the obvious spots. Today, however, the bigger fish are taking on new patterns of behavior. The largest bass tend to be individuals that spend most of their time in solitary isolated spots. These large loners still associate with prime structural areas but they spend most of their lives in obscure spots in the near vicinity, and this is particularly true of bigger bass in pressured lakes.

The best strategy I have found to catch trophy bass in this situation is to fish during periods that cause individual big bass **TO COME TO YOU**! Fortunately, there are times when nature comes forth with all her abundance, and for sharp anglers who anticipate and set up right positions, trophy bass will come right to their doorstep.

During a peak active period, individual lunkers may abandon their neutral holding areas and move to key feeding areas on prime structures. Even though it was resting and conserving energy, it's getting hungry, and when conditions arrive which stimulate activity throughout the food chain, big bass instinctively move to feeding

The biggest bass seem to bite best after the smaller bass have finished feeding. Whenever there is a lull after strong activity, keep working the spot because the larger fish have a habit of feeding during the last few minutes of a peak active period.

areas where they know they can be satisfied in a hurry. Bass, of course, don't have to wait to feed, but maybe an inactive bass was holding where food wasn't available. Active periods stimulate a change in mood from inactive to aggressive. An angler who antici- pates this mood swing can position in a key feeding spot and be in perfect position to intercept them and make a super catch. Positioning in key spots and ambushing bass as they moved in was the secret method employed by many of the early pioneers. Of course, not all individual big bass move to key feeding areas, some stay and become active near their holding area, but enough fish generally show up at key feeding spots during peak active periods to potentially make this strategy produce spectacular catches throughout the year.

Pre-Frontal Conditions

The fact that bass bite best on the front side of an approaching frontal system and bite least on the back side is a truism anglers discover wherever they fish for bass.

While most anglers credit overcast pre-frontal conditions for prompting good fishing and bright, cloudless, post-frontal weather for causing bass to shut off, my studies point to barometric pressure, as having a more important influence on big bass activity. Air temperature, cloud cover and wind direction are only symptoms of a larger weather system, and the barometric pressure associated with the weather system is the key to active and inactive periods.

We like to blame the clear skies and cool temperatures following a cold front for bad fishing, but rather than a limiting factor in themselves, these conditions signal a change in barometric pressure. As the cold front was approaching and the barometric pressure was falling, big bass were biting well, but after the front moved through and the barometric pressure began to rise, conditions became cool and clear, and the bigger fish shut off. Everyone likes to finger the weather, but I believe the change in barometric pressure was the real culprit. Reverse the conditions and this philosophy comes into focus. The same bright, cloudless sky (which was blamed for bad fishing) on the front side of an approaching frontal system can be excellent. One of the best days I've ever had was when an approaching front had stalled a day or so away and the cloud cover hadn't yet arrived. The sun was intense and burning, but the fish were stimulated by the falling barometric pressure and bit like crazy. I caught a bass over 7-pounds or bigger on almost every cast for over an hour!

Barometric conditions are the real cause of big bass activity. Local weather can add a positive or negative influence to active trends that are already set in motion, but local weather is not that important by itself. For example, a heavy overcast on the front side of an approaching frontal system can be associated with high activity, but heavy overcast on the back side of a front generally produces considerably less activity. A cloudy day on the back side of a front may have more activity than a bright cloudless day but the clouds are more of an addition or plus to what's already taking place rather than the cause of activity.

One fact which is often ignored about bad fishing after a front is that most of the fish are already full and satisfied. Just before the front, and possibly for several days before the front, the falling barometric pressure caused the bigger fish to go on a wild feeding spree. But on the next day after the front goes through, conditions got bright and clear and you couldn't buy a fish. What happened is that almost every fish in the lake had completely gorged themselves, and after the front they wouldn't feed. There might be a few lunker fish that for some reason didn't feed well during the pre-front frenzy and might still feed or be caught after the front, but generally not many.

Active feeding is often triggered by an approaching frontal system long before visible changes are noticed. You can't be sure when the fish are feeding but my catches indicate that as soon as the barometric pressure begins to change, some bass become activated and move to key feeding areas, and that can happen long before you become aware that a front is coming in. For example, if a front was coming in on Friday, the fish could already be reacting actively to the changing barometric pressure on Wednesday or Thursday. With a classic pre-frontal condition, cirrus clouds would first move in followed by increasing cloudiness and haze. Each day as the front got closer there would be more cloud and overcast until the skies were dark and threatening just prior to the actual front. But some fronts don't have the expected changes in sky patterns. I've seen days when

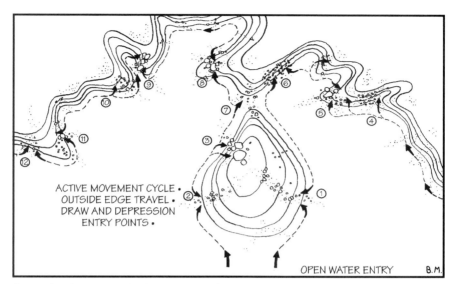

As active bass travel along an outside structural edge, they often pause or hold at key junctures.

1. A small stone/shale lead-in. Big bass normally don't move up on a spot like this, but they might hold at the key depth.

2. A gravel/clam bed lead-in with a slight depression which compounds the effect. More attractive to bigger fish.

3. Key boulders with a slight depression and fast drop. Definitely the prime big bass area on this saddle hump.

4. Slight depression with a cobblestone/hard clay bottom.

5. Small dog-leg point with key elements on outside edge.

6. An undercut shale bank which attracts traveling bass in that area. The saddle hump compounds the effect.

7. Actual saddle structures can be good depending on the bottom composition. Saddles generally have deeper water, more current and firm bottom conditions. If the saddle hump is out of water, wind generated current can make the saddle better.

8. A substantial point where the main rock structure is positioned between the outer and inner edge of the point. Bass tend to approach this spot from the sides rather than the point itself.

9. and 10. is a compound area where one spot enhances another spot. By anchoring in the bay and casting out, or anchoring off to the side and casting parallel, you could work both spots with each cast. Compound spots like this are conducive to a spawning area for big bass. Pre-spawn bass may hold on the rock slide into the draw off point (9), but they would spawn on the flat point (10) which has a clay bottom with scattered cobblestone and shells.

11. and 12. Two side entries on a long flat point. The small clump of isolated boulders(11) on the outer edge distinguishes itself as the key spot. Around the corner at (12) is a windswept undercut bank with hard bottom. Both of these spots can be fished from one boat position.

just a thin whisp of clouds was all the front brought with it, but it was a definite front and strongly influenced a good bite from the larger bass.

A front doesn't have to move directly through your area to be influential. At times your area may get bypassed by the actual front by 100 miles or more, but the barometric changes will still be influential; the skies remain bright and clear, but the fish still react to the barometric influence. Fronts associated with cloudless skies are hard to detect unless you keep an eye on a barometer. Sometimes excellent fishing suddenly stops without any noticeable change. If you study weather maps and watch a barometer you'll usually discover that a front had moved through even though it didn't influence your local weather.

In conclusion, I'd like to say that big bass can be caught at any time of day, but a pre-frontal influence with a falling barometer is the most consistent big bass pattern I know. When the barometer begins to change, nature is telling you something is happening and it's time to get serious. If there's a frontal system moving in, go lock into a key outside spot and fish it hard even if the same spot hasn't produced just a short time before. Conditions are changing and the big fish may be ready to move in. Make every effort to be in the right spot at the right time-a pre-frontal condition is one of the most reliable big fish patterns there is.

Moon Phases

Back in the 70's, San Diego outdoor writer Harlon Bartlett, asked me what I looked for when fishing for big bass, as he was doing an article for Outdoor Life. I told him that I liked pre-frontal conditions and a stable water level. Other than that, it's hunt and peck, just looking and working until you find the fish and a lure and color they'll bite.

"Well there has to be more to it than that?" Bartlett followed. I said, "No, it's just a lot of hard work. Other than that I have my moon phases."

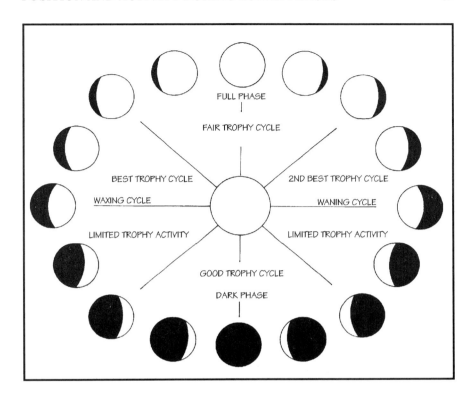

He took notes and we talked about lunar influences and 3/4 moon phases. My moon fishing wasn't as precise back then-usually for numbers of fish I liked the 2 to 3 days prior and after the dark of the moon, and for big fish I liked the 2 to 3 days prior and after a full moon. I hadn't studied it as much back then and I hadn't caught near as many big bass as I have now.

He called me on the phone about a week later and said that he had the article almost done and how he really liked it, but he was going to leave out my moon ideas. When I asked how come, he said it was too "Witch Doctory." He said that although a lot of trackers and commercial fishermen talked about lunar influences there had never been any proof, and he wanted to retain credence to the article.

Since those early days, more and more is being published about the connection between lunar influences and bass activity, but with the exception of spawning season, few writers have grasped the power moon phases can have on year-round bass fishing.

While many doubt that lunar influences have any significant bearing, my records indicate specific lunar energies influence both **ACTIVITY** and **POSITION**. Since 1970-the date I started keeping records-almost 70% of all the 8-pound-plus bass I've caught were taken during full moon cycles. And to get even more specific, almost 75% of all my 10-pound-plus fish were caught on either a 3/4 waxing (rising) or a 3/4 waning (setting) phase of the full moon cycle. (**SEE MOON CHART.**)

Some people believe lunar connections are pure coincidence but my findings are not unlike those experienced by bass anglers from other parts of the country. Even anglers who fish for northern pike, walleye and muskie often catch their biggest fish during identical moon phases.

The intriguing part about following moon phases is the discovery that certain lunar influences tend to **INTENSIFY** activity that is already taking place, and in some cases actually stimulates activity on their own. Take the spawning season for example. In southern California pre-spawn normally begins in late February, and the actual spawn generally takes place throughout March. But there is a time span in March when spawning activity intensifies! On the full moon cycles there will be more big bass in pre-spawn locations than at any other time in March. And the very best time to catch those cautious old females is during a 3/4 moon phase either on the waxing or waning stage. March is a month influenced by the spawn, but the best time in March is influenced by the moon. The full moon cycle stimulates giant bass to a point where they move and bite more aggressively.

The highest oceanic tides occur during full moon cycles when the sun and moon line up on an even plane and work together in a combined force. The 1/2 moon phases, when the sun and moon work against each other, create less gravitational pull and lower tides. It's interesting to note that although full and new moon cycles both create high lunar energies, lunker bass become more active and thus catchable during full moon cycles. For some reason I have never found the same consistency with dark new-moon cycles; for numbers of bass the dark cycle can be better, but the same has not proven true for lunkers. The best big bass feeding activity takes place during full moon cycles, and the best time of the full moon is during 3/4 phases. This reaction can be so dependable I follow tide charts and plan my fishing trips accordingly to the highest tides..

By fishing key outside structures all the time, I discovered that the two or three days around a 3/4 waxing and 3/4 waning moon phase were the two most consistent times each month to intercept large bass on structural elements. Although I might catch a big bass on any moon phase, the 3/4 phase has proved to be the time to catch the unusual trophy-size fish.

If a 5-pounder is considered a lunker in the lake you fish and the lake record is 8 pounds, if you fished a structure that the adult fish were using every day of the month, you probably would catch numbers of 3-to-5-pound bass almost any time there was a good pre-frontal condition, but you might catch several 6-pounders and maybe one over 7 pounds during that same pre-frontal condition on a 3/4 moon phase! Positive moon phases stimulate activity that is already taking place-a good day will get even better, but it has such a power influence on bigger bass, a big bass may even bite during a 3/4 phase when weather conditions are poor. A 3/4 phase represents a time when lunar energies stimulate big bass to move away from their neutral holding positions and move to the outer edges of key structural features. The only reason I know about this moon connection, is because so many times when I caught a "teen" fish, or had a limit of huge bass, after I got home and looked up into the sky, I'd always see a perfect 3/4 waxing or 3/4 waning moon!

Position and Activity

Another thing which may occur during the actual full moon is that sometimes bass feed so heavily during the 3/4 waxing phase, by the time the full moon arrives the fish may have already gorged themselves. In this situation, fishing on a full moon can be similar to fishing on the back side of a frontal system where the fish have already fed and are satisfied. By the time of the full moon big fish activity may have already peaked.

This dandy pre-spawn female fell to a large red crayfish stitched on an isolated edge spot during a 3/4 moon phase. It bit at 11:05 a.m. after waiting three hours without a bite.

As the full moon influences begin to cool off, the moon slides into the 3/4 waning or **EXIT** phase. As bass begin slowing down, they move in from open water chasing and out from shallow water foraging, and they once again start showing in good numbers along outer structural edges. Fishing can be good on a 3/4 waning moon but usually not as intense as on a 3/4 waxing moon. As the moon continues toward 1/2 phase on the waning side it continues to lose energy, and big fish begin dispersing toward their individual holding areas once again.

Successful moon fishing is simply a matter of patterning the moon periods that best suit your style of angling. Anglers who like full moon best will likely prefer shallow water because that's the time when bass fan out over the tops of structures or disperse into the shallows. Night fishermen also like full periods because full moon influences tend to cause a night bite rather than a daytime bite. Full moon is also good for trolling because active bass often roam open water areas off structure in search of shad schools and trolling is one of the best ways to catch them. If you like deep structure fishing, then 3/4 phases will be your best time because they represent the **APPROACH** and **EXIT** stages of structural movements. If you like to fish deep during pre-spawn, you'll want to intercept those fish on structure right at the 3/4 waxing stage. A few days later, when the moon is closer to full, a few individual big fish may get real active and move into the shallows where fishermen using spinnerbaits or surface plugs might do better. If you like to use fast presentations like crankbaits, spinnerbaits or trolling, you're more likely to have success during hot moon phases when the fish are active and chasing, but if you like jigs and plastics then you might have more success during periods when activity is less intense.

Moon fishing ultimately boils down to personal technique and areas fished, and this may be why some people like certain moon phases while others don't. Big bass can be caught on any moon phase and people that are successful have programed their own particular success to a certain moon phase pattern just as I have done. I like 3/4 stages because they represent the best time to catch numbers of big bass in relatively small areas where they are highly vulnerable to precise presentations.

Simply stating that fishing in general, can be good during a 3/4 moon is misleading because the best days for giant bass may not be productive for the bass population as a whole. A good day for big bass might equate into only one or two bites all day, that would be a **GOOD** day, it would mean there is a **POSITIVE** influence on big bass activity even though the rest of the bass population may remain neutral. Pre-frontal conditions normally stimulate bass of all sizes, but that doesn't always hold true with the best moon phases. One or

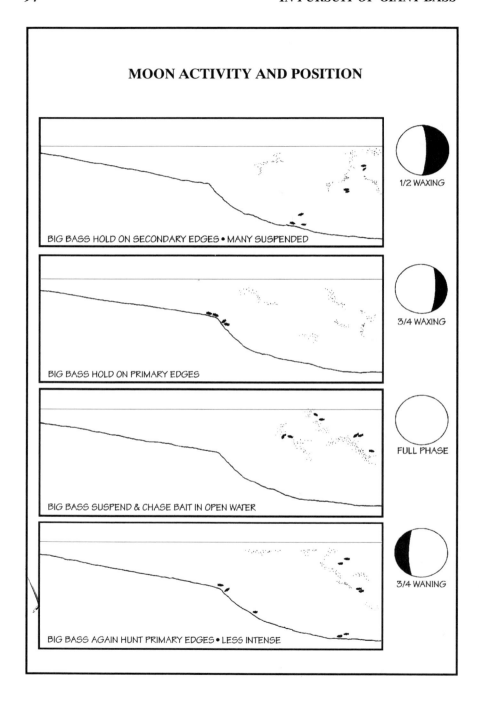

MOON ACTIVITY AND POSITION

two bites may not seem like much, but you have to realize that there aren't that many giant bass in **ANY** lake or reservoir and that trophy bass seldom group in significant numbers.

Timing Is Everything!

When you consider what time is the best time to fish, you have to think of the entire day as an active period. When I fish on a day with a 3/4 moon or pre-frontal condition, I have confidence that sometime during that day the big fish are going to be actively feeding. Initially, I'm not looking for a specific active period because I believe **THE WHOLE DAY WITH THE RIGHT CONDITIONS IS THE ACTIVE PERIOD**. The best time during that day will be sometime from early morning until late evening. Since I can't be sure when the movement will take place, I'll try to find a good big bass spot and fish it all day long. The specific daily active period for that day might only last 30 minutes so I make sure I'm in the right spot to intercept those fish when they move in.

While a certain moon phase can stimulate activity, the exact time of day is a result of many different things and is too complex and varied to predetermine. That's why I don't follow solunar tables. The exact time of day has too many local variables to follow with solunar tables. I'd rather use moon phases to get the best day, and then fish all day to establish the right time of day. There's only one way to find the current daily active period and that's to fish often and stay in-tune with what the fish are doing.

Timing on a spot is critical. There's no guarantee which day will have the most activity, and there can be a fine line between success and failure. You might be fishing exactly on a 3/4 waxing moon, but the best movement of big bass may have already taken place the day before the exact 3/4 phase. I've seen times when a buddy would fish a spot one day and I'd get on the same spot the next day, and one of us would make a great catch while the other got blanked. That's why I always try to fish for three days in a row during a prime 3/4 moon, two days after 1/2 moon, before full on the waxing side, and two days after full, the two days before 1/2 on the waning side. By sticking it out for several days in a row, I give myself a greater chance of

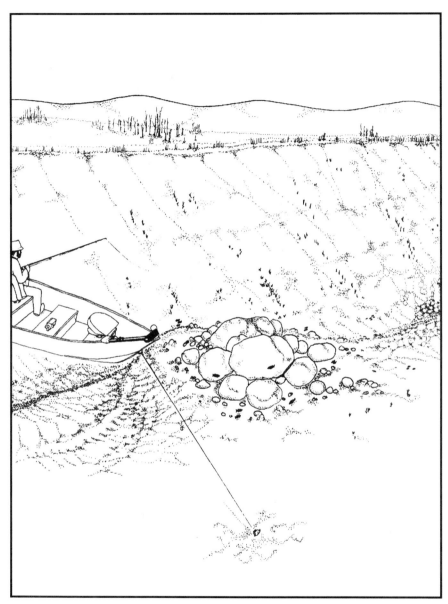

SUPER SPRING PRE-SPAWN SPOT: This illustration shows an angler fishing a spot similar to one that the author fished during one pre-spawn, key target is an isolated rock pile with a close channel that runs parallel with the adjacent bank. Far side of rock pile also drops into deep water. From this one spot alone in just six separate days the author caught and released twelve bass over nine pounds with four over thirteen.

contacting the best movement and making the system work. The same holds true when fishing a pre-frontal condition-fishing for three days in a row before the actual front arrives will give you a better chance than just fishing the very day of the front.

Old timers used to say that bass fishing was better early in the morning and late in the evening. Although much of this philosophy was based on the fact that most fishermen back then only worked shorelines where fishing is often best early and late, even deep water fishing can be better in early morning or late evening. There may be ideal conditions during midday hours but if the fish are on an early morning or late evening bite, it seems like the rest of the day doesn't matter.

When bass are feeding in early morning, the fish may already be working a spot when you get on the lake at first light, so you must approach your fishing area quietly and cautiously. Modern bass fishermen frequently motor close to a spot, cut the big engine and bang down the trolling motor all within a few yards of their target, but this procedure doesn't work for trophy bass. You should have everything ready and ease into a spot as quietly as possible being careful not to bang a tackle box lid or scrape a rod tip on the side of the boat.

When bass aren't biting early or late there's a good chance the peak daily active period will take place sometime around noon. The period from 10 a.m. until 3 p.m. is one of the best times for trophy fish. By late morning, as the sun continues to heat up the earth, subtle changes in air temperature, humidity and wind direction can promote prime activity during midday hours, and you have to stick it out on your best spots even though the sun is blazing and you're covered with sweat.

Sometimes daily active periods are fairly predictable. If conditions remain stable for several days in a row, sometimes the daily active period will be an hour later every day. If you caught bass at 2 p.m. on Sunday, when you fish again on Wednesday the bite should be around 5 p.m. Cyclic feeding cycles normally only occur during periods with stable conditions and they can be reliable until conditions change.

Normally, the exact time of the daily active period is impossible to predict in advance, but certain keys in nature can direct you to a certain spot at a certain time. During the course of the day I would be particularly alert to any changes in weather patterns. Bass are edge-oriented and any weather pattern change could be an influence edge bass would relate to. If I felt or noticed any weather change, regardless how slight or obscure, I would pursue it and treat it as a positive big bass pattern. If I hadn't been catching anything all day and noticed some type of weather change, I would instantly lock into a good spot and fish it hard; that change often signals a big fish bite.

A sudden warm spell, or a very warm humid part of the day that makes you take your jacket or shirt off, is almost always an indication a big bass bite is taking place or about to take place. I don't believe that air temperature has any influence on fish in deep water, but the air temperature is a **SYMPTOM** of something bigger that the fish do feel, like barometric pressure. An approaching frontal system, no matter how slight, pushes warm air and moisture before it and the hot, muggy conditions that make you uncomfortable are a symptom of the condition the fish feel.

All animals, including people, like nice conditions. During a cold day in winter, big bass are generally more active at midday or early afternoon after a bright sun has had a chance to penetrate the water for a while. If bass are holding at 55 ft. and it's a beautiful sunny day, those fish will often move up 5-or-6 ft. But if it's cloudy and cold they may move down 5-or-6 ft. Sunlight penetration has no temperature affect at that depth and I don't believe the movement of bass has any connection with air temperature, it's just something that happens; the bass move up simply because it's nice out. All animals react the same way. A pheasant might hide in cover when it's cold and rainy, but as soon as it gets warm and sunny, it comes out and begins browsing around. Warm, comfortable weather is generally very good for big bass fishing too. Big bass tend to bite well during harsh weather in early spring, but generally speaking, most of my biggest bass were taken during conditions where I didn't need a heavy jacket.

Big bass don't seem to have any noticeable sensitivity to light. I've watched big bass roaming around in clear water when the sun was very bright, and even though there were ample places to take cover, they seemed to enjoy basking in the sunshine.

A smooth glassy surface at times can kill a good bass bite, but a sudden change to a slight ripple can turn bass on like magic. When the surface is dead calm, light penetration is great and everything becomes outlined in detail. It's a poor time for bass to surprise prey, and they can see your line and lure in detail. But when a wind ripples the surface, the ripples cause sunlight to diffuse and a reaction from bass can be immediate. The diffused light makes the fish more relaxed and your line and presentation less obvious.

But wind can be your friend or worst enemy. Big bass like the security caused by strong wind and wave action, but strong winds can also make positioning, anchoring and presentation more difficult. A change in wind direction can cause bass to turn on or shut off because like air temperature, wind direction and strength are only a symptom of an overall weather system.

Cloud cover is often associated with good fishing-subdued or low-light conditions offer concealment from anglers and prey and tend to make big bass more relaxed and catchable-but I have found cloud cover to be no more important than how it fits into the overall weather system. As I stated before, cloudy days before a front can be excellent, whereas cloudy days after a front can produce poor results. But being aware of cloud patterns can put you in the right spot. If a front is moving in and the sky is clear, just a thin band of cloud cover can get those big fish active and moving, and watching this condition develop can direct you to fish a good spot at that time.

In Conclusion

When you're after the biggest bass in a lake you have to spend time and effort and keep after them until you hit the right day; you can't ask them to bite when you want them to. You may think you can predict when they'll hit, but it doesn't always work that way.

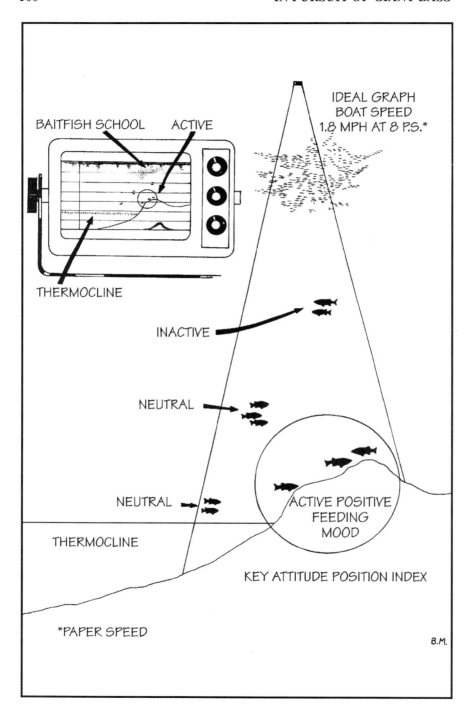

BAITFISH SCHOOL   ACTIVE

IDEAL GRAPH
BOAT SPEED
1.8 MPH AT 8 P.S.*

THERMOCLINE

INACTIVE

NEUTRAL

NEUTRAL

ACTIVE POSITIVE
FEEDING
MOOD

THERMOCLINE

KEY ATTITUDE POSITION INDEX

*PAPER SPEED

B.M.

In reality, you have to fish a lot and spend a lot of time on a body of water to become intimate with current active periods. When you fish the same lake often, you learn from trial and error where and when the fish are biting, and this backlog of current information helps you predict the best daily activity. But when you don't fish often and are always approaching a lake cold without any background knowledge, it takes even experienced anglers time to establish current spots and current active patterns.

The only way to properly evaluate a lake is to fish hard from dawn until dark. You can't give up at 4 p.m. and expect the fish to bite when you're there. Part of being a good trophy fisherman is having the endurance to withstand all the elements and stick with it until the fish get active. A good fisherman takes enough clothing to be comfortable in any weather, and he takes rain gear even on sunny days. A good fisherman copes with strong wind and rain and everything else because he wants to catch big bass on every trip.

A good poker player will always win. He won't win every hand but if you play him long enough he'll eventually get all your money because a good poker player knows what to look for. He knows how to look at you-the rhythm of your hands, how you feel, how many beers you've had, and what your state of mind is. When you get to a point where you start making bad decisions, a good player is going to wait for that moment and take you! A good bass fisherman does the same things! Regardless of how long it takes, he waits out the conditions until the fish are most vulnerable, and when they move up during a peak active period, the smart angler will be in a perfect position to take full advantage.

Big bass fishing is a game of thinking and timing, but you should never let conditions prevent you from fishing whenever you can because the chances of getting the exact set of conditions that worked before is like playing the lottery-there's no way to calculate it. Your next best-fishing-day may have completely different characteristics, yet they all fall into place. You should fish whenever you can and try to establish what works at that particular time.

Having too many concrete, scientific rules could hamper your fishing to a point where you won't go fishing if, for example, the moon isn't exactly right. I have always stated that there is a correlation between certain moon phases and big bass activity, and I believe that intently, but I don't want to influence anyone into thinking that just because the moon isn't 3-days-before or 3-days-after full that fishing would be a waste of time. Bass are free spirits in their world, and too much cause-and-effect thinking takes the freedom out of fishing.

SYSTEM ANCHORING

How you approach a spot reflects how seriously you want to catch a trophy bass. If your goal is to catch the very biggest bass, then you should approach a spot like you were after a hummingbird or sparrow; you would use everything in your power to sneak up on that spot so you wouldn't scare anything that might be there. That's the way to trick big bass consistently on pressured lakes where lunkers are extra-sensitive to unnatural movements and noise.

If there is one single factor which separates making a respectable catch or making an outstanding catch, it's the atmosphere a person creates while fishing. The sensitivities trophy bass have toward natural and unnatural atmospheres can't be stressed enough. Older bass know the natural sounds of a spot, and they can distinguish unnatural sounds fishermen make. The fish might not be able to correlate those sounds with fishermen on the surface, but simply being unnatural is enough to cause them to instinctively go off their feed. Because of these sensitivities, fishing a spot from a stationary position is one of the most important aspects of my big bass system. Anchoring lets you post up on a spot and create a natural atmosphere which allows big bass to feel more secure. There are times when how you handle the boat is the difference between catching a few nice bass or catching the trophy of your life.

Creating a Natural Atmosphere

The birth of trolling motors gave anglers a new freedom of maneuverability unknown in the history of the sport. Anchoring and fan-casting was the way many of the early pioneers fished for bass, but trolling motors allowed anglers to check spots quickly without anchoring, and moving-and-hunting became a more popular strategy than sitting-and-waiting.

THE EFFICIENCY OF THE SMALL FISHING MACHINE:

If thoughtfully outfitted, the small fishing boat can out-perform any larger boat available today. Some of the primary features are:

1. Highly maneuverable in tight places; 2. Slow metering and trolling speed; 3. Stable anchoring in the wind with moderate anchor weight; 4. Low profile and unintrusive silhouette; 5. Efficient fuel economy; 6. Low trailer height, easy launch in shallow water.

As tournament popularity grew in the 70's and 80's, moving-and-hunting evolved into running-and-gunning. Advancements in trolling motor designs and techniques allowed anglers to fish with remarkable speed and efficiency. Fishing fast for active "biters" became commonly accepted as the best way to put bass in the boat.

Fast fishing influenced deep water fishermen as well. Instead of working slowly and carefully from an anchored position, the new breed of bass anglers used trolling motors to get directly over a spot and fish vertically, or to follow contours and cast. After a few vertical checks or passes along a drop-off, if a spot failed to produce the angler would motor off to another spot in search of biting bass.

Fishing fast proved excellent for finding and catching bass quickly, but as more and more anglers discovered how to find prime areas, fishing pressure tripled in key spots. As a direct effect of this pressure, bass began getting harder to catch and in many cases wouldn't respond to standard methods.

Perceptive anglers who realized things were changing began staying away from the fish, making longer casts and took increasing measures not to spook the fish.

Trolling motor companies tell you their units are quiet and don't spook fish, and that may be true compared to large gas engines, but I've been anchored on spots in the middle of an excellent bite when someone came down a bank using a trolling motor on full throttle and their intrusion shut off my fish instantly!

I believe lunker bass react to intrusions similar to the way birds scatter when disturbed. If a bunch of sparrows were feeding in your back yard and you walked out onto the back porch and scared them off, initially it looks like they all flew away, but most birds stay fairly close in the trees and bushes. If you sit down and remain quiet, eventually most of the birds come back. When one sparrow flies down and cautiously resumes feeding, a few more come down, and in a matter of minutes dozens of birds are pecking and scratching just like before your intrusion.

Big bass react to fishing pressure much the same way. After you anchor and remain quiet, eventually the fish become as relaxed as before your intrusion and they begin feeding again as if you weren't even there. The first bite is often the hardest to get, but after one bite it often raises the awareness of other bass and it seems like one bite triggers another.

You can look a spot over with a trolling motor or with the big engine running but it doesn't matter because either way your intrusion will disturb the more sensitive fish. But once you decide to fish a spot, you'd be wise to stop moving around and anchor in place.

Anchoring creates a natural atmosphere. The longer your boat remains in one spot the more of a familiar atmosphere it creates. Consequently, if your boat is in one position long enough, **THE BOAT BECOMES PART OF THE SPOT ITSELF!** The sounds you make become part of the natural environment of that particular spot. The

To compound the effectiveness of an anchor position, care must be taken to align on the exact piece of high potential structure within the overall structure itself.

bass are aware of your presence, but unless you make unusual noises or movements like banging a tackle box lid or scraping a rod tip, even the rhythmic sounds of waves slapping your boat will eventually seem natural to the fish and they will be relaxed and feed vigorously.

Bass will get used to anything as long as it remains in one spot and isn't always changing positions. It's not that you can't catch giant bass from a moving boat, it happens-especially in pre-spawn and spawn when bass are so caught up in the spawning ritual, they become super aggressive and readily bite even with a boat directly overhead-but I'm talking about the rest of the year when attention to the smallest detail is ultra important in getting the biggest bass to bite consistently.

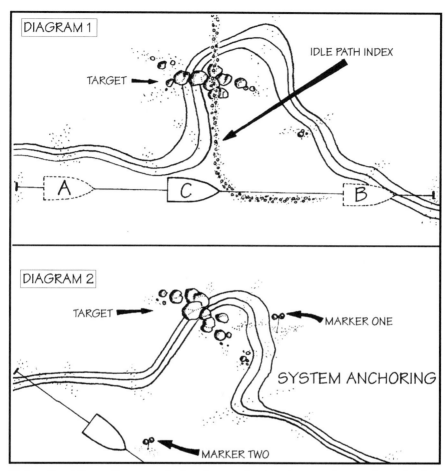

Using the idle path as an index for anchoring is an advanced anchoring method. Once you idle over the target structure, estimate where you want your boat to be in order to cast over the target spot on a long cast, and turn the boat and put it in reverse at that position (C). Back the boat into position (A) first and drop off the first anchor there. Let the anchor rope out, and drop a second anchor at position (B). Let the rope play from the second anchor as you pull back toward (C) on the rope from the first anchor. When you reach position (C), cinch off the first anchor rope, and then tighten and cinch the second anchor rope.

When first learning how to anchor it's often best to use marker buoys. Drop one buoy as a reference for your target area. Calculate the proper anchoring position to fish target effectively on a long cast and drop a second buoy at that spot. Go back and pick up the first buoy, then anchor and pick up the second buoy which should be right beside your boat. Using a marker buoy is great when your target is one isolated rock or stump; it gives you the confidence to know exactly where that target is.

True Angling Potential

If you're satisfied catching one or two bass from a spot then attention to detail won't seem important, but you should always ask yourself, **"WHAT WOULD BE THE POTENTIAL IF I DID EVERYTHING RIGHT!"**

The only way to experience the true potential of a spot is to correctly anticipate an all-day active period and get anchored into position before the daily active period takes place. Ideally, you want to be set up before the time of peak activity arrives, quietly waiting for the bass to move in.

You can't be traveling around searching for fish during an active period because you'll probably miss them. Timing is everything! If the bass are biting early, you can't get on that spot late. If you move in when the active period is in full swing, chances are your boat activity will upset the natural atmosphere of the spot and spook the bigger fish. You might still catch a few but you won't experience the same results as if you did everything right.

I once watched a TV expert fishing Truman Lake, Missouri in summer. He was fishing an underwater hump surrounded by standing timber. His technique was to motor up to the spot, drop the trolling motor right on top of the structure and begin casting a jig and pig. He'd catch a bass or two, leave the spot for about an hour or so, and then return and catch a few more fish. In the final analysis, he said that he was catching all the fish off that spot and by the time he returned a few more had moved in.

You can't assume that just because you can't catch them that the fish aren't there. Ask yourself what would be the potential if you did everything right. Motoring up to a spot and fishing quickly almost guarantees that you'll only catch a few bass on a pressured lake. You can walk right up to a deer in situations where they're used to people, but you can't do the same where deer are hunted! On a day with high activity, where groups of bass are moving in and out of a spot all day long, if you quietly anchored and didn't move, chances are you could catch good numbers of bass throughout the day. By hopping in and out of the spot, the TV expert probably only caught about 25% of the potential catch that could be achieved by anchoring, and he probably wasn't even on the spot during the prime time of day when possibly a giant fish became active and moved in.

It's surprising how few people realize that bass can be alerted by loud noises above water, but we don't have lateral lines; we can't feel the same vibrations they do. We have to put our hands on the transducer just to know that it's sending out vibrations. I don't believe deep water bass are unduly disturbed by above water sounds (although I've seen fish on the surface spook when you yell), but when you fish for giant bass I believe you should be quiet; you shouldn't talk real loud, or make any loud sharp noises whether airborne or not. It may not spook the fish but a loud noise might upset their biting attitude. Maybe it's my own superstition, but I think there's a certain attitude an angler should have when pursuing giant bass. It's a total package. You can't be loud in the boat and expect to have a quiet spot. A normal low conversation doesn't seem to bother a thing, but when you're loudly talking to another angler across water, I think these noises can be felt underwater.

Sometimes I'll just use the weight of the hook to sink a plastic worm when fish are extra finicky. If I throw a weightless worm it may take a minute to sink, but that may be the only presentation a giant bass will hit. This might seem like slow fishing but you have to remember that you're in their environment-you have to give up something. I'm not the kind of fisherman that demands action on every cast, that's not what I'm after. If my presentation takes 15 minutes, that's OK. I'll take as long as it takes and do whatever it takes to make a bass hit my offering. I try to approach a spot and anchor a spot in the way an artist sets up a picture. That's why I get so upset when someone comes close and meters my spot to see what I'm fishing; it's like they just spilled ink on my picture. I might have planned this trip for a week, and then some angler motors over my spot and ruins the atmosphere that took hours to set up. And if I yell at them, they think I'm unsportsmanlike. They don't realize what went into setting up that spot.

Anchoring for big bass parallels hunting for the biggest most cautious buck in the forest. Walking around and tracking a buck in dry leaves would be out of the question because it'll hear you coming.

A better approach is to find a clearing or deer crossing where you've monitored fresh tracks for several weeks and know deer are passing. Once you discover the crossing, you sit in a stand and silently wait for the animals to come to you. The more you cover your sounds and smells, the more successful your deer hunting will be. That's exactly how you hunt for giant bass when you anchor on a prime structure during a 3/4 moon phase or pre-frontal condition. Visualizing the underwater world of bass may be more difficult than reading visible deer signs, so you have to understand things that make up a big bass spot-like bottom composition, security, depth, relationship to deep water-in order to correctly anchor in the right position. If you arrive at the spot late and the movement of bass has already taken place, sometimes an angler with good anchoring ability can quietly slide in without interrupting the feeding activity, but ideally, if you want to uncover the true potential of any spot, you should anticipate the active period in advance and be set up and anchored before the fish move in from their individual holding areas.

Anchoring Equipment

To make anchoring work, it's important to have the right equipment. You're not going to be happy if you drift into a spot and kill a big bass bite because of poor equipment.

System anchoring starts with an efficient anchor. An anchor needs to hold on hard bare bottom like flat shale or decomposed granite, as well as the easier-to-hold situations like a ledge, weeds, brush or soft bottom composition. A good anchor has to grab securely on a flat bottom even in a strong wind; it can't slide or roll.

The most ideal way to anchor is up against the side of a ledge or drop-off. The wind should be pushing the boat toward the drop forcing the anchors to dig deeper all the time. But sometimes you can't anchor exactly in the most ideal position and the wind can blow you off a ledge-this is the toughest situation to anchor. So an anchor needs prongs that have extra grab for those hard-to-hold conditions. The anchors I make lay flat and the prongs and neck dig into the bottom; wind and wave action actually make it dig deeper.

Author's custom-made 18 lb. steel anchor.

Commercial anchors shouldn't even be considered. Anchors such as navy, mushroom and river anchors all slide over certain terrain in strong wind or current. Heavier models (25 lbs. and up) might hold but they're too heavy to raise up and down all day.

The anchors I build hold by design not weight. If the design is right you'll get the best holding power without added weight; the weight just helps the design work better. They weigh approximately 18 lbs. which is fairly comfortable to use all day. My anchors plane better and land softer, and they don't make unnecessary noise caused by sliding and rolling-once they set on the bottom they stay put!

Note how rear prongs plus front tangs assist in bottom retention.

If you're serious about anchoring, you should go the extra mile and have anchors custom made or make your own. My anchors are made from a single piece of 1-inch steel cut to shape. (See Diagram) You can also make very efficient and inexpensive anchors at home out of a 1-gallon can, a sack of concrete, and 1/4-inch steel rods. It's essential to have a quick-release on your anchors for those occasions when it gets lodged under an old tree or slides under a rock.

For anchor line I like 3/4 or 1/2-inch soft braided nylon rope; it is easier on your hands and it has more cushion in case a big bass wraps your line around it. White rope has proven more effective than camouflage green or brown. When a hooked bass sees a brown or green rope, it often confuses the rope for some type of cover and wraps around it. But white is more visible and when bass see a white anchor rope, the color spooks them and they usually avoid it. Never use hard polypropylene rope; it's rough on the hands and bass can easily bust your line on it.

Anchoring is best performed in a small maneuverable boat. A light-weight boat 16 ft. or less is excellent for metering structure and anchoring on fairly short ropes.

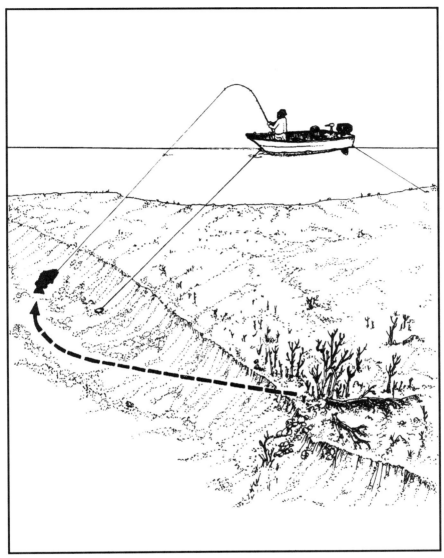

Anchoring so you can cast across a spot and work back along the ledge is the most ideal anchoring position. This position allows the greatest area of high-potential structure to be covered on each cast. Plus you're in a perfect position to play a big bass after it heads toward open water.

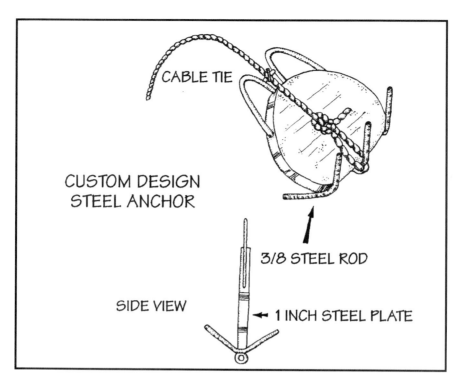

CABLE TIE

CUSTOM DESIGN
STEEL ANCHOR

3/8 STEEL ROD

SIDE VIEW   ← 1 INCH STEEL PLATE

Large, heavy boats aren't suited to precise anchoring. Metering a spot properly for precise anchoring is difficult with a steering wheel (It's much easier with tiller steering), but if a wheel is what you have, you should meter and move into position with a trolling motor. Heavier boats also require longer anchor lines and heavier anchors to hold in place.

To anchor effectively you have to evaluate a spot correctly. You have to determine a subliminal area on the structure and whether it breaks in two or three different directions. When you anchor you want to be in a position that allows you to fish the outside lip of the drop-off because that's where big bass lay. Never anchor with the intention of fishing the entire structure. You should have a specific spot within that area, in mind before you secure the boat. Anchoring should be so precise, you want every cast to hit the spot just right to maximize the potential of each cast.

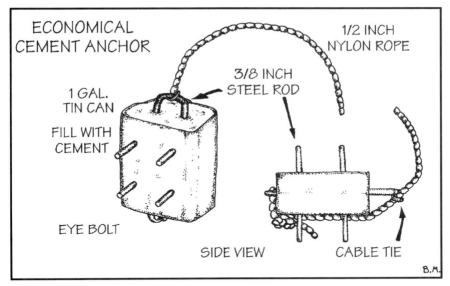

Author's do-it-yourself anchor.

Ideally, you want to be anchored where you can reach the spot comfortable with a long cast. If you aren't making a long cast to reach slightly beyond your target, you're anchoring too close. Anchoring away from a spot allows the fish to relax faster, and a long cast is more conducive to landing huge bass in open water. A giant bass over 13 lbs. has the advantage when hooked on a short line, but on a long cast there's more stretch in the line and it's harder for a giant bass to break off. Once the fish has been worked near the boat, it will be worn down to a point where playing it on a short line isn't so critical.

The next ideal position would have the wind coming directly into the front of the boat. A frontal wind won't move your boat if you're anchored correctly with the right kind of anchors.

Once you anticipate the wind direction and how it will drift the boat, drop an anchor off the back end keeping tension on the rope as it slides through your fingers. As soon as the anchor hits bottom, play out extra slack and tie it off to a cleat at the rear of the boat. At this point, walk up to the front of the boat (or alert your partner) and drop a second anchor. After the front anchor hits bottom, let out about 10-or-12 ft. of slack and tie off. Slowly take up the slack on the back rope until both anchors are holding and retie to the cleat. Sometimes you will have to play more rope off the front and tighten up the back or vice versa, but both ropes should come off the boat at a nice angle when finished.

I like to use as short a rope as possible and still hold. Usually, a properly anchored boat will have ropes coming into the water at a 45 degree angle (45 degrees parallel to the bottom ending at the back and front of the boat). The ropes should be at a similar angle to a comfortable retrieve with a jig and pig. You don't want to let out too much anchor rope because if a big bass makes a long horizontal run around the boat it could tangle and break you off.

Once you're anchored in a good position and can reach the structure with a long cast, it would be wise to exercise patience for the fish to become relaxed or for an active period to begin. Since you don't want to disturb the spot any more than is absolutely necessary, try to remain seated and keep a low profile; standing and moving about can create underwater shadows that may cause fish to spook even in murky water. I've seen occasions where every time I stood up to play and land a bass, my movements shut the bite down for almost 20 minutes. But if I remained seated when playing a bass, I could get another bite quickly, sometimes on the very next cast.

I always try to use live bait or expendable lures like plastic worms when anchored. You can't keep pulling up the anchors and disturbing the atmosphere every time to hang up an expensive crankbait. If you do decide to retrieve your lure, snagged lures can sometimes be collected without too much damage by letting out the anchor ropes and allowing the wind to drift the boat over the lure before pulling the boat back to it's original position. The boat might temporarily spook the bite but if it's a positive active period and you weren't too noisy, the bite should resume a short time after the spot quiets down again.

Retrieve Angle

To fish a spot effectively you have to know how to read it. Sometimes it's best to fish from an angle, sometimes you fish up a draw. If you're fishing a point, sometimes it's best to anchor up on it or off to the side. Sometimes you have to cast across a point and

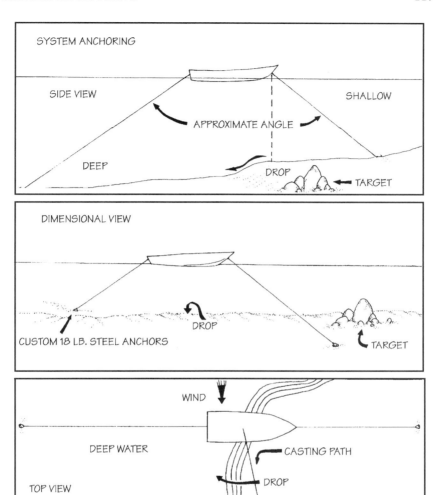

Ideally, the angle of the anchor rope to the bottom should be at about 45 degrees. However, wind velocity and bottom conditions may alter this approach. When anchoring on brush-covered bottom, for example, where you know the anchors will hold securely, you can anchor on fairly short ropes. But in a windy condition with a fairly clean and clear bottom, you'll need more rope. The reason why I tend to use a shorter anchor rope on the shallow side is because I normally approach a spot from the deep side, and I drop an anchor on the deep side first. Placing anchors on the deep and shallow side of a drop-off allows a perfect casting angle parallel to the structure.

make your retrieve come up one side and down the other. Every spot is different and has it's own personality. To extract the true potential from a spot you have you know how to read it so you can anchor in the right position.

The retrieve angle and path are critical because many times a big bass will only hit a bait presented or pulled through a spot in a certain way or angle. If the key break or subliminal spot on a structure happened to be a large boulder and the bass were laying underneath it, the only cast that would trigger a strike is one which comes over and drops by the fish at the right angle. A cast next to the sides of a rock or parallel to the boulder face might not have the same appeal as a bait suddenly dropping right into their face.

Most of the time it's better to anchor a spot and throw out. My most consistent retrieve angle throughout the years for the biggest bass has been working UP a ledge or piece of cover. With the exception of rock piles most structures seem to produce better when fishing uphill. But that doesn't mean your anchoring position has to always be shallow. Oftentimes, I'll anchor off the deep side of a spot and cast across the spot working uphill on one side and downhill on the other. It always seems like the trophy fish are triggered by a presentation coming up a structure or piece of cover, or cresting a spot and just starting down the other side.

When you cast out and work uphill you create a different presentation or look than working down a slope. When you work out from a spot the line lays along the bottom and is camouflaged; when pulling off a spot the line is in the open and easily seen. Working uphill causes your lure or bait to constantly fight the bottom; sticking, popping and pulling on contour and pieces of cover as it moves along. It's a much more difficult way to fish, but a bait which is constantly struggling over and through bottom features is very appealing to big bass.

Working up a slope can actually trigger a strike just by the presentation angle. If a big bass was watching and following a bait that is being retrieved uphill, the fish is decompressing all the time and the feeling in its air bladder is telling it to make a decision soon before the prey gets away because it doesn't want to go much shallower. In this case, the retrieve angle actually stimulated the fish

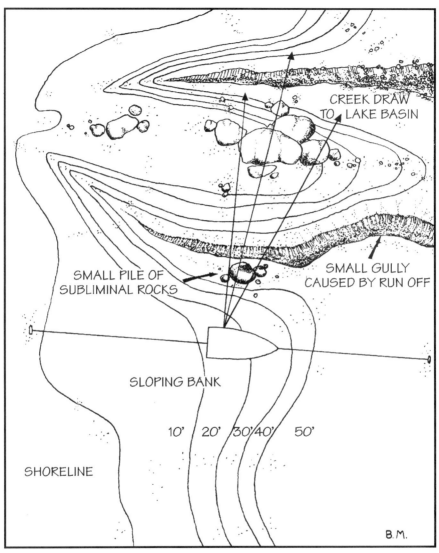

The more you know about a spot the more you can make each cast work for you. After close examination with electronics and extensive casting to feel various bottom contents and subliminal areas, it is determined that the key anchoring position is off to the side of the structure. The key deep water access channels are along the sides of the point and this is where big bass move in and out of the spot; the tip of the point is too flat. By anchoring off to the side, you can reach the channel draw on the far side, come up the draw, over the high spot, down the other side into the second draw, up the draw and over the subliminal rock cluster. Each cast covers a maximum amount of high-potential structure, and may intercept bass in any stage of activity.

into a hasty decision. But if you were fishing out from the spot and retrieving into deeper water, that bass could have followed at its leisure without having to make a quick decision because it feels more secure in deep water. It may follow until it detects your boat and turns off. Maybe the fish didn't actually see your boat but the sound of slapping waves and the boat shadow may have convinced the fish there was something out there that shouldn't be.

Rock piles are the only structures that aren't conducive to working uphill. Retrieving up a rocky structure hinders presentation and you'll be constantly snagged. To fish a pile I'll generally anchor to one side and work down the side that breaks into deep water.

Rather than casting directly onto or directly off a structure, it's often better to anchor off to one side and cast out and across or in and across. Anchoring off to one side creates a retrieve angle which makes hooking big fish more efficient. The problem with anchoring out and working directly off a spot is that when a bass hits it'll run toward deeper water 90% of the time; this means a hooked bass will come right toward you and the hookset could pull your bait straight out of its jaws. When anchored off to one side, however, the fish will still move out into deeper water, but because you're setting the hook from a side angle you'll have a much higher percentage of solid hookups.

Fast Anchoring

Good big bass fishermen have the imagination to perceive all the ingredients that big bass are looking for, and they have the confidence in what they know to predict where the fish will be and when they will be there. A good fisherman may move into a key spot during a good feeding period, and because he is keyed into the right retrieve path and knows he is putting his lure exactly where it should be and is indexing the key spot just right, if he hasn't got bit after half a dozen casts, he may decide that the fish aren't there and move to another spot.

The faster and cleaner you can anchor without wasted time and unnecessary movement, the faster the fish will return to a normal state after you upset the spot. If your anchoring technique is good and you haven't disturbed the spot too much, usually by the end of the second

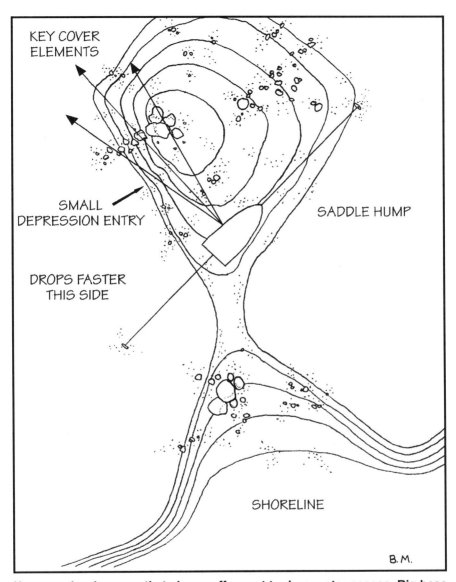

KEY COVER
ELEMENTS

SMALL
DEPRESSION ENTRY

DROPS FASTER
THIS SIDE

SADDLE HUMP

SHORELINE

B. M.

Never anchor in a way that closes off a spot to deep water access. Big bass move in and out from a spot via the best access to deep water, consequently, you never want the position of your boat to disrupt their movements. By anchoring off to the side, a large fish can move in and out freely, totally unaware of the boat.

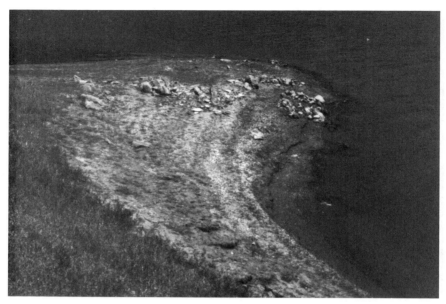

Finger-like projection off the side of a larger point with a hard bottom content, scattered rocks and shells right off the edge of a deeper channel. This is the key feature on the larger structure to target.

or third cast (slow retrieve) the fish should be back to normal-they should be on key spots in the same state as before you anchored. It doesn't take the fish long to regroup if your technique is good.

However, for the novice angler with a sloppier approach, it might take as much as an hour for the fish to calm down enough to bite. For inexperienced anglers who lack the confidence to know if a certain spot has potential, it would be better to sit and fish for several hours to see if any fish move in. Fishing a spot half a day or more may be the only way to correctly evaluate a potential spot.

If you anchored on a spot and quickly boated a 4-pounder and missed another, that would be the time to sit tight for a while. If you didn't get another bite, you might assume that you hit the tail end of an active period or spooked the fish out for some reason, but it would be worth your effort to stay in that spot for an hour or more to see what happens. It could be a day when different groups of bass move in and out all day long. So you have to play it by ear and let your intuition and the activity of the spot dictate how long you stay.

Sometimes when I'm quickly checking spots just to see if there's activity, I may use only one anchor off the back of the boat and let the wind from my back hold the boat somewhat stationary. As long as the wind isn't too strong, it won't push the boat too far to the right or the left. The whole idea is to fish fast and get a general idea if there's biting fish in the area. If I find activity, I'll use the trolling motor, drop the front anchor and cinch them both off. Fishing with only one anchor is an excellent way to check a spot quickly in low-wind situations.

Trolling Motors - When And Where

For using a jig and pig, a crankbait or a spinnerbait, I feel the best approach is with a trolling motor. All these baits are "active" baits and they aren't conducive to a stationary position. I may anchor to stabilize my boat in current or a strong wind, but basically when I use active baits I like to cover ground and work for bass that will strike something that jumps by them.

What about the spooking nature of trolling motors? When fishing active baits you're not constantly on the trolling motor. You use it only to position the boat and keep it in the right place. Most of the time you drift through an area and just kick the trolling motor on here and there to position. Also, you'll be casting ahead of the boat which is less disturbing. The fish that bite active baits are often more aggressive and a boat won't spook them nearly as bad. Active fish bite active baits, and careful positioning with a trolling motor rarely interferes with the bite. But if bass aren't responding to active baits, it's a signal that a more deliberate technique like anchoring would likely work better.

Early in the chapter I mentioned how anglers moving into my fishing area with a trolling motor would shut off my fish. These anglers were moving at high speeds around me and these fish could definitely feel it. Once you create an atmosphere, sustained trolling motor usage at high speeds can spook fish. In other words, the only boat those fish were aware of was the boat coming through. They had already accepted my boat as a natural object in that spot, and the intrusion of the trolling motor is what turned them off. I know this from observing the way they were biting before and after the intrusion.

Troll motoring is one of the best techniques ever invented for bass fishing, but trolling motors only represent a part of the sport -not all of it! Looking for these big fish with just one tool is too limiting. You have to use different techniques at different times, otherwise you won't catch big fish year-round. You can become a specialist, but your technique won't be productive all year. I know some guys who only fish a jig and pig, and when the fish are responding to jigs they really do well. But two weeks later the fish are responding better to anchoring techniques and these guys suffer. To be consistent, an angler needs to do both, and learn when one technique ends and the other begins. A guy who's really tuned-in with a jig and pig will make it work longer and better than a guy who uses a jig only on occasion, but there are times when other techniques completely overshadow a jig.

Controlled trolling should be viewed in the same light. At times big bass will be in situations where trolling with your outboard engine is the best technique. It doesn't mean that at the same time a guy couldn't fish the same water and catch a nice bass on a jig, but when trolling is the technique they want, a troller might outproduce a jig fisherman 5 to 1.

If you really love the sport of bass fishing you should want to know how to do it all. A truly versatile angler strives to find what works best under all conditions. Using a trolling motor is a great technique, but you'll catch more big bass consistently if you learn to anchor. At times, anchoring is the only way to extract the true big fish potential from pressured lakes. Anchoring is a system born of necessity. To use the stitching method properly, you will have to fish from a completely stationary boat with no movement-that's why I believe in double anchoring, it's a technique for a technique.

"STITCHING" THE ULTIMATE STRUCTURE TECHNIQUE FOR BIG BASS

In the early years of plastic worm fishing out West, the popular way to rig a worm was on the back of a weedless jig head or on a jig made with various types of hair. Bass loved worms right from the start, and whenever you found bass they would usually pounce on jig-worm combinations. But using a worm on the back of a jig had drawbacks. First of all, it was hard to work a jig through areas with

Early jig designs with pork trailers. Author made weedguards from orthodontic wire which is finer and more sensitive than commercial wire weedguards.

heavy brush or jumbled rock and I was constantly busting off jigs. Another problem was the fact that big bass could easily throw the heavier jigs. You could land the 2-and-3-pounders, but it seemed like it would never fail, whenever you hooked a big bass it would jump and use the jig as leverage to throw the hook. To counter these problems, I began experimenting with a split shot rig I was using to fish pork rind eels at that time. I'd hook a plastic worm through the nose with a weedless hook that I modified using orthodontic wire (which was much finer and more sensitive than commercial weedguards), and I'd crimp a small split shot to the line about 8 inches above the hook. This rig had immediate impact! Unlike a jig which often hung up on deep structure, the split shot rig was so light it could easily be flipped and popped through thick cover without continually snagging, consequently I could now fish plastic worms in areas where I could never use a jig and worm. In addition, the light rig was hard for bass to leverage out of their mouths and I landed almost every big bass hooked. And as an added bonus, I discovered that bass wouldn't

Pork rind eels rigged on modified weedless hooks were the author's first introduction to stitching.

instantly reject a plastic worm rigged with a split shot as they sometimes did with a worm rigged on a jig. If you fed them line without resistance, a bass might hold onto a split shot worm indefinitely! Obviously, the lighter weight made all the difference, and the split shot rig has been one of my favorite plastic worm techniques ever since.

Because split shot fishing is such a light presentation only the most obvious bites and snags could be felt by working the rig with the rod tip as in conventional worm fishing. To increase my sensitivity or feel, I began holding and retrieving the line with my fingertips. By dragging the worm across the bottom, slowly inching it along with my fingertips, every bottom contour and detail generated into my hand. I now had the ability to feel every rock, stick and pebble my worm came in contact with, as well as every peck, bump and pressure bite from bass. Working the rig with my fingertips was so sensitive I used it as my depth finder and the sensations from the rig became my underwater eyes-I worked the bottom as a blind person and used the split shot rig as my cane. With practice came interpretation skills far beyond anything I had ever imagined when fishing a jig with the rod tip. I could feel the rig pulling uphill over clay bottom, scraping across little isolated rocks, falling off a 2-inch ledge, sticking to moss, even the shaking of the worm caused by a patch of gravel, and the closing of tiny shells as I worked it through an active clam bed. All these sensations were transmitted up the line and into my fingers. How could the finest graphite or boron rod ever compare to trained fingers with a direct link to the ultimate computer-the human brain? Working even the heaviest jig with the rod tip alone only gave me a fraction of these feelings. After further experimentation I refined the hand-held technique into a system of structure fishing which I coined as "Stitching" after the way you manipulate or stitch the line with your fingers.

Stitching isn't revolutionary, it's really an old idea that's been by-passed by modern anglers. Almost every kid who ever fished a small stream for trout or chubs know they can feel the fish bite better by holding the line rather than relying on a stiff pole. Off shore anglers have been using hand-held techniques for years-after casting out a live bait they put their reels in free-spool and hold the line in their hand; when a strike is felt the fish is allowed to run some distance before setting the hook. Holding the line is one of the most basic fishing methods ever invented. All I did was refine the technique for largemouth bass and create a system that applies to structured lake environments.

The disadvantage of fishing with a split shot is that it is a very time-consuming presentation. The rig takes time to sink, and it has to be fished slowly, otherwise the worm rises too far off the bottom. This is definitely not an effective way to cover large areas in a limited time frame. However, stitching is an excellent way to extract the maximum potential from a spot once bass are found. The slow, careful, almost painstaking retrieve is the key! There will always be days when bass thump heavy jig and worms and crush the life out of a spinnerbait with huge blades, but on days when bass turn their noses up at worms fished with heavy sinkers, split shot rigs are deadly. And even on those days when bass hang onto the heavy stuff, a skilled angler can generally catch more and bigger bass by stitching a split shot rig. On many occasions I've moved right into spots vacated by other boats and made big catches with this rig when other people struck out with conventional rigs. But not everyone is geared to fish this way. Personally, I feel the advantages are worth waiting for the rig to sink and the extra patience needed to fish it properly. Bass would hit anything in the old days, but modern fish are more selective; it is these hard-to-catch bass that are prone to hit a super slow presentation inched along the bottom. Your overall system should appeal to fish under all conditions and not just on the best days, otherwise you'll only have one good day occasionally instead of many memorable ones!

The Split Shot Rig

Although my split shot rig appears simple enough, countless hours have gone into selecting the most effective hook, type and weight of shot, and placement of shot on the line. All split shot rigs are not equal, and when it comes to catching trophy bass from pressured lakes, your attention to the smallest details can make a big difference!

Many years ago I was taught an important lesson about the relationship between sinker and drop speed. A friend and I were fishing a spot where we had to work our plastic worms over a ledge and down a drop-off. We were both using the same color, the same line, and the same size hooks, but I was using a #7 shot and his rig had a smaller #3/0 shot. We were in an active feeding period and every time my partner's lure came over that ledge he got a jolting strike. But try as I may, I couldn't catch a single fish even though my worm was coming off that ledge at the exact same angle. Drop speed was the key! As the worms fell off the ledge, the fish only responded positively to the slower drop speed of the #3/0 shot even though they were active and aggressive. Ever since that episode, I've been very conscious of sinker weight and drop speed and I've noticed that a lighter shot will outfish a heavier shot in most cases. Consequently, a smaller #3/0 shot is the backbone of my stitching technique. I may

Stay seated when stitching at all times except to cast and play fish. Staying seated gives you a low profile and keeps the wind from tangling loose line.

use a larger shot when fishing a larger worm, or when bass want a faster drop, but I usually stay with a #3/0 shot for most finesse fishing situations.

The distance between the split shot and the worm is another important consideration. Years of experimenting has shown me that a split shot anchored on the line approximately 8 inches above the worm will produce more strikes and a higher percentage of solid hookups. The sound of a sinker scraping across bottom objects can be an important attractant, especially in darker water environments where bass may rely on sounds and vibrations to first target prey. The ideal split shot position should be close enough to attract bass to the worm, but not so close as to possibly cause a rejection. When a shot is anchored more than 8 inches above the worm, the rig begins to lose the attraction of sound and the worm floats too high. In a dark water situation bass gravitate to the sound caused by a shot scraping over rock. In clear water the distance may not be as critical because it would be visually easier to locate the bait, but even then it's better to

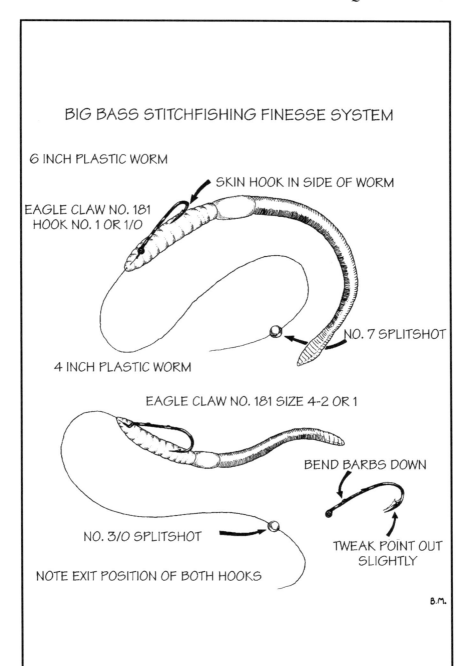

BIG BASS STITCHFISHING FINESSE SYSTEM

6 INCH PLASTIC WORM

SKIN HOOK IN SIDE OF WORM

EAGLE CLAW NO. 181
HOOK NO. 1 OR 1/0

NO. 7 SPLITSHOT

4 INCH PLASTIC WORM

EAGLE CLAW NO. 181 SIZE 4-2 OR 1

BEND BARBS DOWN

NO. 3/0 SPLITSHOT

TWEAK POINT OUT
SLIGHTLY

NOTE EXIT POSITION OF BOTH HOOKS

B.M.

Stitching fools another big one.

have an attractive sound closely followed by your bait. Placing the shot closer than 8 inches may at first seem a better alternative, but a shot in this position also has drawbacks. One reason why finicky bass reject plastic worms with a slide sinker pegged to the head of the worm, or rigged on the back of a jig, is because when a bass inhales one of these rigs the sinker weight doesn't compute naturally in her mouth. But when a bass sucks in a worm with a split shot placed approximately 8 inches in front of the worm, the worm shoots straight into the back of its throat and the bass never feels the sinker. The unweighted worm computes as natural food and they seldom reject it. You might be thinking that the weight of a small split shot surely couldn't make a difference even if the fish were to inhale it, but after years of trial and error I would argue that it does! When the shot is closer than 8 inches the worm may not be inhaled as **DEEPLY** reducing overall hooking efficiency and numbers of trophy bass landed.

Sound is why plain lead sinkers produce more strikes than painted sinkers. Plain lead makes a different noise scraping across bottom features than painted lead, and soft lead makes more of a dead sound than a hard painted surface. My favorite split shots for stitching are old soft-lead shots with roughed-up, gritty textures. Split shots in this condition grab and cling and scrape over bottom terrain producing more sound and giving the worm a more erratic action than smooth shot right out of the box.

Another item that affects this system is how you attach the shot to the line. No matter how carefully you squeeze on a split shot, if you look at the line under a microscope you'll see that you've effectively destroyed that section of line. Pinching on a shot causes a depression in the line which breaks down internal fibers, and there's really no way to control line damage. The best way I've found to eliminate wear and preserve line strength is to crimp the shot to the end of your line **BEFORE** you tie on the hook. Once the shot is secured, hold the open end of line taut with one hand and grab the shot with the other. Now force the shot up and down the line in about 10 inch strokes until the shot begins to slide up and down the line smoothly and easily. The shot should slide but still retain its grip. When the shot begins to slide easily you have effectively worn a groove inside the sinker around the line diameter. Once a groove is made, slide the shot up about 15 inches onto a length of fresh line and cut off the damaged line. Now your shot is anchored to fresh, strong line and you can position the shot wherever you want. This technique will not work, however, unless the slit on the inside of the shot is smooth (split shot with gripping teeth on the split cause severe line damage). I purchase soft shot in bulk with straight slots and no crimping ears. Some national chain stores like Wal-Mart have split shot with smooth slots.

Is all this trouble securing a simple split shot necessary? If you just crimp on a shot as most people do, you not only stand a good chance of losing a giant bass due to weak line, you also risk rejection. If a shot that was secured tightly to the line becomes snagged on the bottom, a bass might drop the worm when it feels strong resistance. The effect you're trying to achieve by first pulling the shot up and down the line is a split shot that functions like a sliding sinker; a

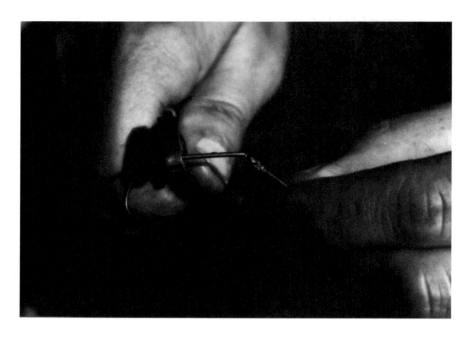

Use ignition pliers to crimp down barbs on Eagle Claw #181 Baitholders.

properly secured split shot should grip but also slide under light pressure. Sometimes after landing a bass on this rig you'll notice that the shot has moved 3 ft. or so up the line. What happened was the shot became lodged behind some bottom object and the fish had time to strip some line through the slot before you were ready to strike. If the shot had been secured too tightly and didn't slip, there's a good chance the bass would have felt resistance and rejected the worm.

There are many fine worm hooks on the market today, but after experimenting with virtually every style available, I honestly believe you'll get better hookups and lose fewer giant bass with an Eagle Claw #181 Baitholder, a hook I have been using for almost 35 years.

A big bass hook should feel like a solid piece of steel and not flex like tempered wire; you can lose a bass the moment a hook flexes and never know why because it instantly springs back to its original shape. Eagle Claw #181 hooks are made of forged steel; they won't

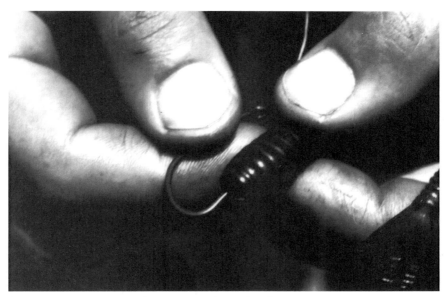

Skin-hooking a Worm—Step #1. Push hook point through nose of worm.

Skin-hooking a Worm—Step #2. Pull hook through worm leaving just the hook eye in the plastic. How far back the hook comes out is dependent on worm length. Pull out about 1/2-inch back with a 6-inch worm, about 1-inch back with a 7-1/2-inch worm, and about 1- 1/2-to-2-inches back with a 9-inch worm.

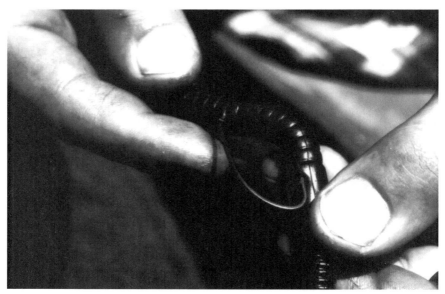

Skin-hooking a Worm—Step #3. Reverse hook. Bend worm slightly forward and skin hook worm on the left side of the worm.

Skin-hooking a Worm—Step #4. A properly rigged worm should be straight with just the hook barb lightly hooked just under the plastic. Always hook along the left side of the worm. The Eagle Claw #181 hook is offset to the left side and it breaks free when you strike, making a solid hookup almost every time.

flex even on a large bass. Be careful when purchasing hooks; hooks from one company may flex, whereas hooks from another company don't.

Because #181 hooks are super strong, you can use smaller hooks even for giant bass. You don't need a 5/0 hook–there's no need to brutalize big fish. Smaller hooks are better concealed and their smaller barbs penetrate more deeply with less pressure. Normally, I'll use a 2/0 hook for worms over 6 inches, a 3/0 hook for worms over 9 inches, and I might go as high as a 4/0 hook when fishing 16 inch worms. For 4-inch worms I'll drop down to a #2 hook or even a #4 if the fish are hook-shy, but if bass are biting a 4-inch worm aggressively I'll probably switch to a bigger #1 hook. But I never use a big hook where bass are pressured and sensitive to details like line or hook size. I'd sure love to fish a lake where the big fish are dumb enough to bite a worm fished with a 5/0 hook and 25 lb. line!

If you're wondering why I prefer baitholder hooks with barbs on the shank over smooth-shanked hooks, it's because the barbs help detect subtle bottom conditions. Even though I flatten the barbs with pliers, the flattened edges still catch fine clay and sand and bits of tiny shells that smooth shanks don't reveal. Minute details such as these give clues that direct me toward bottom compositions that attract big bass and away from those that don't.

Stitching Equipment

Ultra-light tackle is often used for fishing with split shot rigs or little worms, but ultra-light tackle isn't suited for trophy bass. You're not going to land many 14-pounders with a tiny noodle rod and 6 lb. line. A big bass fisherman needs tackle to handle big fish without sacrificing lure presentation. Your tackle needs the flexibility to cast a light rig a long distance on 8, 10, or 12 lb. line and the beef to handle a giant bass in any situation. Virtually all ultra-light rod and reel combinations on the market today lack either the capacity to use heavier line or the ability to successfully play trophy fish.

All my stitching rods are custom made, two-piece fiberglass spinning rods either 7' 6" or 7' 8" in length. Rods made from one long wrap of glass don't have the balance I prefer to play big bass and cast

A seven and a half foot stitching rod and a medium sized spinning reel coupled with a trained touch are the ingredients for the stitching technique.

light baits at the same time, therefore my rods are constructed from two different rod blanks. A good stitching rod needs a slower flexible tip section to generate the whip action necessary to cast a light rig a long distance even into a strong wind, and because most of the pressure that comes from battling a big bass, or setting the hook, is placed on the middle of the rod, a stitching rod should flex parabolically with the power generated from the middle and not solely from the butt section as in fast-tapered rods. The metal ferrules I use to connect my two-piece rods form a heavy center section which absorbs shock and distributes pressure evenly. Having a flexible tip section allows you to play big fish better as it follows every movement when a lunker takes off on a powerful run or shakes its head like a bulldog. Most big fish are lost when the line momentarily slackens between head shakes, but a rod with a soft fiberglass tip more closely follows fighting movements and absorbs the shock of battle better than graphite or boron. Graphite or boron rods recover too fast and actually work against you. Longer rods are more forgiving than short rods and they cover up errors in fighting technique and hook setting. A sweeping hook set with a long rod is much more efficient than a quick jolt with a short rod. I complement the long spinning rod with a Garcia

Mitchell #306 spinning reel. The purpose of this light saltwater reel is casting efficiency. The Mitchell allows me the luxury of anchoring a long cast away from a potential structure, so to lessen the spooking factor, because the extra-wide spool gives me the ability to reach the spot with a lightly weighted worm even with medium weight lines.

My favorite lines to stitch with have rather unique characteristics. The fingertip stitching motion can cause little, inverse knots and loops to develop when the line goes slack, consequently stiffer lines that are not as prone to twisting and tangling as much as softer lines are better suited for this technique. Stiffer lines also have superior resistance to abrasion and hold up better in heavy cover. Abrasion resistance is important in stitching because the line is in constant contact with rocks, brush, and other bottom objects. Before settling on a brand of line. I suggest taking a short length of several different lines and rubbing them over coarse rocks to see how well they hold up. Soft lines abrade easily and lose tensile strength quickly. Your line must hold big bass even when the line is scraping over bottom cover during battle. A stiff line of either 10 or 12 lb. test works nicely. Lines 14 lb. and larger decreases casting distance and their larger diameter can alert bass. Lines of 6 or 8 lb. test have smaller diameters but they tend to twist more readily. I find a line of either 10 or 12 lb. test perfect for stitching. They have the right combination of toughness and strength and their diameter isn't too large to spook wary fish.

The Stitching Retrieve

Although the stitching technique is easy to do once you get the hang of it, the stitching sequence is such a radical departure from other bass methods it may be difficult to comprehend without physically being shown how. With this in mind, I'll talk you through it step by step with the hope that after reading the text a few times you'll have the basics to catch bass by stitching.

Securing the boat in a stable position is the first step and one of the most important. I refined my anchors and anchoring system to make my stitching technique more effective. Your boat has to be double anchored within casting distance of a prime big bass spot. If you use only one anchor or don't secure the boat properly with two anchors, the boat will move too much and you won't be able to detect the subtle line movements of a light bass bite. Stitching is the ultimate finesse presentation and if you aren't anchored in a stationary position you'll miss about 90% of the action. If you're the type of fisherman who doesn't like to anchor, you might as well use a conventional worm presentation because you can't stitch with a trolling motor. Stitching isn't a guessing game like using your rod tip. When done correctly you'll have absolute control at all times, even when the line is slack!

After anchoring in a solid position, cast your split shot rig toward a prime structural area and allow it to sink on a slack line. Make sure the line has no tension as any pressure while the lure is sinking causes the rig to pendulum back toward the boat and settle short of the target. Usually I'll strip off a few extra coils of line after I cast and then sit back and wait until my lure touches bottom. This may be a good time to tidy up or pour some coffee, however, you should begin to retrieve shortly after the lure touches bottom, as waiting too long can create a negative effect. The line should come off the rod tip at roughly a 45 degree angle at most depths, and if you wait too long to begin the retrieve the line may sink deeper than desired causing a poor retrieve angle.

From a sitting position, hold the rod in your right hand (assuming you're right handed) and grasp the line between thumb and forefinger with your left hand about midway between the reel and first guide. In the stitching technique the rod and reel are only used for casting, striking and playing fish. The rod should be pointed **DIRECTLY** at the point in which the line enters the water throughout the entire retrieve. If the rod is at an angle that puts pressure on the line, it's in the wrong position. The only purpose the reel serves is to gather line and hold it out of the way until you get a bite. With the exception of a few slight movements, this is the basic stitching position. It's important to stay seated and keep a low profile because fishing from this position reduces problems caused by excessive wind on loose line. Anglers fishing from a small aluminum boat won't have too many problems, but if you fish from a large bass boat you'll find it helpful to stitch from the back end or lower sections of the boat.

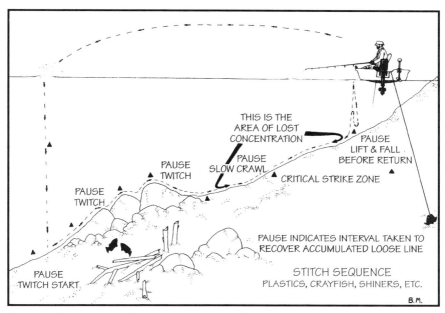

THIS IS THE
AREA OF LOST
CONCENTRATION

PAUSE
LIFT & FALL
BEFORE RETURN

PAUSE
TWITCH

PAUSE
SLOW CRAWL

CRITICAL STRIKE ZONE

PAUSE
TWITCH

PAUSE INDICATES INTERVAL TAKEN TO
RECOVER ACCUMULATED LOOSE LINE

PAUSE
TWITCH START

STITCH SEQUENCE
PLASTICS, CRAYFISH, SHINERS, ETC.

B.M.

The stitch sequence diagram points out how a fisherman pauses at all key junctures throughout the stitching retrieve. The area of lost concentration is the area where you run out of prime structure and you assume that it's a lost cause from that point on back to the boat. This is the area where most anglers don't work their lures as good as they should. But you should always work each cast back to the boat. Sometimes bass don't strike in the key areas and they follow the bait instead. But when they move too far from the prime spot, they reach a point of no return where they either have to take a shot at the bait or let it go. Sometimes you'll catch the biggest bass off a spot in the area of lost concentration.

Sitting also reduces the chance of your body movements spooking bass. Standing should be limited to setting the hook and playing fish, or possibly when making an extra long cast.

When you're ready to begin retrieving, continue to hold the line between the thumb and forefinger of your left hand and bring the lower two or three fingers (I prefer two fingers, middle and third) up and over the line and pull the line down and toward you (see Stitching Sequence Photos). The lower two or three fingers act as one, and when the line is pulled down almost into your palm, briefly let go with the thumb and forefinger and grasp a new section of line. Once the new line is secured between thumb and forefinger, release the line held with the lower fingers and let it fall straight between your feet

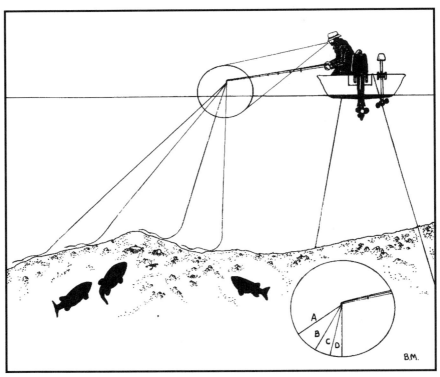

Watching the rod tip is a necessity in stitching. Any twitch or line movement up or down or off to the sides is a signal that a fish has struck your bait. Another important element of line watching is the line angle as it can tell you where your bait is and what it's doing at all times. Angle (A) depicts the line tension caused when your bait is coming uphill at distance. Angle (B) is a little more vertical as your bait reaches the top or crest of the structure. (C) represents a bait coming over the top of the crest and down the other side. And (D) represents the more vertical look of the line as it drops further down from the crest closer to the boat.

toward the floor of the boat. It sounds complicated but with a little practice you can stitch with your eyes closed. The basic stitching movement includes three simple steps: 1. Grasp the line with thumb and forefinger between the reel and first guide; 2. Bring the lower two fingers up and over the line; 3. Pull down gently with the lower fingers, take hold of fresh line and let go of the old. The transition between steps two and three is a very fast movement. You don't want to be fiddling with the line where a bass might feel you. Step two is the "feel" and "twitch" position. Your hand should be in the feel

Assuming you're right-handed, start by holding the rod with your right hand and grasp the line halfway between the reel and first guide with the thumb and forefinger of your left hand. (The little finger of your right hand holds the line tight to the spool throughout the retrieve.)

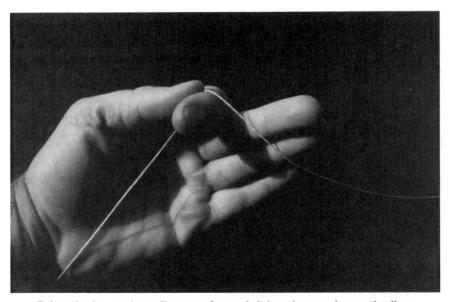

Bring the lower three fingers of your left hand up and over the line.

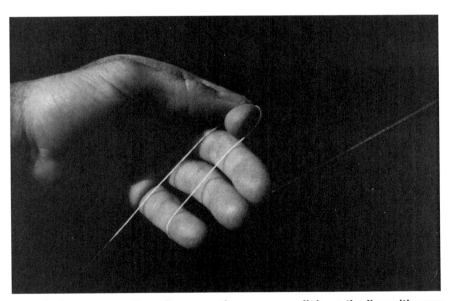

With the lower two or three fingers acting as one, pull down the line with your fingers until they are a few inches from your palm. This is the "feel" and "twitch" position when you let the bait pause in one place. If you feel a bite or see line movement, releasing the line from the lower three fingers instantly gives the fish a few inches of slack line so it doesn't feel you. The line should be pulled down slowly as this is the point where you move the worm along the bottom.

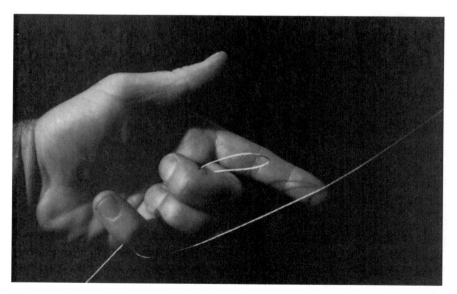

When you're ready to move the bait once again, pull the line with the lower two fingers further back and regrasp a new section of line with thumb and forefinger.

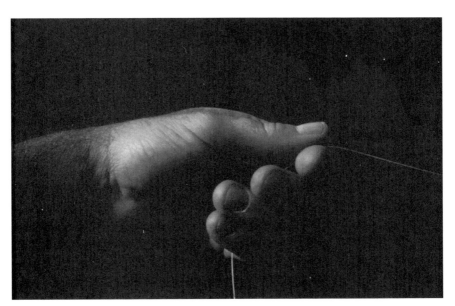

Holding the new section of line with thumb and forefinger, lift the lower two fingers dropping the old section of line, bring them over the new line and pull down to the "feel" position once again. The transition between 4 and 5 is very fast - you don't want to be caught switching positions when a bass bites. The goal is to drop the line and to begin slowly pulling down on fresh line as quickly as possible.

position most of the time. The feel position allows you to detect the most subtle bites and to instantly give the fish slack line when you do.

I often stitch with the bail open on my spinning reel. Sometimes a big fish grabs the lure and runs, and with the bail open I can instantly give it all the line it needs. I press the little finger of my right hand tight to the spool to prevent line from unraveling. Before retrieving, I like to leave one large coil or drape of line hanging from the first guide down to the floor and back to the reel. This allows me to slowly work up to the bait in case a bass has already taken it on the drop. Once I start the retrieve, I'll stitch in about 4 or 5 ft. of line, stop, close the bail, reel up the slack, open the bail, put my little finger back on the spool, leave a drape in the line from the spool to the first guide, then I'll start a new stitching sequence. After about 4 or 5 ft. of loose line gathers at your feet, stop stitching, pick up the loose end and hold the line tight to the rod above the reel with your rod hand, and crank up the loose line under tension. This will eliminate loose line from building up on the spool and hopefully prevent future casting foulups. Never let line accumulate on the floor as it leads to troubles and tangles. Beginning stitch fishermen may be so concerned with other things, they let excessive line build up on the floor, and it always seems like they get a bite when the line is snagged on a shoelace or wrapped around a rod butt. Get into the habit of letting only a few feet of loose line pile up before reeling it back up. I normally let only 3 or 4 coils of line drop before reeling it up. This is doubly important during a strong wind.

The biggest mistake I see most beginning stitch fishermen make is retrieving the line too fast. Each stitching sequence only moves the bait about 4 inches along the bottom, but if you stitch too fast the bait will not be as appealing. Working in inches at a slow, painstaking speed is what separates stitching from all other techniques. Creatures which big bass feed upon move slowly 90% of the time, and that's how you want your presentation to appear. Ultra-slow is the speed of nature in freshwater lake environments, and ultra-slow is the speed pressured bass often respond to best. A worm quickly moving across the bottom, or in a steady up-and-down motion, has no resemblance to anything big bass normally eat, and the last thing a big bass wants pressured bass often respond to best. A worm quickly moving across the bottom, or in a steady up-and-down motion, has no resemblance to anything big bass normally eat, and the last thing a big bass wants is to chase after prey that's quickly moving away. Chasing is a small-bass trait that uses energy without guarantee of success. The hunting practice of trophy bass is to capture prey which is totally unaware of their presence, and the best way to trick these fish is to slow your presentation down to match the slow pace of nature.

Retrieving a bait with frequent pauses is a trick that is deadly on big bass. As you stitch your worm across a structure, periodically stop retrieving and let the worm lie motionless. At times big bass simply will not respond unless the lure is absolutely motionless. And there's no time limit as to how long you should pause; you'll have to experiment to see what triggers a strike. Pausing gives a bass that's been lurking on the other side of an object the time to move over to your bait; it's heard the sound of the split shot and now you've given it time to sneak up. Big bass love to sneak up on prey unnoticed, and you have to give them the chance. This is why you often get a bite on the second cast to the same spot. When fishing small plastic worms or tiny live baits, keep in mind that these baits need to be fished with frequent pauses. Small baits emit less sound and create less disturbance, and bass have a harder time homing in on them; bass have to stop more and concentrate on picking up the signal.

The best time to pause is in the feel position with the line pinched between thumb and forefinger and under the lower fingers. You have just pulled the bait a few inches and now you can pause in this position as long as you like. Once you become familiar with a particular spot, a sharp angler will identify the subtle breaks which always hold the fish best. Experience teaches you that when your lure falls off that little ledge or falls off that snag, that's the time you always get a bite. Once you establish these prime big fish spots, you can give your lure a nice pause in the highest percentage areas. And you can pause longer because you have confidence that a big fish might be examining the bait. Pausing gives you time to reel up the slack and when a fish bites you'll be ready to set the hook instead of retrieving up coils of line.

Hold little finger of right hand on edge of spool to keep line from looping off in the wind.

Another trick I use when my bait is in a prime area is to twitch the line with my middle finger. This only makes the worm jump a few inches, but a little twitch can sometimes make undecided bass pounce on a lure. Adding a little jump to your retrieve is especially effective on northern largemouths.

Correct stitching may seem like a long drawn-out process but the fact is you purposely want to slow your retrieve and take your time. You should be slow and deliberate in everything you do. Largemouth bass in heavily fished waters often get into a kind of rhythm to presentations that are commonly used, and a retrieve that is out of the ordinary can completely change how these conditioned bass respond. A new retrieve can make cautious bass bite like they've never seen a lure before. That's why it's important to work extra slow in pressured lakes. Stitching is a subtle approach that the fish are not used to seeing; it's a completely different action than every other plastic worm that quickly hops through a spot. The stitching action is so different that I've caught dozens of bass off spots where conventional rigs have caught none. I've seen the same response when trapping wild animals; the first few were easy to trap, but then it got hard as the other animals instinctively reacted negatively to traps. I don't give bass as much credit as animals with larger brains, but there has to be a connection there. We really don't know how smart bass really are. I only know for sure that bass fishing isn't getting easier, and as more and more people take up the sport, big bass are going to be increasingly harder to catch. People keep releasing greater numbers of small bass that become very instinctive and cautious when they reach adulthood. That's why the stitching technique is made to order-you're using a presentation that in most cases the fish have never seen before, and big bass in particular find that very appealing. It's no wonder a good stitch fisherman can often score big in waters noted for poor fishing.

The trigger appeal of a bait moving slowly and naturally is the reason why straight worms are more effective for stitching than plastic worms with curly tails. Many fishermen think that if a plastic worm doesn't wiggle enticingly it won't catch bass, but from the standpoint of catching the biggest bass, the opposite is more correct. My all-time favorite worms are made by Delong, Creme, Burke, and Mann's Bait Co., and all are straight worms with no built-in action of their own. But a straight worm with a do-nothing action is precisely the action big bass prefer most of the time. Minnows and crayfish don't twist when they move; their whole body turns at the same time, and that's how a plastic worm should move to fool cautious lunkers. Delong is perhaps the stiffest worm on the market, but its attractiveness comes from the subtle natural movements a straight stiff worm makes as it bumps and deflects off bottom objects slowly fished 8 inches behind a split shot. Big bass find this action much more irresistible than a tail which swings wildly back and forth.

Another interesting fact about plastic worms is that stiff worms catch just as many bass as soft plastic worms. Delong worms are so tough it's hard to pinch off a head or tail, but bass love that texture. I think a chewy mouthful is more natural to bass than biting something with the texture of jello.

The Bite

Once you master the basics of stitching and are free to concentrate on the feelings transmitted up the line, a whole new world of
detail suddenly comes into focus. As you inch and pause your split
shot rig across the bottom, vague structural details now become
crystal clear. The outside edge of a point isn't just a point anymore;
it has areas of hard and soft bottom, an old stump hanging over the
break, and a small area of broken rocks on a high spot. Your fingertips
will feel everything your lure comes in contact with, and after
spending a few hours stitching a spot you'll uncover the subtle
structural variations big bass use.

Practice gives you the ability to recognize exactly what your lure
is doing at all times. You'll be able to distinguish the pull caused by
a rock as a different feeling than the pull caused by a piece of stick.
You'll be able to tell if your lure is dragging over a clay bottom or
over a cobble stone bottom. And you'll be able to feel the most subtle
big bass bites. There's always a distinctive flavor about the resistance
caused by something alive, and with practice you'll be able to quickly
distinguish a snag from a fish. Most bass bites, however, are not
extremely difficult to recognize. Any unusual feeling can be a bass
and should be treated as such, but a big bass normally makes one
distinct thump or tug when it strikes a slow-moving or stationary bait.
Generally speaking, you won't feel a "tap-tap" that's so common with
small bass; a big bass usually opens its mouth and sucks in the lure,
and you'll normally feel one distinct thump or tug. Aggressive bites
are easy to distinguish even for an inexperienced fisherman, but many
bites are much more subtle. All you'll feel is a slight but distinctive
tug from something alive. Your worm might have just come over a
little limb and as soon as it starts to fall you feel that telltale "tug" as
a bass intercepts the bait. Lucky thing you're feeling the line with
your fingertips because the first thing you'll realize after catching
bass stitching is that you might never have felt some of the bites if
you were fishing with the rod tip.

The size of the bait often determines the strength of the bite. Bass often strike a big crayfish hard, but at the same time they might take a small crayfish so lightly you can hardly detect the bite. The same holds true for plastic worms. A long worm or a thick-bodied plastic bait like a lizard are often struck with a vengeance, but the bite on a 4-inch worm in the same spot may be subtle. I believe bass strike with enough force necessary to subdue whatever they attack. It's important to notice how bass bite because the flavor of a bite may be an indication of activity. If you're fishing during a pre-frontal condition or during a good moon phase, a sharp thump might be generated by an aggressive fish, but that same fish during an inactive period might take a bait with a minimum of force. If you had several aggressive bites on successive casts, it might be a good time to put down the stitching rod and use a faster presentation like a crankbait. Sometimes a crankbait will catch more fish faster, and sometimes a crankbait will produce the biggest fish, but on many occasions after catching a few fish on crankbaits I'll go back to stitching and find a slow-moving bait far more appealing.

In stitching you have to be a line watcher. **HOW YOU HANDLE THE LINE AND HOW CLOSELY YOU FOCUS ON THE POINT WHERE THE LINE ENTERS THE WATER IS THE MOST IMPORTANT THING IN STITCHING.** Where the line enters the water is your **STRIKE DETECTOR**, and that point should never be interfered with. Never raise or move the rod in any way that causes the line to move; your rod has to stay rigid and pointed directly at the bait, even when you stop to reel in the slack. By watching the point where the line enters the water, an experienced stitch fisherman can detect every subtle bite and acquire the ability to notice bites that can't be felt. A slight line movement to the right or left or down into the water are all indications that a fish has your bait. Sometimes a big bass will grab the lure and attempt to circle an object and move toward deep water, and the only indication that this is happening is an unusual amount of slack in the surface line. Even aggressive bites sometimes can't be felt. A fish might strike hard causing the line to jump out of the water; it was a solid strike visually but you never felt it.

When I feel a bite or see the line move, I instantly release the line from my lower fingers and give the fish slack so it won't detect me. If the fish moves off quickly, I'll release the line from my thumb and forefinger allowing the line to pay free. If the line picks up speed, I know the fish has it and I'll throw the bail and set the hook. But if the line is only moving in inches, I'll continue to hold the line between thumb and forefinger and add a little resistance trying to make the fish take it better. When you add a little pressure to the line, one of two things will happen. Either the fish will pull harder, which is my signal to strike, or it will drop the bait. If the fish drops the lure, it means the bass didn't have a good hold and it dropped the bait to reposition it better. When a bass drops the bait I just leave it sit. The fish will usually come back, and when it takes the lure for the second time, she'll take it well and you'll have her. So in the end you get her both ways. But I always like to add a little resistance to the line after a bite just to finesse the fish into taking it better.

Crankbaits and other active baits often trigger strikes while bumping and ricocheting off objects, but in stitching you never want to pull so hard as to make the worm slide off the hook; you want to preserve the look of the worm so when it comes over an object it has the best appeal as it sinks straight down to the base of cover. That's why it's always best to finesse a stitching lure through bottom cover rather than ripping them free.

When you feel a steady pressure that isn't moving, your lure is probably snagged. However, I always take my time and add a little pressure to the line to see what happens next. If the resistance is caused by a bass then the added line pressure will likely cause the fish to move with the bait, but the resistance will stay the same if it's snagged. Even when snagged I'm never in a hurry to move the bait. After all, the lure is in a prime piece of cover and sometimes a bass will root it right out of the snag. Some of my biggest bass were caught by leaving a lure lie still after it became snagged.

When it's time to free the lure, raise your rod high overhead and gently bounce the tip back and forth from side to side. If that doesn't work, pop the rod tip up and down with a jiggling motion. Don't be

Delaying before you set the hook gives a bass time to swim away from potential trouble.

in a hurry to break the line as bass often strike the moment it pops free. If all attempts fail, grab the line above the rod tip and pull slowly until the line breaks above the knot.

Setting the Hook

Everything written about worm fishing says to strike as soon as you feel a bite or the bass will spit out the worm, but when a bass takes a worm on a split shot rig there's no need to hurry. If you do things right and don't let the fish detect you, it will hold the worm indefinitely. Waiting before you strike lets the fish take the worm more deeply which promotes better hookups and a higher percentage of fish in the boat. Waiting also teaches self control which will help you play a giant bass more efficiently.

After I feel a bite or see the line move, I close the bail and begin reeling up most of the slack. On days when bass are real sensitive they may drop the worm if any resistance is felt, so I never reel up to a point where I actually feel the fish. I stop just short of causing the rod tip to bend. One of the benefits of a split shot rig is that bass don't

When casting over potential obstructions, it's a good policy to let the fish run a little before setting the hook. In this diagram, a big bass has intercepted the bait on the edge of a large boulder. If you struck right away, there's a good chance of busting the line on the rock. But by knowing that big bass always move off toward deep water, you can let it take about 10-or-15 ft. of line and move into a position where your line angle will clear the rocks when you strike. You'll have a better angle to strike and play the fish free of obstructions. And even if your line was caught in a little rock crevice, the new striking angle would help break it free of the crevice without breaking your line.

quickly reject them, and even if the fish struck during the end of a stitching sequence with several coils of line laying on the boat floor, there's normally ample time to reel up all the slack and prepare for the hookset without rushing. If the bass doesn't feel you it'll normally swim toward deep water with the worm. Watch for line movement and direction as you reel up the slack. I let the fish run just long enough until I get the line straightened out and where I'm in a comfortable position to fight the fish. When I'm a fraction of a reel turn from contacting the fish, I set the hook. Instead of a hard jolting strike, I've had much better results setting the hook with a smooth, solid upward sweep. Starting just below waist level, I'll make solid contact with the fish at some point from the starting position to the end of the sweep straight above my chest in the 1 o'clock position. The sheer body weight of a huge bass might break a medium test line with a jolting strike but because of the way I rig plastic worms the initial set needs no more force than is necessary for the hook to break free and penetrate the mouth. It's easy to hook bass using live bait because the hook comes out easily, and it should be the same with plastic worms, yet most conventional rigs make worm fishing more difficult. I developed my way of skin hooking plastic worms to eliminate this problem. A big hook needs more striking power, but in my system I use smaller hooks and skin-hook the worm which eliminates the need for an exaggerated hookset. I don't mean to say that I don't set the hook hard. There's great leverage in the sweep set of a 7-1/2 ft. rod, plus you have the momentum of the fish. A smooth, strong, upward sweep hooks the fish almost every time.

Usually, one good set is enough as the first powerful run a bass makes will finish burying the hook, but if you feel that you didn't get a good initial set, sweep back a second time but only when the fish is pulling away from you-setting a second time while a fish is swimming toward you can rip out the hook. If a bass is taking line steadily before you strike, the initial set should be about half as hard as you would strike on a stationary fish. Also, use less force when fishing live baits; the hook doesn't have to break free of tough plastic and the smaller hook needs less force to penetrate.

When you miss a fish on the initial strike you can cast back to the same spot and the same fish will usually bite again. If you can't make solid contact it's better to miss the fish clean. If a big bass gets off after it's hooked you're through, but if you miss it altogether on the strike and the worm pulls smoothly out of its mouth, it may actually stimulate or antagonize the fish, and you can often catch it again on the next cast. That's another reason why I went to longer rods-the greater strike/line-takeup ratio.

Is all this detail in setting the hook necessary? The purpose of this book is to teach the reader how to catch giant bass consistently, and that includes times when fish are hard to catch. In this section I'm describing a hooking system that produces when bass are very cautious where they might drop the bait an instant before you set the hook. If you tighten up on the line to feel for a bass before you strike and the bass feels you, the muscles in their throat can relax and the hook will pull out through their jaws. Ideally, you want the fish to take the worm as deep as possible and hold the worm with their throat muscles. Every muscle should be taut, otherwise you'll hook them in the lips and there's a good chance they'll come up and throw the hook. The ideal hooking area is inside the roof of the mouth. Leaving a minute amount of slack in the line and striking without ever feeling for the fish is the way to make a cautious lunker hold tightly to a worm. Why spend all your time and effort locating bass and triggering a strike if you're going to look at setting the hook as something less important? Every aspect of big bass fishing should be constantly refined until the most efficient methods are found and that includes setting the hook.

The Advanced Course

The purpose of a detailed method like stitching is to uncover isolated targets and subliminal fish-holding breaks seldom found with electronics or conventional fishing methods. The advanced course in bass fishing is to first find these spots and then target your casts to the cover-free areas around them.

The advanced course of bass fishing is tricking a trophy on a spot with relatively little cover to make your worm move erratically. On cover-free spots you have to impart all the action yourself. Picture that big bass just sitting there eyeballing your lure. How would you work it? Twitch it, stop it, crawl it, jump it. Try to impart a movement that will make it strike. This is the concentration and mental attitude that makes an expert big bass fisherman.

For example, there might be a lunker holding near an isolated stump, but bringing your lure up and over the stump in a conventional manner may not trigger a strike. The fish might only react to a presentation worked along the sides or along the base of the stump without actually coming into contact with the stump. Sometimes a lure hitting the stump first will actually spook them out. Few anglers realize the triggering effect of different retrieve angles but experience has shown me that the right angle can make all the difference. Fishing

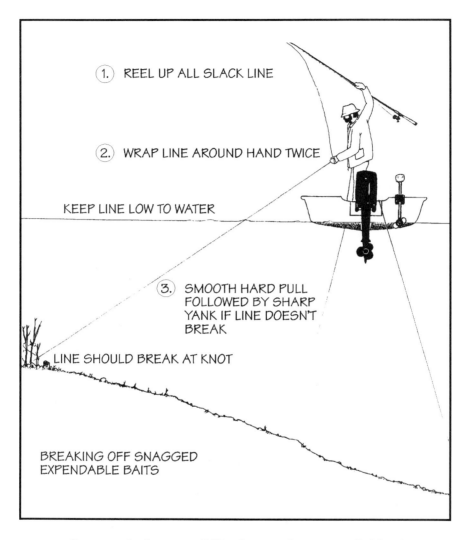

a cover-free area is the most difficult part of structure fishing because there's nothing to index or relate to during the retrieve. A prime cover-free area may only have a little depression, some tiny stones, a few isolated sticks or a minute clump of weeds, consequently there's not much to grab and pull on your lure letting you know you're fishing the right area or are even in the ballpark. You don't have the convenience to work into a bottom object and say, "There it is; I'm coming over the stump right now." When you try to fish down the side of a stump without actually hitting it first, it's hard to tell if your lure is right beside it or some distance away. Anyone can tell if their lure is coming over a rock or down the side of a channel-those things are basic-but working a clean bottom with absolutely nothing to index or focus on is very difficult. You have to fish the spot long enough to mentally visualize exactly where everything is, and once you locate a potential piece of cover you have to line it up with shoreline sightings, then direct your casts to the right or left of those sightings. This is the only way to accurately know if your lure is coming down the side of an object without actually making contact with the object first. At times, however, that's exactly the presentation lunker bass want. Most anglers who fish fast look for places that cause their lures to hang up, and then they slow down and fish the cover. But that's not how to stitch these subliminal big bass spots. You have to anchor and deliberately fish around the cover using shoreline sightings to direct your casts.

Another problem with fishing a cover-free area is that there is nothing to cause a plastic worm to dart and fall in an enticing manner. You'll have to supply all the action to the lure yourself. Instead of simply dragging the worm across the bottom, picture in your mind that a big bass is in pursuit and watching your lure moving along. How would you work that lure if you thought a 16 pound bass was right on the verge of taking it? That's how you fish a cover-free spot. Twitch it, crawl it, jump it, stop it, all the way to the boat. Make believe a huge bass will pounce on it with every new movement. The ability to fish a cover-free bottom and trigger bass through your skill alone is the ultimate achievement in plastic worm fishing and the advanced course in big bass fishing.

As incredible a method as stitching is, it can be frustrating and even impossible to learn for some people. High strung anglers who have to move all the time may have a hard time developing the patience for stitching. If an angler thinks plastic worm fishing is slow, you can imagine how hard it will be to sit and work in inches. Stitching is not for everyone, but if you take the time to learn how to do it properly, stitching is just about the most deadly structure technique-especially for giant bass.

PLAYING AND LANDING GIANT BASS

Large bass usually make one last dive right under the boat. Keep cool and just put on a light steady pressure, she will eventually come up to the surface where she can be easily netted.

The sight of a huge bass clearing the water two or three times can make even the most composed angler turn to jelly. When most experienced anglers play a nice 5 or 6-pound bass they aren't afraid of losing it because deep down they know they'll probably catch more, but when you hook a giant bass, and it comes up and jumps, you suddenly are struck with the thought that you may never hook a fish that big again in your entire life! And that thinking causes you to treat that fish differently than how you'd normally play a good bass. It makes you freeze up and do the wrong thing at the wrong time. Time after time, I've seen huge bass lost by anglers who tense up at the wrong moment.

Contrary to popular opinion, a bass over 10 or 12 lbs. is not more difficult to land than a bass of 6 or 7 lbs. A bass over 12 lbs. is certainly stronger and more savage, and it'll bust you off in cover much more easily. But giant bass are very predictable in their fighting habits, and if you learn to anticipate their moves and prepare before you catch one, you'll find that landing them is no more of a problem than any good size bass.

Rule #1. **NEVER TRY TO TURN A GIANT BASS REGARDLESS OF WHERE IT'S HEADED, UNLESS IT IS A LAST DITCH EFFORT TO TURN THE FISH FROM AN OBVIOUSLY DANGEROUS OBJECT**. The one thing I learned long ago about big bass is that once hooked and started off the bottom they seldom go back into heavy cover. In most situations where a big bass breaks off in cover, it was the angler who pulled, or coerced, the fish into a bad hangup by exerting too much pressure. I know this statement sounds a little far out, but I must again remind the reader that I'm describing an outside structure situation and not heavy cover in shallow water. In a structure situation you'll normally catch a lunker bass on outlying spots near deep water, and if given a chance, a big bass will generally move deeper rather than head for shallow cover. One of the problems with playing a giant bass is that you can exert too much pressure and if you hook it in the wrong spot the hook can pull out. Huge bass have extreme pulling power but they don't have a mouth to go with it. Their mouth, in relationship to their size, has fragile spots. The jaw is tough and firm, but there are spots within the mouth where a hook might easily pull free, so you must prepare for lightly hooked fish. When a giant bass is headed for cover, the tendency is to freeze up and apply more pressure to stop it, and this is when a hook is most likely to pull out, a bass will bust your line, or it will become hopelessly snagged. But if you loosen the drag and allow the fish to go where it wants, nine times out of ten it'll move away from cover toward deeper open water if your boat is not in its path. The way I anchor, I always allow a big fish access to deep, open water. Anchoring is a part of my big bass system that guarantees a high percentage of success. If the spot has a lot of heavy cover, I'll anchor so I cast parallel to the spot and fish along the deeper edges. Normally, once the spot settles down, the fish will move out from dense cover to the edges, and when I hook one it'll swim out

When a big bass is hooked on the edge of an outside structure, they instinctively move toward open water. Anchoring is a part of big bass fishing that guarantees success. Always anchor in a way that allows fish access to deep, open water. Experience has proven that when you let a big bass go where it wants to go, the percentages are much greater for landing that fish.

toward open water. Personally, I'd rather have a big fish bust me off in cover than trying to stop it by applying more pressure. Experience has taught me that when I let the fish go where they want, the percentages are good that I'll land it, but if I try to stop a bass that's moving toward cover, the percentages are just as good that the fish will get off. Only bad things happen by pulling on a giant fish and trying to stop it.

Playing Giant Bass

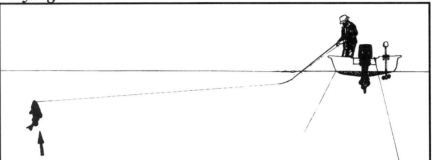

When a big bass is coming up to jump, push your rod tip into the water the moment you notice your line rising toward the surface. Hold the rod steady, stop reeling, and simply let the rod exert a steady, even pressure. A drag that is set to give just enough line at the critical moment will save a big bass from throwing the hook on the jump.

Rule #2. **ALWAYS LOOSEN THE DRAG.** I've found, over a period of many years, that you need to play giant bass with a fairly loose drag. I use two drag settings on my spinning reel, one for the hookset and another for playing the fish. The hookset drag is strong without much give. However, once I hook a big bass I hold the fish with a steady, even pressure, but at the same time reduce the drag to the fighting position. Then, when the bass takes off on that first big run. I just let it swim toward deep water and let the smooth drag pressure wear it down. When you first set the hook, you want to hold the fish right there. **DON'T BE IN A HURRY TO MOVE THE FISH TOWARD YOU.** While the fish is momentarily disoriented, that's when you adjust the drag to a looser setting. A fraction of a second later, the bass will take off on a strong run, but the reel will be properly adjusted to apply the best pressure. Setting a drag just below the breaking

Sixteen pounders are rare trophies indeed, many hours are required to find just the right area that is suitable to the lifestyle of these huge fish.

strength of the line is suicide for playing a giant fish. The drag should not be ridiculously loose, but it should be well below the breaking strength of the line. The drag should not have a great influence on the fish. Most of the forces that the fish pulls against should come from the flex of the rod and the drag of the line on the guides. The reel drag is simply used as a safety clutch so the bass can't possibly bust the line with a sudden surge.

Some anglers choose to backreel when playing bass with a spinning outfit, but I feel that backreeling is not a particularly effective tactic when playing giant bass. The flaws in backreeling are evident when a huge bass comes to the surface. All giant bass normally jump at least once, except in the coldest months. A huge bass may tire quickly when jumping, especially if it's carrying a lot of belly fat, but a jumping fish is dangerous because when a giant bass clears water and shakes its head it's liable to toss out the hook. Once a bass clears water, there's no way even the best loose-action fiberglass rod tip can follow every movement as the fish shakes its head, and in that split second an airborne bass can exert enough pressure to throw the hook. The situation calls for some drag pressure, but it's difficult to achieve the right amount of pressure at the critical moment when backreeling. If I'm playing a big bass and see the line rising toward the surface, I put my rod tip in the water and hold the rod steady. I stop reeling and just let the rod exert a steady pressure. Doing this puts just the right amount of pressure on the line where a big bass can pull a little line on the jump. The pull is almost undetectable, but with a loose drag and the rod tip in the water, the system gives just enough line to save the fish. If the drag was set too tightly, or if you were backreeling and failed to instantly give line because you froze up when you saw how big it was, the hook might be shaken out or pulled free on the jump. That's why I favor fighting giant bass with a drag over backreeling and why I like to use a two-drag system over the popular line setting just below breaking strength. Always make sure before you start fishing that the line pulls smoothly and hasn't set, or stuck, from lack of use. You should never have to grab or pull the line above the reel with your hand.

Rule #3. **ALWAYS NET A GIANT BASS**. The closer a big bass gets to the boat the greater the chance of losing it. After jumping a few times and making one or two wide arches around the boat, a giant bass will begin to tire, but during the fight it may have weakened the line by rubbing across some brush or rock. Sometimes a big fish will make one or two last-bid dives right under the boat. You've fought her all this way, and everyone has always told you this is where you're going to lose her. And to make it worse, you've seen how big she is! She jumped ten feet from the boat and you're thinking, "She's down

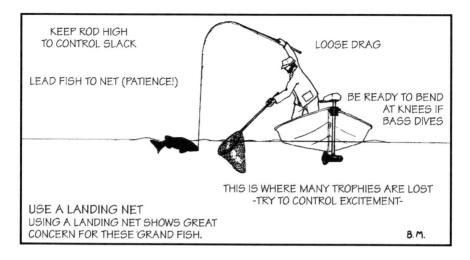

KEEP ROD HIGH
TO CONTROL SLACK

LOOSE DRAG

LEAD FISH TO NET (PATIENCE!)

BE READY TO BEND
AT KNEES IF
BASS DIVES

THIS IS WHERE MANY TROPHIES ARE LOST
-TRY TO CONTROL EXCITEMENT-

USE A LANDING NET
USING A LANDING NET SHOWS GREAT
CONCERN FOR THESE GRAND FISH.

B.M.

there and so close. She'll get hung up on something–I can't let her go!". But as I said before, never try to stop a big fish, especially around the boat on a weakened line. Just let it run with some resistance and it'll come right back up. Once it comes to the surface, work the tired fish toward the boat and slip the net under her.

I always net large bass; save grasping the jaw for the small ones. I use a large dip net with a medium handle and sink it about halfway in the water. Lead the bass into the net headfirst and place her gently on the boat floor. Calm the fish by covering it with a wet burlap sack or place it immediately in the livewell.

There are many things a guy can do to give him confidence, and I always keep a landing net at my feet. The net is moistened and folded and always kept in the same position. When I'm fishing alone I can reach down and place the net between my knees. With the net in the water held between my knees I'm ready for anything, because I've had times when bass were fighting hard near the boat and there wasn't any way to look for the landing net. But a net between my knees is my security blanket. Once I was working a big bass toward the net and she jumped, threw the hook, and landed in the net-the fish weighed 15 pounds! Before I began holding the net with my knees I blew a very large bass that shook off as I was groping for the net. Holding a net with your knees is just another of the many advantages of fishing from a smaller boat where you're closer to the water.

Avoid pumping a giant bass. Keep the rod up and wear the fish down with a smooth, steady drag pressure. Always keep the same fighting angle on the fish. If you play it from one side and then from another, you risk the hook pulling out if a bass jumps or pulls from the opposite direction. If you must change the fighting angle, keep the rod low rather than high. There are times, when you must pump a big fish up and out of the stuff, also in deep water when you want a big fish off the bottom quickly.

Rule #4. **PRACTICE ON SMALLER FISH.** You rarely get a chance to practice on giant bass, so your practice must come from playing 5, 6, and 7-pounders. Play the fish like it's a 15-pounder. Practice setting the drag after hooking a fish to where it only takes a split second to adjust the drag as loose as you want. You have to automatically set the drag to the point where a giant bass won't cause problems. Anchor each spot to allow the fish to move freely into deep, open water, and when a 5-pounder jumps, practice placing the rod tip in the water and letting her pull on a light drag.

How to Work an Active Spot

When bass start biting, the serious big bass angler will try to catch as many as he can while the active period is in full swing. The time when big bass are vulnerable in a certain spot is generally short,

Trophy bass are best landed with a landing net. Get in the habit of using one by practicing on smaller fish.

and you have to be ready to take advantage of the time given. You have to assume that you're going to catch a bunch of good fish the moment you get that first bite, and you have to work as quickly and deliberately as possible. Even during a prime active period the fish may not feel that the spot they're working is good enough for them to stay (absence of prey, boat noise, etc.). The fish may have just come in to prospect a spot, and the only reason they stay is the fact that you are presenting a lure or live bait to them and are catching them. There has to be something out there to hold their interest, so in this situation the faster you can get your lure back out there and hook another fish the better off you are. Catching one fish after another creates an activity and momentum on the spot. Buck Perry used to write about the same thing. He would drop a fish in the boat and make another cast as quickly as possible when he intercepted an active feeding spree; he wouldn't even stop to put them on a stringer and sometimes had five bass flopping on the boat floor at the same time. As soon as I get a big fish in the net, I lay it on the bottom of the boat and cast back to the fish. As the lure is sinking, I put the fish in the livewell and get everything ready in the boat. It's important to make that time (when the lure is sinking) work for you because you don't know how long the active period will last.

I approach big bass fishing with a total picture of what I'm after. My goal is to catch five lunker bass, or one of the very biggest fish I possibly can. I've worked out my tackle and techniques to accomplish this, and I follow a routine to help eliminate possible screw-ups. I'm not going to stop and gloat over a 14-pound bass in the boat when I might miss an 18-pounder that's still out there. I've seen guys stop fishing because they wanted to weigh in a big fish at the dock, or because they were too excited to keep fishing, but their sights were set too low; it was the biggest fish they ever caught and consequently they were through for the day. On many occasions I've moved right in on a spot when an excited angler left with a good fish and caught several more big ones. Most people are oriented to believe that giant bass are loners, but there could be a number of big ones on the same spot. We can't be sure if they're a school fish or simply individuals vying for the same spot, but huge bass do accumulate in certain areas during primary active periods. Some people are going to say that taking bass fishing as serious as I do takes all the fun out of the sport, but I represent the fanatic only because I'm trying to find the ultimate way to catch most of the biggest bass possible. You don't have to be the best golfer to enjoy golfing, and you sure don't have to be the best fisherman to enjoy bass fishing, but I believe an angler ought to be aware of what the ultimate potential of the sport can be, so when he gets into a good spot during an active feeding spree he'll know how to effectively take advantage of the situation.

When working a spot with active bass, it's also important to remember what factors turn off a positive feeding mood. If you play a big fish too long in a prime spot, or if you lose a big one and it returns to the prime area, sometimes that will spook the rest out or shut them off. There's some type of alarm factor at work, whether they secrete some type of fear enzyme or simply react to the unnatural body language of a hooked fish. Bass know what's natural and what isn't, and I believe it's the sight and sound of a struggling fish that turns the others off. Fish at times will shut each other down, and it's something to be aware of. You can release a fish on the other side of the boat and point them out in the opposite direction. Usually it takes a while for the released fish to regain its composure, and it will swim slowly down and not really influence the spot negatively. On a day when the bass are really positive and feeding, hooking a fish may actually cause the others to feed even more aggressively. Fighting a big bass and allowing it to burst and thrash through an area can stimulate the other fish into a frenzy, but be aware that if you lose that fish it'll probably be the last bite you'll get for a while.

Author is shown here with a giant bass caught on a secret plastic worm which he developed years ago as the perfect stitching worm. For more information contact Lunker City Fishing Specialties. (See reference section)

HOW TO CATCH INACTIVE LUNKERS

Never assume that just because you're fishing during a post-frontal condition, or during any other influence people associate with bad fishing, big bass are impossible to catch because activity is shut down. Active and inactive periods don't necessarily mean some giant force has enveloped everything all at once. An active period, for example, doesn't mean that all the fish are feeding at the same time. Maybe certain fish were unsuccessful when all the others gorged themselves with food, or maybe the timing of these fish wasn't right and they missed linking up with a roaming school of shad? Whatever the reason, all fish don't feed at the same time, and some may be a little more active and catchable than others even during the worst conditions.

Also, consider that a bass always can be tempted into biting; its just in their nature. Although it has just been on a feeding spree, if you put something good to eat in front of it chances are the bass won't pass it up. Bass don't have the mental capacity to figure out when their next meal will come, consequently, even the most inactive fish may take advantage of an easy, or tempting, feeding opportunity when it presents itself.

Again, the key to catching inactive bass is fishing the right spot. We all tend to move around and look for new areas when fishing is slow, but fishermen seeking quality fish should do the opposite. The same spots that produced the best before an inactive period would remain the key spots to fish when fishing is bad. Big fish attract to certain areas because all the conditions are right (bait, structure, seasonal conditions, etc.) and a simple inactive period generally won't move them far from that spot; some bass will probably suspend and others may move to isolated cover near the key feeding area, but they probably won't move too far. You have to know of a spot that is currently producing, or at least have an idea of where to fish from your backlog of information, so you can have the confidence and patience to fish inactive bass correctly. Generally, when fishing is slow I may only fish one or two prime spots all day long. It would be too hard to exercise enough patience to make a spot produce if you didn't have confidence that the spot was currently holding fish. The secret to catching bass on the bad days is to find the key spots during the good days. It's difficult to leave a spot when the fish are biting, but that's the best time to check for new spots. The more spots you find that are currently producing, the more options you'll have when fishing is tough. On a day when the fish are very active, I'll always allow at least a few hours for checking new spots.

If you were able to take the top off a lake and look at the fish during an inactive period, you'd be surprised how many big bass would be laying in one position at the base of a boulder, stump, or weed patch. Big bass retire to isolated holding areas when in a neutral or inactive mood. These areas are hard to fish because you have to know where they are or at least have a general idea from past experiences. Your presentation has to be right on the money because the fish won't chase. It's not like fishing an active period when the fish might disperse throughout a general area. If the spot was a large, underwater bar, for example, you would stand a good chance of intercepting a large bass at any one of several key breaks during an active feeding period, but when the fish settle into their inactive holding areas your presentation will have to be much more precise, and you'll possibly have to goad the fish into biting. The fish won't move far to take a lure, but they might be made to hit by repeatedly putting a bait right in front of them.

Once I was fishing a structure on Lake Sutherland during a period with low fish activity. I knew the location of an isolated bush on an underwater point, and I knew there was a good chance a big bass might be using the bush because I hooked a good one there some days before. It was a big bush on the edge of a drop-off in 12 ft. of water. The bush was on the deep edge and had a small rock cluster at the base. Working up to the bush from an anchored position, I busted off at least six crayfish snagged on the bush. It must have had crayfish hanging all over it. Finally, I rigged a 9-inch purple Jelly worm and was able to work it through the bush and pop it over the top. On the first cast, as soon as the worm came over the bush, I got a bite and set the hook on a 12 lb. 6 oz. largemouth. It was a neutral period and the fish was buried in the cover. But the plastic worm enabled me to get to the fish without becoming fouled. Neutral bass can be caught, but you have to put it right in their face.

Tough conditions call for patience and open-minded presentation. If you haven't got a bite after an hour on one spot, your first inclination is to think that the fish aren't there, and the lack of activity convinces you that it's time to move to another spot. However, in most situations, when bass aren't biting on a proven spot, it doesn't necessarily mean the fish have moved, it simply means they're inactive. If the prey is still there and the lake environment hasn't changed dramatically, there's no reason for those fish to move. A lot of times they'll just sit there and watch everything in the world go by, and you'll swear the spot is void of bass, but there are times when a good angler can coax a bite and all of a sudden have a big one in the boat.

An inactive bass is like a person that uses the drive-up window of a fast-food restaurant on a cold, rainy day. He doesn't really want to go out, but because he's hungry, he's willing to reach out and take a bag of food. That's exactly how some bass are after a front. They won't actively chase prey, but if your offering happens to come close enough, sometimes they'll stretch out and take a shot at it.

Inactive bass frequently tap, or bump, a lure and then reject it. When a bass taps a plastic worm, for example, and then drops it and won't hit it again, you have to assume that that fish can be caught with the right presentation-it was active enough to hit once, and it should still be active enough to respond again, if you can figure out the right presentation. Rejection is a signal to re-evaluate your technique. Try switching to a lighter line, a smaller lure, a different color, a different retrieve angle, or change from an artificial to live bait. Usually, the best presentation for inactive fish is a finesse presentation worked through the key spot over and over again. My favorite technique for this situation is stitching because I can anchor in a way to present each cast accurately to the key spot, and the super-slow speed is ideal to goad the fish into hitting.

**Post-frontal lunkers can be caught if you fish the
key spots with lots of patience.**

Active bass usually position in a way relative to the normal traffic
flow of prey species on a particular structure, but sometimes when
you present a lure or live bait from a direction different than the fish
are used to seeing, the difference may be enough to trigger them to
bite. At times fish won't respond to a presentation coming across a
structure in the same path all the time even though it's a proven angle.
If you notice that you always fish a certain spot from the same
direction and you aren't drawing strikes, consider working the spot
from a different angle (different from the way prey moves on and out,
and from the way people normally fish it). Because the biggest bass
are hard to fool, sometimes it's important to try something different
instead of the matching-the-hatch philosophy or matching the direction of prey specie movements. Finding the subliminal spot is always
the big-fish pattern, but a presentation from a different direction that

the fish are use to seeing prey move through that spot might draw a positive reaction from a neutral fish. Using a familiar angle that bass are used to seeing may be better suited for crankbaits or some type of lure that imitates the prey they're used to seeing. But when you're stitching with live crayfish or nightcrawlers, for example, you might be using a bait that is completely alien to that particular water. You might be fishing a live crayfish at 22 ft. in a place where natural crayfish seldom go during that time of year. In this case you're not trying to match the habits of any natural prey, but you're trying to provoke a positive response by using something different.

A lot of times, inactive and neutral bass are in areas where prey doesn't go in the first place. An inactive bass might be holding under an isolated stump on the side of a ledge at 22 ft. but when that fish gets active and begins to think about feeding, it might move up to the edge of the ledge at 10 ft. And in this respect, fishing for inactive bass can be, in some ways, more efficient then trying to catch very active bass. Inactive bass will often hold tight to their isolated holding areas and it seems like nothing will move them. Being neutral or inactive doesn't necessarily have to do with feeding, it can also mean the fish are not moving and don't want to move. A holding fish can take a lot of disturbing without actually moving. So in this sense, inactive bass can be easier to approach than active bass. You could theoretically make noise and drop your anchor right next to one without moving the bass from its spot, whereas, the same procedure might entirely shut down an active feeding period. Because inactive fish are so stubborn about moving, it gives you time to work the spot over and over with different lures and live baits fished from different casting angles. Rather than working on a fish in the feeding area where it might become preoccupied with all sorts of feeding opportunities, you actually have an inactive bass cornered where all it has to do is concentrate on your offerings going by. Neutral holding areas rarely have prey sources and they're away from the competition of other bass.

There's little luck when fishing for inactive fish, sitting on a proven spot and waiting the fish out is the best method I know of.

HIGH PERCENTAGE TECHNIQUES

Anglers who know how to catch big bass don't waste time using lures or live baits which seldom produce. Years of experimenting have taught them which techniques are most likely to catch big bass during each seasonal period. Even though they remain open to new patterns, they know what techniques offer the highest percentages for catching trophy fish. They know that to search for big bass with ten different patterns in mind won't do any one pattern justice, and they know that if they fish hard all day with only a few high-percentage lures or patterns, they may not get the strikes but they're willing to sacrifice bites for quality fish. Most consistent big bass anglers rely on only a few proven techniques, and when you limit your tackle selection to only a handful of things, you have reached a point where you are sure about the lure, color, and pattern you're going to fish in each situation.

Part of being a productive big bass fisherman is subtracting all the things that don't work. You do this on a short-range and a long-range basis. The short range is finding out the current patterns on the water you're fishing, the long range is your backlog of knowledge and experience that point you in a certain direction at various times of the year. Over the years certain patterns stay with you, and every time you see the same situation you recognize patterns that work and those that don't. Some lures and patterns rarely produce giant bass (the percentages are too great against it happening), so you eliminate those from your arsenal. Occasionally, you might enjoy the abilities it takes to use these lures and techniques, even though you know there's a very slim chance of catching a huge bass with them. Surface lures are a prime example. Surface lures are fun to use, but on certain lakes the chance of catching a trophy bass on a surface lure is almost nonexistent. In this case, you would eliminate surface lures from your backlog except for a few isolated situations. That's why successful big bass anglers cut their arsenal down to the absolute essentials and leave the current fads and hot new lures to the rest of the fishermen. It's understandable why many fishermen are not willing to make this sacrifice because fishing with the latest colors and innovations is enjoyable. And it doesn't rest well with lure companies when you tell them only five colors in two sizes in their entire line are good big bass producers. That doesn't mean that someone else couldn't make another part of their line produce, but the lures you trust are the colors and patterns that you have found most effective, and you stick with them because they work in your area.

Discovering what lures, or combinations of lures, produce best in each individual lake is one of the biggest secrets in big bass fishing. Every lake can be different, and nobody knows why. There are lakes that are better for jig and pig fishing, and it has nothing to do with cover density or water clarity, there's just some ingredient that makes it a better jig lake. Some lakes are good plastic worm lakes, while others are good for live bait, and there can be certain times of the year when plastic worm lakes become good live bait lakes and vice-versa. These are the strange happenings which make big bass seem so elusive and what trophy fishing is really all about. You may never know exactly why bass do what they do, but staying abreast of the various lake patterns, and the changes in these patterns, is a big part of successful big bass fishing.

If a lake has a history of being a good jig and pig lake, a good big bass fisherman might take an assortment of jigs and pork rinds in all sizes and colors, but I'll bet when he gets into a prime area during a good active period he'll tie on his favorite size and color because a good big bass fisherman always plays the best percentages. It's important to stay with a proven slot. You might experiment with new lures and techniques because you want to increase the slot, but regardless of how many you add, you always boil them down to the best handful. It goes for colors, blades, jigs, crankbaits, and everything you use. Your goal as a big bass fisherman is to reduce your tackle selection to the most effective lure and technique, and once you find them you play them for all they're worth. You believe in

**Figuring out the high-percentage pattern is the key
to making consistent catches.**

those patterns because they always work for you, and when they fail, you begin experimenting to try and find a pattern current with the times and abreast of the active feeding periods; in other words, the colors and lure combinations that work on that particular lake at that time of year. It's hard work and takes complete dedication, and not everyone is willing to do it, but big bass anglers stay with it because they love the sport and the feeling inside that **THEY** made it happen when they make an outstanding catch.

Bass fishing is a percentage game and it's even more so for big bass. You always try to play the best percentages even if it only means one bite a day. When you go fishing you try to figure out what is your best chance on that particular water for catching a giant bass. You examine all the options available and all the techniques that have proven successful for that particular water at that time of year. This is why it's so important to become intimate with the waters you fish. Over the years an experienced angler may have a great backlog of information on many different lakes, but for anglers who are just starting to learn, it would be better to fish only a few lakes and learn them well. The same philosophy applies to learning a few different techniques. The beginning angler shouldn't buy dozens of different lure types, he should buy a few lure types and learn to use them well. So when you go out on any body of water you use the high percentage rule. You select the best method that has a successful history, or that has worked well for you at that time of year in the past. You work that method all the way through; even if you don't get a single bite all day, you stay with the high-percentage technique. As a big bass fisherman you shouldn't say, "I'm not getting action, so I'll try something else." That's the difference between trophy fishing and just fishing for bites-a trophy angler is not looking for a particular pattern that works on one particular day like a tournament fisherman; a trophy angler stays with the all-time proven patterns whether they catch fish or not. I know this philosophy may sound wrong to some anglers, but you're not fishing for a type of bass that's constantly changing, when you hunt for giant bass. You're looking for that percentage fish, and as a big bass fisherman you know those percentage fish are going to hit a certain technique at a certain time of year. In other words, if you haven't got a bite in 3 hours, you might change spots, but you probably wouldn't change techniques because you know from your backlog of experience what those big fish should hit. All you do is concentrate on the right spots and wait for an active period. When the fish become active, you'll more than likely catch them on the proven technique. Not catching fish simply means the fish are not active.

Big bass fishing is not switching colors every fifteen minutes when you're not getting bit. Switching colors reflects a lack of confidence in what you're using, and a belief that the best color is a shifting, mysterious subject. Fact is, big bass like certain colors. Big bass prefer certain colors, and the colors they like best may not appeal to the majority of smaller bass that are in an active feeding mood at that time. You might be using a worm color that you know from experience is real good for big fish, but it might have little appeal to the majority of other fish that are hitting that day. You might be throwing a proven worm color on a prime structure and catch nothing, and at the same time watch another angler limit with 2-and-3-pounders with another color. That's the confusing part of trophy fishing. But you stick with the proven slot, or color, and when the big ones become active and move in, it'll be your turn to catch a huge fish whereas the angler throwing the small-fish color may catch nothing.

When it comes to catching the biggest bass from deep structured environments, my experiences reveal that the most productive or highest percent lures and live baits are: shiners, crayfish, plastic worms, jigs and pigs, spinnerbaits, and crankbaits, in that order. Jigs, spinnerbaits and crankbaits are terrific big bass lures, but from a year-round high-percentage basis they all fall short of stitching prime structures from an anchored position with either live baits or plastic worms, and this is especially true of lakes with lots of fishing pressure. And that's not to say that your chances aren't as good with other techniques. Take fishing with the popular floating, diving minnow lures for example. With so many people using these lures, there's going to be a ton of big bass caught on them, but success with these lures is deceiving. Wide usage gives the appearance that they're a great big bass lure, and they are, but as a single fisherman throwing these lures all day, your chances of contacting a giant bass are not as good as an angler stitching a prime big bass structure. Unless conditions are such where the larger fish are in the upper 4- or-5-ft. of water (such as the spawning season), fishing with a floating, diving minnow lure will not be as effective as fishing deep. It's the same reason why I haven't talked about fishing with surface plugs, because surface and sub-surface lures are marginal big bass producers in structured lakes. And you can get good shallow-water how-to information in almost any bass fishing publication. I hate to judge any lure, or reaction, by the spring shallow-water season, because spring is a time when almost everything works. Ten guys fishing ten different lures at different depths might all have success on the same lake. But the title of a "high percentage" lure or technique is determined by results over the course of an entire year when viewed under all conditions. If you limit yourself to crankbaits, spinnerbaits or jigs, you might catch big bass at certain times, but these would not necessarily be the highest percentage big bass baits all the time. Trolling is a good example of a high percentage seasonal technique. In early summer after the fish have finished spawning and prefer a faster bait, speed trolling with crankbaits becomes **THE** high percentage technique. When bass are active and moving, such as during a stable pre-frontal weather pattern, speed trolling crankbaits can be devastating, whereas a slower method like stitching might be too slow for the larger fish. To be a successful year-round angler, you must be aware of the high percentage techniques and not waste time on patterns that don't work. I use spinnerbaits, crankbaits and jigs when conditions call for their use, but the highest percentage technique for catching the most big bass off structures, from the standpoint of year-round consistency, is stitching from an anchored position with either live shiners, crayfish or plastic worms. Crankbaits, spinnerbaits and jigs become secondary or alternate approaches.

Some anglers say, "But I don't like to fish one spot. Stitching is maddening; it's not fishing it's brain surgery!" Everyone's different, but I'll bet many anglers would really enjoy stitching, trolling or fishing with live bait, if they experienced for themselves how successful these techniques can be.

FINDING THE RIGHT COLOR

The thrill of catching a really big bass lives with you for a lifetime.

A friend and I were having a great evening catching bass, one on almost every cast, and it was getting dark. Earlier we tried several colors, but the fish would only bite a purple worm. I had different colored worms separated in shirt and pant pockets, and when I broke off a worm I would reach for the appropriate pocket and get a new one. After a period of time the bass stopped biting for me, but to my surprise my friend who was fishing only 4 feet from me kept catching fish. I shrugged my shoulders figuring the fish had just shut off in my angle of the spot. But after we got back to the dock and were loading the station wagon, I slid the rods in from the back with the rod tips pointed toward the front seat, I turned to say something to my partner and saw one purple and one black plastic worm dangling from the rods. Then it hit me what happened. In the darkness I had mistakenly tied on a black worm after busting off a purple worm. And the bass could tell the difference; they could distinguish colors in practically no light at all! That happened over 15 years ago, and it really opened my eyes to how important fishing the right color is in bass fishing.

Color is one of the most important features of an artificial lure. There are many colors that will catch bass, but only certain colors catch giant bass. Small bass might strike any color, that's one reason why they are easier to catch, but big bass are more selective. Sound and vibration may initially attract bass, but the color is the first thing it sees, and if that color doesn't compute favorably, it won't stimulate a positive response from a giant bass. Even with a fast-moving crankbait or spinnerbait, where you'd think color might not be critical, a big bass might rush out to investigate the vibration of a lure, but if it sees a color that triggers a negative reaction, the fish won't strike.

Finding the right color, in many cases, is the missing link which elevates an angler from a good bass fisherman to a good big bass fisherman. Your skills may stay at the same level, but when you find a color that the bigger fish like, the appeal of your presentation dramatically increases in the eyes of the biggest bass. There can be a number of different color patterns that work, but usually there is only one or two colors, or color combinations, that for whatever reason, big bass prefer best. Once a preferred color pattern is established, the pattern can last for weeks or even the entire year. A heavy spring runoff or dramatic change in temperature may alter a favorable response to a certain color, but generally speaking, a good color will remain good for quite a while. On some lakes a color preference won't change for years. Why they like that color has to do with the whole makeup of the lake environment, and finding that color is everything.

Did you ever watch someone fish with a light meter? With every cloud shift or wind change, they lower a probe and say, "The meter says blue; Now it says green; Now the needle is between purple and red." With each new reading, the angler digs into his tackle box for a corresponding color. Switching colors may prove effective for small bass because a small bass is the size that will bite practically any color just out of curiosity, but constantly switching colors has no bearing on big bass fishing. Light meters indicate what colors are most visible under various light conditions, but meters can't tell you which colors the big fish prefer. There is no sure way to predict which colors will work on a particular body of water. Even waters within close proximity can have totally different color responses. The only way to discover the best color is to fish the right area with all the proven colors. It takes time and effort, but once a color preference is found, those colors become your confidence colors, and you stay with them; you don't keep changing color with every shift in the wind or sky condition.

Let's say you have located several big bass spots on a particular lake, and after several trips during good active periods, you have discovered after experimenting with all your best colors that the bigger bass really like two worm colors-a brown worm with a black stripe, and a plain black worm. These two colors would become your confidence colors, and you'd have them tied on at all times. You stay with brown and black although you keep rotating in other colors for comparison. Fishing remains good all year and you catch lots of big bass. By fishing the same spots all the time, it becomes obvious that when you're catching bass the fish are simply not active and moving. And when they do get active and you begin catching them, they always bite brown or black. For some reason the other colors just don't produce strikes. This scenario is what an angler learns after pursuing big bass for decades. Big bass only respond consistently to certain colors, and the only way to find those colors is to fish the right spots when the big fish are active, and experiment with all the proven colors. After a bite slows down, you may be able to switch colors and stimulate a few bass that weren't responsive to the color you were using, but usually when the action slows on a productive color it means the active period is over.

When using a finesse presentation, like the stitching technique, everything has to be right. When a big bass moves up to a plastic worm and eyeballs your lure, you can bet your life that worm has to look right or the fish won't hit. That's why when I find a productive color I don't stop experimenting with color. Big bass have great color perception and definition. Even when deep in murky water, where you wouldn't think bass could distinguish subtle color variations, different hues of even the same color can make a big difference. I once took clothing dye and dyed a batch of blue, purple and brown worms until they were so dark they all looked black. To the human eye you could hardly see a difference, but the bass picked up the difference instantly! I fished each color side by side with the others on a good spot during an active period, and the only worm the fish would hit was the brown/black color. Then I used the brown/black worm next to a straight black worm. Again, the fish only wanted the brown/black worm. I've witnessed subtle color preferences many, many times. I've even seen bass prefer a translucent worm over an opaque worm of identical color and vice-versa. So it's important to keep experimenting. A productive color may become your bread-and-butter presentation, but experimenting with different shades of the same color may produce even better.

Another consideration, when selecting color, is the type of lure. A color that works for spinnerbaits and crankbaits may be totally different than a productive color in a plastic worm. If I were fishing a lake with muddy water, I might select a yellow/black crankbait, a chartreuse spinnerbait, and a blue plastic worm. All are proven choices, yet they all have different colors. But if you mix these colors, their productivity would likely decline. A blue crankbait, or a yellow worm, would likely produce poor results. No doubt confidence in certain combinations would be a factor, but some colors definitely work better on certain lure types.

Abstract Elements

When trying to fool a bass, I think it's important to understand that bass normally feed by focusing on abstract elements. Bass don't count how many tentacles a creature has, or a lure has, before it decides to strike, they're not intelligent enough for that. But they do feed by focusing in on key elements which can be very subliminal in effect. It could be as small as a spot on the side of a baitfish. The baitfish are moving fast trying to escape, and bass really don't have time to examine them too closely. All they know is that they ate something that tasted good, and it had a spot, so next time they look for something with a spot. Shiners don't have spots, and if bass are feeding on shiners, they might react negatively to a lure with a spot because, in that situation, shad might be viewed as harder to catch

Bass are sensitory creatures that feed primarily by sight and sound. They have great eyesight and can see black, white and color. Each eye sees independently - one can move forward while the other moves back.

and less predictable. Bass are used to seeing certain signals in nature. It could be the spot of a shad, the green flash of a shiner, the colored spots of a trout, a silver flash, a gold flash, or whatever, but all these abstract signs in nature signal different things to bass. Some promote a positive strike reaction, and some signals turn bass away. The important thing to realize is that your presentation does not have to be an absolute replica of what fish are feeding on to promote a positive strike response. Your presentation only needs to be a characterization of something real. All you're trying to do is find something that will stimulate a predatory response, and it doesn't have to closely match anything bass naturally feed upon. That's why lures don't have to be photocopies of live prey. In fact, crankbaits with photo finishes of real crayfish, or real baitfish, have proven my **LEAST PRODUCTIVE** colors for big bass, and I think that is a testament to my belief that bass feed by focusing on key subliminal elements that do not have to closely imitate real food. The early paint jobs, found on the old-style Bomber plugs and Buck Perry's Spoonplugs, such as yellow Coach-dog, and a white body with a red head, were effective because they were made by people trying to characterize a moving lure into an overall effect. They weren't trying to paint a detailed portrait, they were trying to create an effect that would trigger a positive response from the fish. Many of these colors are still available today because they continue to catch bass. All you need to do is find a color that triggers a positive response, and it could be a weird color that has no resemblance to anything alive. Nothing in nature that I know of looks like a scuppernong worm, but there are times when the fish absolutely refuse to hit any other color. Big bass sometimes feed like grazing cows. A grazing cow doesn't eat all the grass, it moves from clump to clump over the entire pasture. Bass often feed the same way on a prime structural element. They often have so much to choose from, when they begin feeding they just move around at random picking and pecking, they don't have to eat everything in their path. Your presentation may seem to you like a dark shape moving across the bottom, but a big bass might analyze the size, speed, color and relationship to the path of normal bait flow. If that fish doesn't feel right about something in your presentation, it simply moves on to something else that looks better. That's why when a fish bumps a plastic worm but rejects it, you can often throw another color to the same spot and it'll take it. Initially, the bass was interested in the worm but the color was wrong. A different color promoted a different response, and the fish just wasn't smart enough to correlate the two.

People tend to associate grey and brown as natural colors, but that's not necessarily true. A natural color can be bright green, bright blue, bright pink or yellow! All these colors are already in nature, you just have to look closer to see them. If you examine a dried crayfish shell under a microscope, you'll discover that crayfish are not just green or brown or red. A red crayfish, for example, isn't straight red, it's more of a purple-red, and there's a lavender in the red too. An examination of shad and shiners reveals vivid blues, greens, pinks, and practically every color of the rainbow in the pigmentation of their translucent skin. Some people say that there isn't color intensity in nature and that natural colors are drab and camouflaged, but I would counter that there is so much color reflected from the side of a shad, or shiner, in bright sunlight, it's almost unbelievable. Nature has brilliant color, and at times the bigger bass will focus on these colors, in an abstract way, even though they don't appear natural to the human eye.

I was once catching a good number of 2-and-3-pound bass on tiny green crayfish, but when I cast out a brown worm I caught the biggest bass in the area on the first cast. Before that, I was rotating between crayfish and a green worm, and I never had a hit from even a small bass on the green worm. So there had to be a positive triggering effect with the brown worm, and it was different than the triggering effect of green crayfish. The brown worm was the same size as the green worm, so size wasn't the trigger. Normally, you'll find the bigger bass responding positively to only one or two colors, and the productive colors will be linked to a major food source in some subliminal or abstract way. Once you become aware of this correlation on a particular lake, you can use this knowledge to your advantage. For instance, I know from past experiences that when big bass start feeding on crayfish in winter, I have better results using purple, lavender, bright green and brown colored worms; these are the colors that seem to have a correlation with crayfish. And when bass feed more heavily on shad, I consistently get more strikes on black and rootbeer-colored worms. I know what they've been feeding on by the condition of their teeth. Bass feeding on crayfish usually have smooth jaws, but when their teeth are razor sharp, stomach contents usually reveal shad.

Seasonal Colors

While it's true that hot colors may produce throughout the entire year, the colors bass respond to best can also change from season to season. The colors that work best in winter are often different than colors that are productive in summer. Everything is more brightly colored in summer-green plants are vivid, and flowers have brilliant color. In the underwater world, summer creates bright healthy weed growth, gives bluegill bright coloration, and makes the dark markings on bass darker and more distinct. A wide variety of plug colors work in summer, including yellows, oranges, greens and golds. During late fall and winter, however, the environment changes and the colors of nature become subdued, blanched and very drab. As the water color gets more of a whitish hue in winter and everything has a softer, more pastel look about it, it's often better to use subdued colors that the fish are programed to seeing. The same colors that worked in summer might still produce in winter, but you should switch to shades of those colors that are more drab and subdued. Instead of a blue worm, try a blue with a lot of white that gives the blue a pasty or frozen look. Instead of a dark purple worm, use a light magenta worm. Winter is a good time to soften the appearance of crankbaits and spinnerbait blades with a coating of nail polish (a subject I'll cover in the chapter on "Crankbaits").

Bright colors start producing again in early spring. Although the environment is still cold and drab, bass seem to instinctively sense that conditions are beginning to change, and for some reason bass become more susceptible and less spooked by colors that are brighter and more outrageous. Brightly colored spinnerbaits that produce a lot of flash often create strikes in early spring, but the fish would likely snub the same lure in the dead of winter.

Low Light Colors

Bright colors show up better in murky water or low light conditions, but I don't think it matters if a fish can see chartreuse farther than another color under low light conditions. Generally speaking, yellow or chartreuse plugs work very well on big bass in murky water, but I don't think it means anything to a big bass that it can see chartreuse from farther away. Chartreuse happens to be a good plug color in murky water, and it happens to be visible too. But yellow or chartreuse plastic worms are one of my least productive big bass colors in murky water. Red is another worm color that rarely works in murky water, yet a splash of red can make spinnerbaits and plugs much more attractive.

I think the most important factor in selecting color in murky water is simply finding a color the fish like. If you find a color that bass like, you won't have any problem getting bites regardless of the water color. It's not a matter of bass seeing a certain color from a long distance, bass move to a lure because they sense the vibration or sound. Once a bass homes in on a lure, color comes into play, but the color still has to compute right-if the color isn't something bass are used to seeing or feeding upon, then a big bass may let it go by.

Smaller bass might strike from impulse or curiosity, but a giant bass, which is more sensitive and aware, might instinctively reject the wrong color whether it is highly visible or not. A shad or shiner basically has greens, blues, pinks, silver, and sometimes even yellow colors in its body, so when I use a plug or spinnerbait, I would try one or all of these colors in any water color. You discover the most productive color by experimenting with all your proven best colors, and a positive response to certain colors will likely vary with each individual lake. Color patterns frequently overlap, but just saying one color is more visible under low light conditions doesn't really mean anything in big bass fishing.

A brown or black plastic worm is especially productive in murky water and low light conditions, yet I'm always hearing anglers say that fish can't even see it. You shouldn't care if a bass can see your lure or not because bass have other ways of finding prey. When you work a color with low visibility, you're working with all the instincts of nature; you're using a subdued color, you're working quiet, and you're making the bass work for it. And a giant bass is used to working for it; it loves to hunt, hunting is part of its game. If you skin-dive in water that is full of sediment, where visibility is inches, you may not see anything from far away, but as you get close to an object every detail comes into view. There is always some light present, even at depth in murky water, and a bass can see everything close in perfect detail. Bass can still see, but turbid water reduces their vision to the little environment surrounding them. They can't see very far to the right or left, so they concentrate on their small circle of vision. Even though a stitched plastic worm has little sound or movement, when the worm penetrates that sphere of vision it immediately stands out. Once your lure enters that sphere, then it's just the bass and your lure. If the worm color computes in a favorable way, a giant bass might jump all over it. I've found that brown or black worms often compute well in low light conditions, and both these colors can promote vicious strikes when you stitch them slowly through a big bass spot.

Establishing a Color Preference

The first thing I do when fishing a new lake is seek information about color. I don't really care about depth or the currently "hot" lures, I can find my own spots and figure out the patterns, but I really like to know the best color before I go out. If I see a guy come in with a big fish, the first thing I ask him is what color it hit. My experience usually confirms whether he is telling the truth or not. Color is important to know beforehand because you rarely get enough practice with lunker bass to establish any kind of color pattern in the first day or two on a new water. Knowledge of the best color only comes after fishing the same lake often.

On the first trip to a new lake I'm really not thinking about making a great catch, all I'm trying to do is get at least one bass over 4 pounds to bite. If I can catch an adult bass on an outer edge spot in deep water then I know the color the fish bit is important. There's something about the bottom composition, the color of the water, the light refractory at that depth, and there's something about the color-prey relationship at that depth that triggered a positive response to a certain color. Once I get that first bite, I'll stick with that color. Catching a small bass up in the shallows would likely be of little benefit because the same color, more than likely, would not trigger the bigger fish in deep water. Generally speaking, if I fish a good outer edge spot my chances are good that when I do get a bite it'll be from a quality fish. But if I caught a small bass in deep water, there would be two questions going through my mind: 1. This spot might not be a big fish spot; and 2. Not only is the spot wrong, but I'm probably using the wrong color. But if I were to catch a bass over 4 pounds from that spot, then I would assume that it's a good spot and I would have faith that the same color will trigger big bass on different spots all over the lake.

If the lake has several good-looking spots I would not go from spot to spot trying to establish a pattern. I would rather add up all the ingredients of each spot and then pick one spot that looks like the best big fish spot in the entire lake or the section of the lake I'm fishing. I also might pick a spot that has a history of producing lunker bass.

Generally, I try to fish a new lake during a good moon phase or pre-frontal condition, but if activity is slow I'll stay longer on the best-looking spot.

The system I use to find a color preference is to anchor on the best-looking spot and use all my proven colors until I get a bite. I generally try to establish a color pattern with a plastic worm. I may switch to a live crayfish if there's absolutely no response to worms, but my goal is to first establish a big bass color, so I just keep rotating all my proven colors until the fish decide on one they like.

I like to use the activity of dark moon phases to establish color preference and productive areas. A dark moon phase is not a particularly good time to be looking for giant bass, but you almost always have more activity on a dark moon phase from smaller fish. I'm not saying that all the bass will be real active, but you'll have a better chance to catch numbers of bass off structures on dark moon phases because the bass population as a whole is more active. There will be active periods on dark moon phases and fishing will get better during these times; these are the times when you try to establish a color preference. I don't like to fish a new lake during a prime 3/4 moon phase because although a 3/4 phase is a prime period for catching a giant bass, a 3/4 phase can be a bad day for the rest of the bass population. I try to establish the color preference on a dark moon phase when fishing for numbers is best, and then I camp on a prime structure during a 3/4 phase when bass fishing in general is slow. I'll fish a prime big fish structure with the proven color and fish it hard all day waiting for a giant bass to become active and move in. If you find a spot that produces 4-and-5-pounders on a dark moon, it'll probably produce 8-and-9-pounders on a big fish moon. A 5-fish limit of 15 lbs. on a dark moon might translate into a 5-fish limit of 32 lbs. on a 3/4 moon. That's why it's important to fish a new lake as much as possible. If you fish the same lake at least once a week, you'll be able to establish the locational patterns and color preference. You'll fish the bad days and good days, and you'll learn something every time and get closer to what the fish are doing. You'll learn their feeding cycles and become more intimate with the lake with each trip.

Beyond the Visible

Because the eyes of bass have both rods and cones and because their low-light vision is so acute, many scientists believe bass have the ability to detect a longer span of color separation than humans. If bass can see colors we can't, and if we become aware of those colors, it might be possible to make more productive lures even though we can't distinguish the color ourselves. I suspect that there is a good chance that bass can decipher colors that lie in the infrared and ultraviolet ranges. I know this sounds far out, but it might be the reason why some lures work better than others. You can have two identical plugs, and one always out-fishes the other. Anglers always gave credit to super fine tuning, and there's no doubt that a plug running perfectly straight has great attracting abilities, but two plugs can run the same and one still out-catches the other; maybe the real reason is that the color is different?

Presently, I'm experimenting on ways to actually discover what bass see. If you go into infrared there are a lot of colors our eyes cannot detect. But you can find these colors with black light, fluorescents, and radiation. Colors can be created from many things that will fluoresce under normal or artificial light. Radiation from the sun can fluoresce certain colors that we can't see. In my work as a Dental Ceramist, I make teeth that not only fluoresce under black light but under natural sunlight as well. Eventually, I hope to create a plug that will fluoresce under natural sunlight much the way sunlight illuminates through a transparent shad. If bass can detect that color, it may be the color they see in baitfish that is lacking in the most translucent paint. The reason why I believe this may be true is because I have plugs made with old silver paint that work better than the most natural-looking silver Rapala or Rebel. There may be something in the old lead pigment that fluoresces under normal daylight that we can't see.

The spectrum of white is so great, two people can be using the same white lure and have completely different colors. White is a neutral color, and not being able to tell the radiation factor in either white or black, it's hard to tell what color you actually have when using white. If bass can detect a radiation spectrum that we can't see it might account for why certain white lures produce better than others of the same color. When I paint a lure white, I'll make a dozen of them to see if there's a preferred color spectrum. When I discover a batch of white paint that the fish like, I'll paint all my lures with that color white.

The whole subject of color perception is fascinating. Bass are truly amazing creatures, and they're much more complicated and sensitive than we would like to believe. Every time I read an article about someone who thinks they have bass all figured out, I just shake my head and snicker because the more you dig into this sport the farther you seem to be from getting to the bottom of it all.

PLASTIC WORMS

Even after hundreds of variations in styles and colors that have evolved over the years since they were first introduced, the plastic worm still has the same phenomenal big bass appeal that I found them to have in the very beginning. The appeal factor comes from it's versatility, and it's versatility makes the plastic worm the highest percentage bait you can use for giant bass in a structured lake situation; no other artificial lure or live bait has a better percentage of consistency than does a plastic worm. Worms can be rigged so they don't hang up, and there's nothing that will go through cover and work structure better than plastics. Besides their locational versatility, plastic worms also have the appeal of a wide range of colors. You can keep changing the color until you find which worm color appeals to the bass on any particular day. And once you find the best color, then you can key in on the big bass areas and experiment to find what size worm they're responding to best.

From a year-round standpoint, plastic worms are super-consistent because of their appeal to neutral fish. I think active, neutral and non-active fish is simply a state of mind. Obviously, activity has a lot to do with general feeding habits and the programs fish get from nature such as barometric pressure, moon phases and all the things we discussed concerning active periods, but I think bass are neutral more often than any other stage and therefore catchable most of the time. There has to be very severe condition to make fish totally inactive, and a very favorable condition to make them totally active. Consequently, the greater majority of the time when you're fishing, bass are in a neutral state and can be provoked into biting given the right stimulation and persistence. Plastic worms have a proven record for catching bass in all stages of activity, and they're particularly effective for neutral bass. You can actually work a worm in a way that will provoke a strike from fish that otherwise wouldn't bite. Many anglers never grasp the true potential of worm fishing because they aren't willing to work hard enough to generate a bite. Most

13 lb. 11 oz. beauty caught on 16 inch plastic worm.

modern anglers have been conditioned to fish fast even when using a worm. A dozen casts to one spot is adequate to check it, so the current thinking goes. But if you want to catch neutral bass, and catch bass when activity is slow, you'll have to fish much more deliberately. Fishing fast won't aggravate neutral bass into hitting; you have to slow way down and leave the worm in one place longer. Even experienced stitch fishermen sometimes get caught up in the "fish fast" syndrome. It's easy to pull into a good spot that has been producing well and fish a worm too fast because you're bursting with confidence and you expect so much from the spot. You're so pumped up you may totally miss the timing, or speed, the fish want on that particular day. There are days when the fish want a worm to sit absolutely still for long periods of time, and the more neutral they are,the longer they want that worm to sit in between movements. I've often left a worm lie in one spot for several minutes and then had a bass pick it up. It's very important to use a pause, or sitting technique, when fishing is slow. When I come across a situation where bass aren't responding to a proven retrieve, that's my signal to work a worm with long pauses. A jig and pig might be the next highest percentage bait, depending on the time of year, because you can fish it slowly and deliberately, but even then you can't methodically irritate bass into striking a jig like you can with a plastic worm. You can leave a worm in one spot and the movement from the bait alone can promote a strike reflex from the most lethargic bass. Even though there is some movement in the skirt of a jig, when a jig is at rest on the bottom it basically becomes a non-moving object. But when you rig a plastic 7-to-8-inches behind a small split shot, the worm will float slightly off the bottom, and it will move and twitch with the subtle underwater currents even when at a standstill. This action irritates neutral bass into striking, and it's one reason why my stitching rig has proven so successful.

Most people don't give plastic worms the credit they deserve. People who use live bait, for example, tend to treat live bait as the ultimate presentation and ignore the appealing qualities of plastics. But I've had times where I totally outfished live bait fishermen with plastic worms, even though they were overlapping my casts and using live crayfish and shiners in the same area. Live bait is not always the answer, and it's important to understand that a plastic worm does not have to represent anything alive. The color of a worm doesn't have to match the brown color of a crayfish or the silver-grey of a shad. All a worm has to do is have an effect that stimulates some type of positive reaction from the fish. The goal should always be to stimulate a positive response no matter what you use. The stimulation comes from a total effect that includes size, action and color. Bass feel the vibration, they see the color and motion, and the total effect clicks something in their brains that says, "I've got to have that!" But the stimulation doesn't necessarily come from a worm that looks like anything the bass are currently feeding upon. If you consider a jig and pig the closest lure resembling a live crayfish, this is nonsense because the only thing that looks like a crayfish is another crayfish. If you observe a crayfish and a jig and pig side by side in a fish tank,

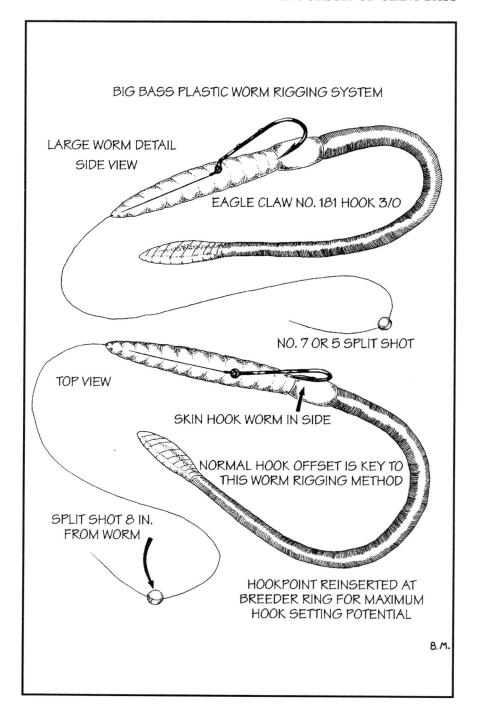

BIG BASS PLASTIC WORM RIGGING SYSTEM

LARGE WORM DETAIL
SIDE VIEW

EAGLE CLAW NO. 181 HOOK 3/0

NO. 7 OR 5 SPLIT SHOT

TOP VIEW

SKIN HOOK WORM IN SIDE

NORMAL HOOK OFFSET IS KEY TO
THIS WORM RIGGING METHOD

SPLIT SHOT 8 IN.
FROM WORM

HOOKPOINT REINSERTED AT
BREEDER RING FOR MAXIMUM
HOOK SETTING POTENTIAL

B.M.

you're really underselling the intelligence of these fish, even with their small brains, if you think a crayfish and jig and pig look alike. But when a bass sees a jig and pig being pulled along the bottom, kicking up little clouds of mud, the clouds of mud and the lure combine to create an **ILLUSION** of a crayfish. The illusion, or total effect, is what stimulates a positive or negative response. But the illusion doesn't have to look real to promote a strike. Even if the fish are feeding on crayfish, you still might catch them better with a plastic worm simply by creating a more stimulating effect that couldn't be created by using a live crayfish. I've often found that it's more important to figure out the stimulation than trying to match the creature the fish are feeding upon. Plastic worms stimulate by their action, size and color, and their ability to penetrate areas where bass hold. For these reasons, worms can produce strikes when no other lure or live bait can. And with all the hundreds of options in style and color, there's just no other lure that offers a higher percentage for catching big bass than a plastic worm.

Worm Color

In another chapter I discussed the importance of finding the right color, and finding the right color is probably more important when fishing a plastic worm than with any other lure. A big bass may have only seconds to decide whether to strike a spinnerbait or crankbait, but it can eyeball a plastic worm as long as it likes from close range. And the color of the worm will have a great impact on whether or not a big bass will hit it.

When I first fish a new spot, I normally use a 6-inch worm and try that size in each of my ten best colors. I'll lay all ten on the boat seat and go right down the line making one cast with each color. I might make a few casts with a particularly good color, but once I establish the proper casting direction and retrieve path I'll generally make just one cast with each color. If you're casting to the right spot on the structure and the fish are there, you'll normally get a bite, or some signal of activity, once you cast a worm with the color they want. If I was privileged to acquire some accurate knowledge on what worm colors had produced big bass from this lake in the past, I would

Big bass can be very size selective. This 11-pounder fell for a 6-inch worm.

probably stay with that color and begin to switch to different sizes before changing color, but if it was a new lake where I didn't have accurate color knowledge, I would experiment to establish a color preference before switching sizes.

Author's Personal Favorite Big Bass Worm Colors
Black
Blue (blue with a green influence)
Brown (also cinnamon)
Purple (burgundy wine color)
Green (dark emerald green)
Rootbeer (scuppernong)
All other colors used are spinoffs of these basic colors.

I like the black and colored stripes on Delong worms, but I don't know if the stripes are important or not. The stripe may stimulate by creating a combination of color such as: a black stripe on a brown worm, or a blue stripe on a cinnamon worm, but I think the stripe also adds to the overall action. A black stripe on a brown worm gives the worm an illustrated movement. When the worm bends, the black stripe illustrates or intensifies the motion. Colored stripes are most important when used with a clear worm. Clear worms take on the overall color of the stripe. A clear worm with a blue stripe, for example, turns the worm a clear blue. Clear worms with colored stripes create a translucent, minnow-like color which seems particularly effective in clear water situations. Delong is one of the few worm companies that will custom color to order. I enjoy experimenting with new colors, and you never know when you'll discover a productive color only you will be throwing.

Black is probably the best all-around color for big bass. If an angler would use it long enough, I'm sure he would catch a giant bass on black if he fished the right spot at the right time. Black is one of the few colors that seem to work all across the country for both Florida and northern strain largemouth bass; black is even good for big smallmouths.

The only way to find the best color for big bass wherever you fish is to experiment. Remember that the colors that catch the most bass may not necessarily catch the biggest bass. When you catch a bass over 4 pounds on an outside structure, the color that tricked the fish is probably one of the better big fish colors on that lake. Stay with that color and experiment with different sizes before switching to a different color.

Worm Size

Bass either want a big bait or little bait, and it has nothing to do with any condition or phenomenon. Sometimes bass want big shiners and at other times they want little shiners; sometimes they want big crayfish and sometimes little crayfish; sometimes they want big plugs or big plastic worms, and sometimes little ones work best. And this size selectivity has nothing to do with season or any correlation I can think of. I've caught big bass on large and small live baits, and large and small artificials during every season. There's no way to accurately predict what size will work best because there's no way to tell; **IT ALL DEPENDS ON WHAT THE BASS WANT!** It's like a light goes on and every big fish in the lake suddenly wants 9-inch worms, and two months later they want 4-inch worms. Sometimes they'll eat 16-inch worms, and these times generally coincide with larger live bait preferences.

Over the years I've noticed a few trends in seasonal size selectivity. During a severe post-frontal condition, even big bass are more apt to take a smaller lure or live bait; the fish are in a finicky mood and they don't seem interested in pursuing larger prey. Bass in the middle of summer and the coldest parts of winter often respond the same way-they tend to react more sluggishly and prefer smaller lures and smaller live baits. The interesting part about size selectivity is that the size of the lure or live bait bass respond to best may be totally unconnected with the size of the prey they're feeding upon. In winter, for example, the bass may only bite small crayfish. But at the same

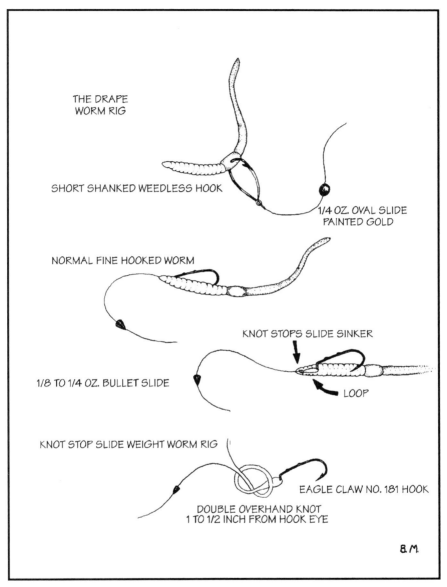

THE DRAPE
WORM RIG

SHORT SHANKED WEEDLESS HOOK

1/4 OZ. OVAL SLIDE
PAINTED GOLD

NORMAL FINE HOOKED WORM

KNOT STOPS SLIDE SINKER

1/8 TO 1/4 OZ. BULLET SLIDE

LOOP

KNOT STOP SLIDE WEIGHT WORM RIG

EAGLE CLAW NO. 181 HOOK

DOUBLE OVERHAND KNOT
1 TO 1/2 INCH FROM HOOK EYE

B.M.

Specialty Worm Rigs: *The Drape Rig*—**This is an excellent searching tool. Drift it or fish it fast to quickly check a structure. Use up to a 3/4 oz. oval sinker when checking deep water.** *Knot-stop Worm Rig*—**Excellent for fishing heavy cover. Instead of using a toothpick to anchor the hook in the worm, a double overhand knot keeps the sinker from pushing the worm down the hook. The double overhand knot is strong—I've successfully landed bass up to 14 lbs. on this rig.**

time, they have large crayfish in their belly. But they won't bite a large stream-caught crayfish, they only respond favorably to small green ones. I've found that bass often prefer big lake shiners in winter and spring, but in summer they favor smaller shiners and if you use a large shiner in summer they'll often just kill the shiner but not eat it. Why these things happen is anyone's guess, but it really doesn't make any difference because it's not important to know why. When the bass are feeding on small green crayfish, an angler might generate a strike from the biggest bass in the area by using a large red dad. So as a big bass fisherman, I would always take a healthy supply of crayfish in all different sizes whenever I fished with crayfish, and the same rule applies to plastic worms.

When I first fish a new lake, I start with a plastic worm in a size I'm more apt to draw a bite from bass of all sizes. In summer that would be a 4-inch worm, and any other time it would be a 6-inch worm. When I talk about a 4-inch worm I'm referring to a thick-bodied 6-inch worm cut down to 4-inches. You don't want a delicate, thin-bodied 4-inch worm; short and meaty is what big bass like. I'll prospect with these two sizes until I get a bite from a decent fish, and once I establish a color preference, then I'll experiment more with size.

Normally, once you find the productive color, there will be a certain size in that color which will draw the most bites. I call this the "standard" worm size for that lake at that particular time. If I was getting bites from decent fish on a 6-inch worm I might experiment with a bigger worm to see if it would attract bigger fish, but I would never drop down to a 4-inch worm. I might drop to a 4-inch worm in summer or after a severe frontal condition, but even then if the fish were biting a 4-inch worm then that worm would be the standard size making a 6-inch worm a big worm. Once you find a productive size (the standard size) you can work up but never down; you only work down in size if a 6-inch worm, for example, was not drawing strikes. If the bass were in a positive mood, they might take a 7-1/2-inch worm over a 6-inch worm, but very seldom will big bass respond better to a 4-inch worm if they are generally taking 6-inch worms. If I was fishing a time of year or weather condition where a 4-inch worm was the standard size, I would have another rod rigged with a 6-inch worm

Sinker Position Makes a Difference

There's a big difference how line comes off a plastic worm and the way the worm appears to fish. To a bass observing a worm rig, the actual start of the line is the point where the line connects the sinker to the boat. If the line starts at the head of the worm top, bass may instinctively reject the worm if it notices a line stretching up at an angle from the bottom. But a worm dancing horizontally some distance behind the sinker can completely kill that rejection attitude because the fish concentrates more on the worm and away from the line. A horizontal line 8 inches behind a split shot is enough to cause bass to lose instinctive rejection. Being at a different angle, the worm appears not to be a part of what's going on in front of it. A bait is always more attractive when the line is camouflaged horizontally along the bottom.

Top — Line very obvious when coming directly off plastic worm.
Bottom — Nice bottom hugging effect as line trails split shot.

of the same color to periodically check to see if I couldn't tempt a big bass that wasn't responding to the 4-inch worm. But if 4-inch worms were the standard size, you might as well leave the 7-and-9-inch worms back home because very seldom will they go from a 4-inch to a 9-inch worm.

Paying attention to worm size is important when you're after big fish. It helps if you focus on how they act and respond. Sometimes they only want 9-inch worms, and sometimes they only want a 16-inch worm, and they'll yank the rod right out of your hands when they do. Sometimes they won't bite a 9-inch worm, or even a 6-inch worm, and you have to drop down to 4-inches to get any kind of interest. So bass fishing is a mystery, even to people that know a lot. You might go to a new lake and cast a 6-inch worm all day with the idea that it should appeal to the widest range of fish, but when you only catch one 2-pound bass, you convince yourself that if you had used a 4-inch worm you might have caught more fish. But then you meet a guy at the dock with a big string of bass from 2 to 4-pounds, and he says he caught them on 9-inch worms. He also says that he caught them from four different spots, which means the fish were biting all over the lake (including the prime areas you were fishing), but you only got one small fish. No matter how you look at it, it was a day when the fish wanted 9-inch worms. There's no reason for it, it just happens. And that's what you're up against when you pursue these fish. It took me years to figure out that there is no under-standable correlation to half the things big bass do. But it doesn't matter why they do it, all you have to know is that these things happen. Bass can be extremely size- conscious as well as color-conscious. If you get locked into a certain size or a certain color, you will only get certain results, and you will blame the times when you're not catching fish on exterior conditions when, in fact, the fish may have responded to a worm of a different size or color much better. A spot isn't properly checked until you experiment with all the options.

NATURAL BAIT

Many of the early bass fishing pioneers detested the use of live bait, however, the pressure on the lakes back then was nothing like it is today. Nowadays, fishermen are using more refined techniques and the fish themselves are a lot more sophisticated. Educational magazines like Fishing Facts and In Fisherman have always appreciated the benefits of trolling and using live bait, and I think this is a healthy approach for people who want the maximum enjoyment from this sport. A person can be a purist but they should never close their eyes to productive ways of catching bass. Ruling out live bait fishing as being unsportsmanlike, or assuming that it somehow lacks the skills or ability that it takes to use artificials, is a grossly unfair

If you stay with artificials when the big fish want live bait, you might miss the best fishing of the year.

assessment of this method. Each year some of the biggest bass are caught on bait and if we hope to stay a step ahead, we're going to need a variety of methods to compete.

Years ago when I first started experimenting with live bait; plugs, spinnerbaits and plastic worms, were my primary tactics. Sometimes on those days when fishing was tough, I'd use nightcrawlers as a secondary bait. As I experimented with other live baits, I reached a point where live crayfish became my primary bait at certain times of the year. Using live bait proved an eye-opening experience. Not only did live bait produce sometimes when artificials didn't, but I began to learn more about how giant bass relate to structure. I noticed that there are spots where artificials work better and there are spots where live bait works better. It was also interesting to learn that very few spots produce with both artificials and live bait at the same time. I came to the conclusion that it was the structural configuration of the spot itself that generally caused this artificial/live bait selectivity.

Plastic worms, for example, work best in areas where the bottom structure and cover is sufficient to promote an appealing worm action. Plastic worms work best when they are sticking to and deflecting off subtle variations in bottom terrain, or climbing up and falling off objects. But on flatter terrains which lack these important bottom elements, plastic worms become less effective. Even when you cause the worm to move erratically by working the line with your fingers, there are spots where bass just don't find a plastic worm appealing.

On these spots I've had much greater success with natural bait. Bait is ideally suited for structural areas with flat, clean bottom features, obviously it doesn't work well in areas where the cover is too thick because it constantly gets snagged up. But on featureless areas or at least reasonable amounts of bottom cover, live baits can entice and stimulate bass with their natural actions. You can let a crayfish walk around in a natural way, and if a big bass is cruising that flat, it will hear those tiny movements and home in on the crayfish. A stationary plastic worm might trigger bass within viewing distance but a stationary worm doesn't have the drawing power of the subtle clicking sounds of crayfish. When I discovered that the largest bass often relate to these flat subliminal areas throughout much of the year, I began working these spots more with natural bait

Proper handling of trophy fish can guarantee a successful release.

and in most cases my catch ratio increased. Just because you can't catch bass off a spot with a plastic worm doesn't mean they're not there. Sometimes using natural bait can make all the difference in the world.

Another lesson using natural bait has taught me is that there are certain periods throughout the year where live bait will totally out-produce artificials of any kind. Stitching a live crayfish during pre-spawn on deep structures adjacent to spawning flats can be devastating. Anglers are targeting the use of this technique on the lakes north of Los Angeles, and several giants have been taken with live crayfish during the spring in the last few years. Crayfish also work well in the dead of winter, and shiners in the heat of summer, when you can't buy a big bass with anything else. I'll talk more about these special periods in the chapters on seasonal patterns.

I guess what using live bait boils down to is a question of ethics. A bass that is properly handled and unhooked carefully will survive with no more trauma than one that was hooked on any other method. I've caught and released many bass that were hooked with live bait and I feel confident that they made it. You must respect every bass you catch regardless of the size and take the time to remove the hook properly. Remember that hooks are hooks whether they are in a plastic worm or pinned through a crayfish and they both can end up in the lower throat where they can do damage.

CRAYFISH - Big Bass Bait Supreme

Some species of crayfish are found in practically every region of the country, and whether you fish lakes, reservoirs, rivers or ponds, live crayfish really appeal to big bass whether they be largemouths, smallmouths or kentuckies. Live crayfish can be the great equalizer stimulating bass to bite in extra-clear water and after the passage of the most severe cold front. Crayfish are such an exceptional big bass bait, it's not surprising that so many anglers have decided to take advantage of them.

Crayfish Facts

Crayfish are very prolific and may take over a pond or small lake in short order if predators are limited. Females can produce hundreds of eggs which they carry under their tails until hatched. Young crayfish, and crayfish that live predominantly in cooler waters, tend to have pale green hues with speckles of black. They may also have slight reddish tints in their pinchers (this coloration is most common in winter and early spring). As water temperatures begin to warm in early summer, pale green hues give way to dark green before changing to light brown or a light reddish brown. By the time they reach

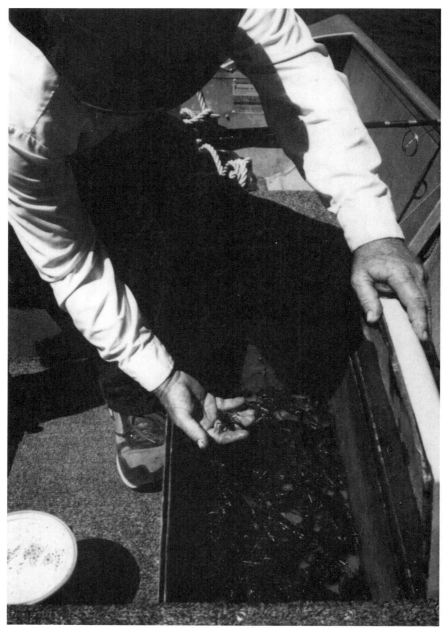

It isn't unusual for a big bass fisherman to carry several hundred crayfish in various sizes and colors.

adulthood, many crayfish turn a bright dark red. Some crayfish become so red or so green, they almost look black . I believe a certain alkaline content is responsible). After hibernation, crayfish emerge pale green and the color cycle begins again. Black specks on the back shell and pinchers usually remain regardless of color.

Crayfish typically feed at night and they eat almost everything (alive or dead), but minnows are a favorite food which they capture by snatching them with their pinchers. Crayfish can be extremely cannibalistic when food is scarce.

Crayfish have excellent vision and they are very light-sensitive, which is one reason why they prefer to feed at night and hide during daylight hours. Similar to alligators and crocodiles, their eyes reflect light which may help predators find them under low-light conditions. Bass also find crayfish by homing in on the distinct clicking sounds crayfish make as they crawl around.

As crayfish grow they shed their hard outer shells becoming very soft and vulnerable in the process. During the shedding and rebuilding stage, crayfish hide and become somewhat dormant until their new armor hardens. When adults reach the red stage, they grow slower and shed less. Crayfish often hibernate in burrows on mud or clay banks, and they seem to instinctively know when the coldest winters are coming.

Care and Handling

It's important to keep your bait fresh and lively as they will trigger the most bites. When a crayfish is strong and trying to pull away all the time, it creates a stressed body language which big bass react to. A healthy crayfish hooked correctly should stay lively for a long time. However, they can become limp and lethargic if the water is too cold or if they stay submerged for long intervals at deep depths. Crayfish can breathe in or out of water, but they can become tired if fished too long without a rest.

When tended properly, crayfish can live quite a while in captivity. I've personally had some for almost two years in my holding tanks at my home. It's a good idea to separate crayfish by size (big

Author uses smooth overhand cast when using fragile natural baits. This technique allows maximum casting distance and is less traumatic to the bait itself.

and small and green and red) in two containers. Add only a few inches of water and feed them lettuce to keep them active and alert and to give them a nice fresh smell. Crayfish will die if overcrowded.

Temperature changes can make crayfish dormant, so I keep mine in outside holding tanks to acclimatize them. In winter, the water in my tanks remains the same as the lake temperature, or possibly a little colder, and my bait stays lively no matter how cold lake temperatures get. If you buy them from a warm baitshop, your bait may go into shock when it hits the water.

There is no truth to the myths that bass won't eat crayfish with big pinchers, or that they won't eat big red hard-shelled crayfish, preferring soft-shell crayfish instead.

Nature makes crayfish in all sizes and textures, and bass eat them all. But there are times when size is a factor. In winter, small-to-medium green crayfish work best. Large red crayfish seem to work best from early spring through October or November. But you never can tell when a different size may trigger a reluctant fish. Sometimes when bass are biting small green crayfish well, using a large red crayfish might stimulate the biggest fish in the area. Usually larger crayfish, 3 inches and up, are most attractive to bigger bass, but if the fish aren't hitting these I'll switch to a smaller crayfish before changing to a lighter line. Because I keep crayfish in holding tanks at home, I'm able to use bright red crayfish in early spring when all the native lake crayfish are green. There are times when bass prefer these "red dads" and often I'll be the only one throwing them on the whole lake.

Fishing With Crayfish

Because there are so many different ways to work them and so many different situations, fishing with live crayfish can be a real art form. But it's like any other lure, success comes from boat positioning and making the right cast.

Crayfish generally work best when hooked through the beak or through the tail. When beak hooking is desired, run the hook up and under the pointed piece of shell between the eyes and carefully ease the barb out about 1/4 inch back. The pointed shell is brittle, and you must carefully wiggle the hook through without cracking it. For tail hooking, start by turning the crayfish on its back. Notice that the tail is divided into several segments with a black vein running down the entire length. Insert the hook between the last and second-to-the-last segments and bring it out the top of the shell while being careful not to pierce the tail vein or the crayfish will quickly die.

Each hooking position gives crayfish a different look and action. Hooking through the beak doesn't affect their ability to swim, as they swim by kicking their tails. When you slowly stitch a beak-hooked crayfish through a spot, you actually walk them slowly along in a natural way, yet they still have the freedom of tail movement. The nice thing about beak hooking is that when you work them toward an area where they don't want to go (like a spot with a big bass), they'll constantly try to resist. If you feel excessive kicking and struggling activity, the crayfish is telling you there's a bass nearby. I generally work a crayfish from one end of a spot to the other, and just pull them along like a dog on a leash until they're intercepted. But if it starts kicking, I'll stop stitching because there might be a bass there (they don't twitch and kick for no reason). At this point, I'll pull it a

Crayfish crawl forward naturally and can be led like a dog on a leash by hooking them through the beak. If disturbed, such as by a predator, they will use their strong tails to dart with short surges to swim to safety.

little forward, let it kick back, pull forward again, and let it kick back — this is the sequence you work in one spot to antagonize a big bass into biting; it is the stimulation live bait can produce that can't be duplicated in any artificial lure. Beak hooking works best during pre-spawn, spawn and early fall. Beak-hooked crayfish have more action and are easier to work through rocks and up ledges, but the shell needs to be hard to support this hook position. If the shell is soft, it's better to hook them through the tail.

Tail hooking is a completely different presentation because you're working crayfish through an area in an unnatural way (tail first). Tail hooking camouflages the hook better but it doesn't allow the tail to kick as freely. Tail hooking seems to work best during late spring, summer and the dead of winter. This method is especially good in clear water or when fishing long points and flats without too much cover. Crayfish hooked through the tail sink slowly, and letting a tail-hooked crayfish sink slowly through the fish is an excellent way to catch suspended bass.

Even though I believe beak hooking crayfish to be the most effective way to fish these baits, there are times when tail hooking should be seriously considered; when bait is green and fragile, when bass are being hooked lightly on the lip, when bass are taking the bait on the sink, and when bass just simply want them hooked that way. When properly tail hooked, crayfish exhibit a more subdued and restricted action but it does not injure them seriously.

For most crayfish I like to use a #4 Eagle Claw Baitholder hook in bronze. I tie the hook directly to the line with an improved clinch knot and make seven turns instead of the standard five to help cushion the knot. In situations where I'm fishing a very small crayfish, where the bass are hesitant to strike, or where I'm fishing structure where it's very hard to work the crayfish through, I'll drop down to a #6 O'Shaughnessy No. 9174 Mustad hook. I'll bend the point out slightly to get a better hooking angle.

Finessing a crayfish over and through rocks and bushes can be difficult with an exposed hook, but I never use weedless hooks because they make the bait less effective. Weedless hooks can ruin the effect of the bait and seem to trigger negative responses from cautious bass. You'll catch bass with weedless hooks, but my records show that exposed hooking is much more effective for big bass. With

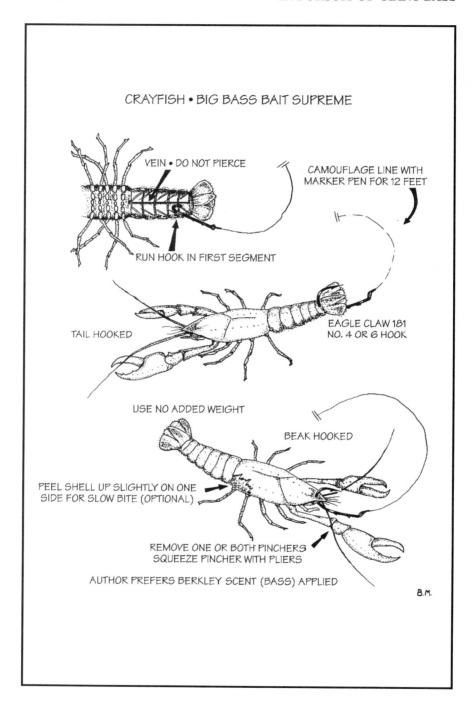

CRAYFISH • BIG BASS BAIT SUPREME

VEIN • DO NOT PIERCE

CAMOUFLAGE LINE WITH
MARKER PEN FOR 12 FEET

RUN HOOK IN FIRST SEGMENT

TAIL HOOKED

EAGLE CLAW 181
NO. 4 OR 6 HOOK

USE NO ADDED WEIGHT

BEAK HOOKED

PEEL SHELL UP SLIGHTLY ON ONE
SIDE FOR SLOW BITE (OPTIONAL)

REMOVE ONE OR BOTH PINCHERS
SQUEEZE PINCHER WITH PLIERS

AUTHOR PREFERS BERKLEY SCENT (BASS) APPLIED

B.M.

Breaking off a claw makes a big crayfish appear disoriented and vulnerable. But never pull off a claw or the crayfish will die. Squeeze the base of the claw with your fingers or pliers and the crayfish will release the claw and seal the hole naturally.

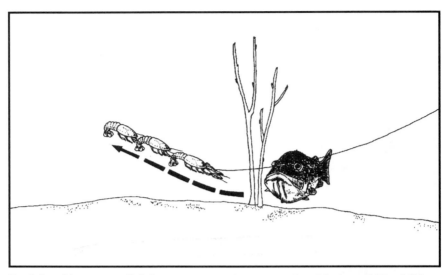

Beak hooking a crayfish is a great way to aggravate a big bass into striking. You work the crayfish forward and when the bait becomes alarmed it darts back in short spurts which means it stays in the area longer. Beak hooking is a deadly springtime technique.

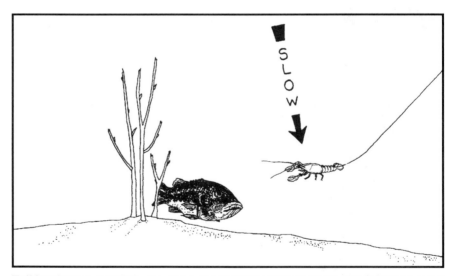

Tail hooking a crayfish creates a slower fall which is more conducive to bass that eat crayfish on the sink. Tail hooking hides the hook better and can be more effective than beak hooking in some waters. Tail hooking tends to be a better winter technique, though there can be times in any season when bass prefer crayfish hooked through the tail. Plus, hooking through the tail may be the only way to fish crayfish with softer shells.

California big bass angler Gene Dupras displays Lake Hodges record largemouth that went 20 pounds 4 ounces. This magnificent trophy is the largest bass ever taken in California from a non-trout planted reservoir. It may quite possibly be the biggest since the world record.

Storage tanks at home always insure that you'll have a healthy supply of fresh lively bait.

an open hook you have to learn how to finesse a crayfish around and through cover, and this is ultimately a much more attractive presentation.

I also never fish a crayfish with a sinker, even in very deep water or high winds. Crayfish are most effective when you can gently tug and work them over snags and hangups. This cannot be done if the crayfish is weighted down. Weight also interferes with the natural kicking action which is an important strike stimulant. Crayfish will sink straight down to any depth as long as you give them plenty of slack and exercise patience.

Regardless of how I hook a crayfish, I often break off at least one of the pinchers on my crayfish. Pinchers are their number one defense, and with two pinchers a large crayfish can be a little too aggressive for some fish to bite. But with one pincher, they use more tail action instead of relying on pinchers for protection. It also upsets their balance slightly and seems to trigger predatory instincts in bass that something is wrong. Sometimes I'll break off both pinchers and these crayfish will twitch and pull away from everything - at times this action is just what the bass want. Taking off their pinchers

Crawdad-catching Equipment - Note headlamp, hip waders, bucket to carry catch, net with 6' handle, and small hand scoop.

Being a nocturnal creature, the best time to catch crayfish is at night. Work up the creek so as not to rile the water in front of you.

reduces the overall size of the crayfish and they cast farther because they tend to curl their tails under their bodies and cast like a bullet. A pincher has to be squeezed and removed just right, or the crayfish will lose body fluids and die. When a pincher becomes damaged or when they lose one in a fight with another crayfish, a small flap of shell membrane flips down and closes the hole as the claw is broken off. If you crush or pull off the pincher before the crayfish realizes it's been hurt, body fluids leak out of the hole and it will die. You have to squeeze and crack the claw carefully with your fingers or pliers, and the crayfish will release the arm and seal up the hole naturally. Some crayfish give up a claw more easily than others; use persistence until reluctant ones get the message. But always see if you can get them to release their pinchers naturally. If you do break them off, the crayfish is only good for about one cast before becoming too weak to fish effectively.

Fishing crayfish is most effective from a boat securely positioned with two anchors. The wind should be at your back or to the side so there is constant pressure on the ropes. I use the same stitching technique that I use with plastic worms, but stitching a live crayfish requires more finesse. You never should pull a live bait so hard that it pops over and away from cover like you might a plastic worm that has become snagged. Try to ease the bait over cover with as little trauma as possible. Ease it over and let it fall straight into the prime areas next to, or at the base of, the cover. Stitching a crayfish becomes an art form because they get hung up easier and it takes a lot more practice to get good at it. When you pull a plastic worm off a drop-off it goes straight down, but a crayfish may not fall straight down; it might kick back up on a ledge or kick off to the side. You never really know for sure what it's doing, consequently when you use crayfish there's a totally different think process involved.

I like to anchor within a long cast from the target and work the crayfish up and over, or up and across the sides of the prime structures. I seldom anchor out and cast onto a spot except during winter months when bass may locate at the base of a structure such as the base of a rocky point (anchoring out allows you to fish outer structural areas more vertically). But I generally like to work crayfish over and off, or over and down a structure as much as possible because it's easier to work crayfish off rocks and brush instead of up and through the cover; it's a better live bait presentation and it makes them do a lot more hopping when they come off a spot. Plastic worms work best when fished uphill but it's difficult with crayfish, so it all depends on what you're using.

Fishing with an exposed hook means you can't effectively fish crayfish in a spot with extremely dense cover, but by anchoring the boat off to the side of the spot you can cast to the edge of the cover and work along the margin of the spot and down the ledge. The crayfish might get momentarily hung up on the outer perimeter of the cover, but it will still be in a position where a giant bass might intercept it for a majority of the cast.

To cast a crayfish properly, first allow the bait to hang down from the tip about 2-1/2 ft. This allows the weight of the crayfish to bend the rod as it is gently cast. Care must be taken to make smooth casts as to not tear the hook out of the bait. After casting a crayfish out and over the prime target, strip out about 4-or-5 ft. of line to make sure the bait sinks straight down. Sip some coffee and let it sink to the bottom before starting the retrieve. I work crayfish with the same stitching method I use for plastic worms. You can stitch crayfish at different speeds, although very slow with long pauses is usually best. Make sure the bait stays on the bottom the entire retrieve. If the crayfish comes over a rock and free swims where you lose feel, stop and let it sink back to the bottom before continuing the retrieve.

The first cast with a crayfish can tell you a lot about a spot. Pick a nice medium-size crayfish that's highly active and cast it well over the intended target. Medium crayfish sink fairly fast and can be worked back fairly quickly. How the crayfish acts will tell you how aggressive the fish are and how dense the cover is. You don't have to give the crayfish the same action you would give a plastic worm, just pull or walk it through the spot and let it talk to you through the line. If the crayfish tugs and acts nervous throughout the retrieve, assume there are bass at various locations, or a bass is following it, even if it didn't get bit. Sometimes a kick means the crayfish saw a rock and jumped into a little crevice, but generally they don't kick unless a bass is close. When the crayfish gets active and you feel short light jerks, stop stitching and let it sit for a few seconds. If nothing happens, continue the retrieve but begin by stitching very cautiously as a big bass may already have the bait and is just holding on. If the crayfish is acting nervous but you aren't getting bit, one trick I use to stimulate reluctant bass is to twitch the line in a series of short sharp tugs. This makes the crayfish jump wildly and can provoke some hard strikes.

Crayfish have their own individual action as all live baits do. They not only move, they also cause sensations in the line that resemble a bite. Many people believe that live bait is easier to work than artificials because bait has its own built-in action, but working a crayfish or any live bait can be very confusing because you have to interpet the action of the bait. With a plastic worm, for example, you don't have that-one little twitch or tug is an indication of a bite, but with a live crayfish it might not be. The bite of a bass might be intermingled with a series of natural kicks, or the bite may register as a complete absence of activity. One single tug might mean a bite, but at other times when you'll feel a whole series of twitches and tugs and it doesn't mean you've been bit or are about to get bit, it can also mean a clam just nailed it on the foot. So in this sense I find it easier to fish with a plastic worm than with a live crayfish. When you get good with crayfish you will learn how to work around the natural movements of the bait. Only experience teaches this.

Since it's difficult to interpret the bite of a bass from the kick of a crayfish, the beginner should treat every twitch as a possible bite. The safest way is to lightly hold and watch the line after every unusual twitch until you learn how a bass feels. A bass can feel like a number of different things, but when a big bass bites you'll usually feel one distinct "pop" and the line may suddenly tighten or slacken. Recognizing this pop or tap can be confusing when it is in conjunction with natural bait movements. You might feel-tug, tug, tug, and then a distinct tap. The first tugs were the crayfish trying to get away, but then the crisp pop was the bite. Sometimes you'll feel-tug, tug, tug, and then a complete absence of resistance.In this case a lack of feeling after crayfish activity means a bass has intercepted the bait and is moving towards you, or off to the side. If you're not sure you had a bite or not, check the condition of the bait. When bass bite plastic worms they often leave teeth marks in the plastic (rough slashes).

With a crayfish, you check for minute cracks in the shell. A bass generally sucks a crayfish right in; they don't hold it or mouth it, they turn it around and it goes down backwards with the pinchers facing out. If the shell is badly crushed or if you're left with just a crayfish head on the hook, it probably was the work of a catfish.

After a bass strikes a crayfish, the line may begin moving off in a steady pull or you'll notice the line jump. Don't be in a hurry to strike. Reel up the slack and allow the fish to take a few extra feet of line (I usually let them run about 8-or-10 ft.). A good rule is as long as it takes to clean up the loose line. Raise the rod tip slowly and carefully, always watching the line, and as the line begins to tighten and the rod tip starts to bend, swing up with a firm smooth hookset. It's important to make sure that the movement of the line moving off is uninterrupted. The line shouldn't be jerking. A jerking line means a bass is trying to reposition the crayfish in its mouth or dropping it and picking it back up. Jerking indicates that the bass doesn't have it good, but when the line quits jerking and starts moving slowly and smoothly, that's when you can set the hook with confidence. But don't break the rod, just set the hook with a smooth even swing.

The biggest secret to fishing with any live baits and with crayfish in particular is the ability to work them through snaggy area. You'll never achieve anything positive if you're constantly breaking off bait on every other cast. Bass often strike right after a bait is recovered from a snag, so it's important to practice the following; Most snags occur as the crayfish is coming over a piece of cover. Stop retrieving the moment you feel any line resistance. The pressure may be a bite, in which case the line will jump or move. But if the bait is snagged, stopping the retrieve will allow the crayfish to work its way over or around the object naturally. Sometimes when they run into a hole or under a ledge, you can set the rod down and let the crayfish crawl out by itself. If that doesn't work, I'll hold the rod tip high and work it in tiny twitches trying to make the crayfish jump free. When a crayfish kicks itself loose, sometimes a bass will strike it the moment it breaks free. Crayfish come through cover better when hooked through the beak. Beak hooking allows the bait the freedom to kick themselves free.

Always work with a line that best suits the conditions. I normally use 8, 10, and 12 lb. line for crayfish. As a general rule, the smaller the crayfish or the deeper and clearer the water, the lighter the line test should be. I use grey, pink and clear line in winter and early spring when the water is a clear to gray color, and green, blue and brown line for the rest of the year. I never use gold or fluorescent lines for anything. Another tip to consider is marking the line with a big black magic marker a few feet above the hook. Just a few color patches here and there can help break up the lines appearance; it can make a difference when fishing is tough. Also as a concluding note, I have to recommend the use of Berkeley Strike (bass). I squeeze some on my hands, rub them together and then apply some to the hook and about three feet of line above the hook. Then I handle the crayfish. I have proved to myself that this really makes a difference.

Texas-rigged Nightcrawlers

Most anglers fish weekends and can't always fish when conditions are most favorable, but one bait that usually produces activity when nothing else seems to work is the old reliable nightcrawler. Nightcrawlers are impulse baits and their seductive, squirming action often attracts catfish, walleye or bluegill as easily as a bass; it always seems like something is biting a nightcrawler. But crawlers have a special attraction and I've seen many days following a severe cold front where the only lure or live bait that would draw any kind of response was a nightcrawler. Some excellent bass anglers use nightcrawlers almost exclusively because they often produce big bass under a wide variety of conditions.

Nightcrawlers must be kept cold both at home and in the boat. They must be firm and lively to attract big bass; sick or wilted crawlers don't work. Take along plenty, and change baits after every cast or two. I like to use nightcrawlers during cold water periods because the bait stays firmer, casts better and has a better action in the water for a longer time. Crawlers work in warm water too, but they tend to wilt much faster.

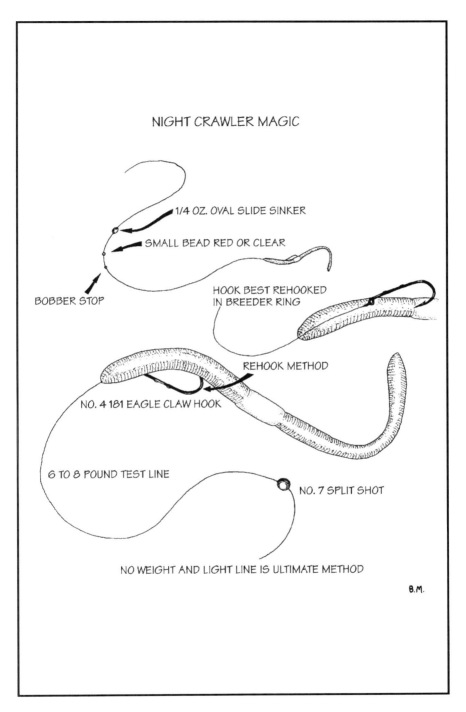

NIGHT CRAWLER MAGIC

1/4 OZ. OVAL SLIDE SINKER

SMALL BEAD RED OR CLEAR

BOBBER STOP

HOOK BEST REHOOKED
IN BREEDER RING

REHOOK METHOD

NO. 4 181 EAGLE CLAW HOOK

6 TO 8 POUND TEST LINE

NO. 7 SPLIT SHOT

NO WEIGHT AND LIGHT LINE IS ULTIMATE METHOD

B.M.

I always hook crawlers Texas-style. I use a #4 Eagle Claw 181 bait hook and bring the hook out through the head and re-insert it back into the breeder ring. Texas-rigging also helps keep the crawler from breaking off on a long cast. Crawlers work best in sparse cover, but when Texas-rigged it's surprising what you can work them through.

I fish nightcrawlers with the same stitching technique I use for plastic worms and crayfish, and fish from a boat securely positioned with two anchors. I anchor closer than normal because long distance casting with crawlers is difficult. I use my normal spinning outfit with either 6-or-8-pound line, and lob-cast rather than whip-cast. Start with the crawler hanging about three feet below the rod tip and lob it gently out and over the spot. I rarely fish crawlers with any added weight as the combination of light line, lively bait and no weight is what ultimately tricks bass that don't respond to other presentations. If, however, it becomes a problem in deeper water, a light shot can be used. Be sure to pull loose coils of line from the reel so the crawler sinks vertically rather than swinging back toward the boat due to line tension.

Once the crawler reaches bottom, I'll stitch it a few inches and then let it sit for about thirty seconds. I'll repeat this stitch-and-pause sequence all the way back to the boat. Many times a strike will come when the crawler remains in one spot, and frequent pausing also guarantees that the unweighted crawler will be working along the bottom. A strike usually feels like a sharp tap or thump, and the line will pull away smoothly and sometimes rapidly.

One interesting thing about the appeal of nightcrawlers is that the biggest bait doesn't always equal the biggest bass. Medium crawlers can catch big bass, and sometimes the larger crawlers don't work as good as the medium size. But you judge the size of a crawler different than a plastic worm because the crawler will stretch out underwater. Crawlers of any size, however, must be fat and healthy or they won't appeal to larger bass.

Nightcrawlers are excellent baits but they aren't necessarily a cure-all. Sometimes bass will be more stimulated by a certain color in a plastic worm that a live crawler can't give you. I've seen hundreds of times when bass would strike a plastic worm and would totally ignore a live crawler.

Basically, I use nightcrawlers as a secondary or supplement bait. I never go out and just throw crawlers. I use other baits first, and only use crawlers as a backup. My first choice is generally to stitch a spot with a plastic worm or live crayfish, but if these didn't work then I would fish the spot with a crawler. For smallmouth or kentucky bass, my primary bait might be a crawler but I feel big largemouth are better influenced with plastics or crayfish. But nightcrawlers have their place, and for triggering strikes from neutral bass holding tight to isolated objects, there are times when nothing works like a lively crawler.

Wild Shiners

There probably isn't a deadlier bait for big bass than live natural shiners. Florida is well known for having outstanding live shiner fishing, but few regions other than Florida and California have adopted this excellent method even though shiners appeal to northern largemouth and hybrids as well as Florida strain bass. However, it's important to try and get shiners native to and living in the water you are to fish. Wild shiners have better color, smell, and they seem to be more aware of the danger, making their movements more nervous and therefore more appealing to the predatory instincts of giant bass. Shiners raised in captivity don't seem to have the same appeal.

Catching Shiners

Catching wild shiners from the water you intend to fish not only gives you a more efficient bait, the catching can be great sport in itself. Some anglers catch shiners with throw nets but I enjoy catching them on hook and line.

Shiners school at different depths depending on water temperatures and food sources. In spring they move shallow to spawn in the back ends of finger cuts, coves and sloughs. Shiners spawn on banks

This angler is about to make another cast with a nice medium size shiner, he is checking to see if the shiner is still lively enough to swim unassisted to the bottom, often a small splitshot must be added to the line if the shiner is tired.

with hard bottom, and a shallow flat with a slight drop-off would be an ideal place to begin your search. The structural habits of shiners are similar to largemouth, and if you find a hard-bottom shelf with little clumps of weed, wood or rock next to deeper water, you should be in business. Spring and summer is the easiest time to catch shiners in structured lakes because the shiner schools can usually be found anywhere from inches under the surface to about 12 ft. deep. I usually switch to live crayfish in fall and winter because shiners normally move deeper where they are more difficult to locate and catch. Shiner schools register as bunches of thin lines on a flasher and dense, solid grey masses on paper graphs. A good fisherman can track them just like bass. Shiners frequently travel with shad, but for some reason shiner schools usually hold under shad schools.

Because shiners are a roaming fish, once I find a good structural area with shiner activity I'll chum the spot and stay long enough until the shiner schools find the food. I'll anchor about ten feet from the spot using two anchors just like stitching for largemouth. Shiners spook easily and you don't want your boat swinging over them. Standing up a lot on a bright day also tends to spook them.

Chumming a spot (sprinkling prepared bait into an area to attract fish) is an excellent method to stimulate shiners into a feeding frenzy. Add canned dog food (chicken Alpo) to a large coffee can and mix with water until it gets soupy. Mix in rolled oats to thicken (Quaker Oats) and spray out several handfuls over the spot. Don't overdo it, however, use just enough to get their interest. Use polaroid glasses to see if any shiners begin flashing on the chum as it slowly filters toward the bottom. Once a school finds the chum, they usually gather in large numbers. Make sure chumming is legal in your area and only use biodegradable products.

To catch shiners, I use a little ultra-light rod, 4 pound line, and tiny #14 and #16 gold treble hooks. To assemble the shiner bait maker rig, which is the heart of this shiner catching system, you must first tie a small gold swivel to the end of the main line from the reel. Next, add a small 1-1/2 foot leader to the other side of the swivel. To the loose end of the leader, tie on one of the gold treble hooks. Below the swivel, about 2 inches, tie on a small dropper leader 3 inches long and add the remaining treble. The drop leader needs to be shorter so

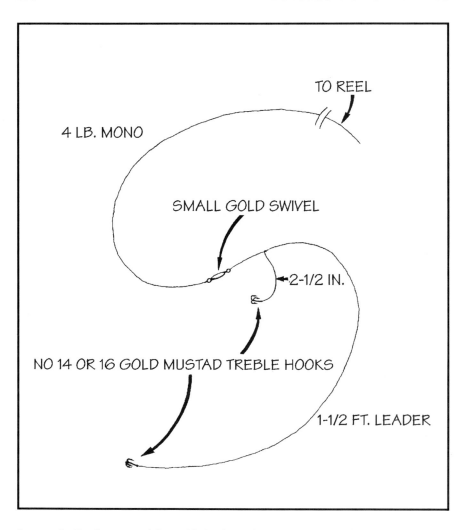

it won't foul up on it's self during the constant whip casting technique. You can use the larger hook on the bottom line. I sometimes add a tiny piece of nightcrawler to each hook, but when shiners are feeding in a frenzy they'll bite the tiny gold hooks without adding any bait.

Since this rig has no added weight, I use the whip action of the light rod and a fly line technique to whip the rig out about 6-to-8-ft. to the spot. Watch the line as the rig sinks slowly through the shiners. Set the hooks whenever the line twitches or flicks out. If I can't see

Wild golden shiners appear to emit an oily scent which becomes airborne when they become active near the surface. This odor can be detected by the angler in search of these elusive bait fish and aid in their discovery.

any line movement, I'll count down and set on different counts: count to three then set, count to four and set, count to five, etc., all the way to the bottom. Shiners may suspend at any depth, and once you determine the best count you can stay with that depth. Re-chum every now and then to keep their interest. Shiners can be harder to catch when free-swimming (that's when counting works), and I've had my best results when the school settles along the bottom. A vertical jigging action right under the boat produces the big ones when shiners are deep. Occasionally a big bass may take advantage of the feeding activity, and when bass move into the area the shiner bite stops like someone turned a switch.

Compared to shad, shiners are easier to keep in captivity, but big shiners consume lots of oxygen, and the trick to keeping them healthy and active is to use a large container that's well oxygenated and not overcrowded. Shiners should also be kept cool. Adding ice to the water slows them down and they use less oxygen; it also makes them more lively when they're used in warmer water. A piece of cheesecloth over the top keeps them from jumping out. And one final note: use a couple of stone aerating pumps rather than your baitwell circulating pump; the bait is less traumatized and it is less noisy when fishing a spot.

Stitching Shiners

Plastic worms and live crayfish are only two of the many presentations that fit into the stitching system. You can use the same stitching technique for live shiners but it's a little different because you have a swimming creature. You have to work a little slower to keep the shiner working along the bottom. Often I'll attach a split shot about 16 inches or so above the bait, similar to a plastic worm rig, but I may go to a larger or smaller shot depending on the size of the bait. Add just enough weight to slow the shiner down and restrict its movement. I generally use a #4 bait hook for shiners of all sizes, but I may drop to a smaller hook when using small-to-medium size bait. Too big a hook can ruin a shiner's big bass appeal in a pressured lake. Big bass usually take shiners head first, so I prefer hooking them through their lips. Run the hook point in from under the lower jaw and up and out through one of its nostrils. I never alter this hooking procedure. If I'm missing fish, or the shiners are coming back with scales missing or gouges on their sides, I'll switch to a smaller bait or a smaller hook. Also, I might try leaving it in one place longer without moving it. But I would never use a hook over a #1 for casting and working them on a spot. You can get just as good a hookset with a small hook, but you'll have to be more particular about when to strike and how long to let the bass take the bait. Larger hooks may be needed to work heavy cover, but a structure situation needs more finesse even with the appeal of a wild shiner.

After you make a cast and the shiner begins to sink, it will swim against the resistance of the weight on the line. Swimming against resistance gives the appearance of being in trouble, and bass often strike these struggling shiners as they approach the bottom. When a bass intercepts a shiner on the sink, the rate at which the line has been

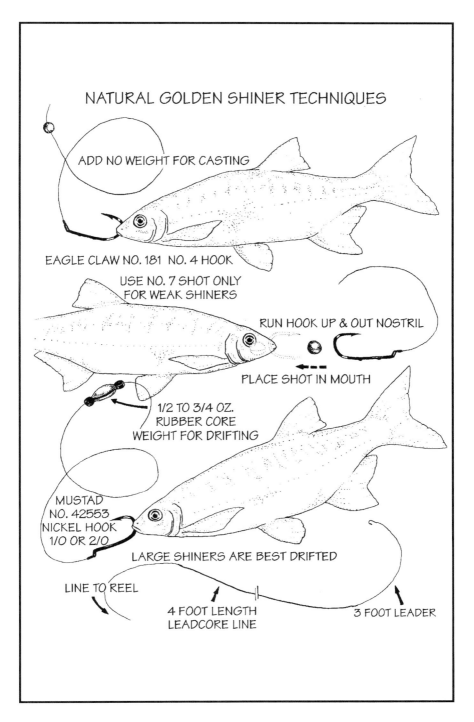

NATURAL GOLDEN SHINER TECHNIQUES

ADD NO WEIGHT FOR CASTING

EAGLE CLAW NO. 181 NO. 4 HOOK

USE NO. 7 SHOT ONLY FOR WEAK SHINERS

RUN HOOK UP & OUT NOSTRIL

PLACE SHOT IN MOUTH

1/2 TO 3/4 OZ. RUBBER CORE WEIGHT FOR DRIFTING

MUSTAD NO. 42553 NICKEL HOOK 1/0 OR 2/0

LARGE SHINERS ARE BEST DRIFTED

LINE TO REEL

4 FOOT LENGTH LEADCORE LINE

3 FOOT LEADER

sinking will speed up and sometimes keep right on going. This is the signal that the bass has the bait good and you should strike immediately.

I work shiners across the bottom just like I would a live crayfish. I stitch them very slowly for about 4-or-5-inches and give them a nice long pause in between each new movement. Shiners learn quickly to swim toward line tension, and pausing frequently makes them lose their direction. Stop, have some coffee, and wait 30 seconds or so before continuing the retrieve.

Sometimes a shiner is too active and lively to appeal to a large bass. A big bass estimates how much energy it will take to catch potential prey, and if the shiner looks too fast the bass may lose interest. I often tap a lively shiner on top of the head with my pliers to disorient it. This confused, vulnerable action seems to trigger reluctant fish. When a bass approaches, the shiner will struggle to get away but the split shot will hold it back. This struggling action is usually too much for a big bass to resist. But you can't use a shiner that's dead. You might catch a walleye jigging and twitching a dead shiner but not a big bass!

Stitching is an ideal method for working shiners through structure and cover because holding the line lets you monitor the attitude of the bait. If a shiner begins to twitch wildly but then suddenly all actions stop or you feel a thump you better get ready, a bass usually has it. Let the bait sit and don't do a thing. Some bass rush up and grab a shiner to disable it but then drop it. Just let the bait sit. That bass knows the shiner is hurt and may return. If nothing happens after a minute, twitch the line a few times with your finger. If a big one is watching, those twitches will look like a last dying wiggle. When a bass finally takes the bait, the line will begin to slowly move away. Let it run through your fingertips, and when it is moving out at a smooth and steady pace, reel up all the slack and sweep the rod tip up smoothly as you set the hook but do it with authority. Another trick I've learned over the years that greatly insures the successful hooking of a big bass is to always add a little tension to the line before a bass firmly takes the bait. When a bass feels that added tension, they think the shiner is getting away and it stimulates them to grasp it better and work the shiner deeper into their mouth. By the time you're ready to strike, the bait will be farther into their mouth and a better hooking area.

I always use either 10 lb. or 12 lb. test line for fishing shiners provided the spot doesn't have extensive brush or timber. In heavy cover I might use 15 lb. line, but never heavier. The trick to fighting big fish in cover is to let them make the first move. After setting the hook, just hold the fish with steady pressure (without pulling) and they will usually swim off to the side or up off a potential hazard. Once they clear the trouble spot, that's when you can put on the pressure.

Drifting Shiners

Drifting with wild shiners on a rubber core sinker rig is an excellent way to search for bass in deep water. Drifting shiners can be deadly when bass suspend off the edges of deep flats and precise structural edges, and drifting can be an ideal technique during winter when bass refuse to hit trolled plugs. Drifting doesn't work well in summer, however, it is basically a cold-water technique that works best when bass are below 20 ft. deep.

My drifting rig is similar to those used to fish shad for deep water ocean stripers, but the rig is also deadly on big largemouth with wild shiners. I place a rubber core sinker about 5 ft. up the line and use a weight from 1/4 oz. to 3/4 oz. depending on the size of the shiner, wind speed and how deep I want to fish. The sinker should be light enough to give the bait maximum action but heavy enough to keep it on the bottom. A sinker which is too heavy constantly digs into the bottom and hangs up. A sinker with the proper weight should bounce along the bottom or lightly scrape across the bottom. I like a larger #1 or #2 hook for drifting because deep fish often take shiners aggressively and you're more apt to strike quickly; a larger hook seems to be more effective in this snatch-and-grab situation. I like medium-to-large shiners from 5-1/2-to-8-inches or larger for drifting because bass are less likely to reject a larger shiner in winter once they take it. It's best to use as light a line as possible, but because you often have to set the hook on a fairly long line, I wouldn't go too light. I use from 12 lb. to 15 lb. test depending on the conditions and the size of the bass. Usually 12 lb. line is plenty.

Once your shiner is securely hooked through the lips, pay out the rig behind the boat at a 45 degree angle until it hits bottom. Drift with the wind and use the trolling motor to precisely follow structural contours and to slow, or increase, the drift speed. Make the shiner move in a slow, natural swimming motion adding an occasional jump or twitch. Let out a little line if you don't feel the sinker working the bottom. The sinker should touch bottom at least every now and then to let you know you're on the money.

When a bass grabs the shiner, hold the boat with the trolling motor and monitor the direction of the fish as it pulls line through your hand. When the line is moving smooth and uninterrupted, put the reel in gear and set the hook. Once you hook a bass, coordinate the spot with shoreline sightings or use a marker buoy for reference, and re-drift the spot. Sometimes approaching from a different angle may produce better.

Few bass anglers drift with wild shiners, but it can be amazingly productive in deep water situations. Drifting shiners might be an ideal cold water technique when targeting big bass in highland reservoirs of the central States, or the deep glacial lakes of the upper Midwest and Northeast.

Free-Swimming Shiners

During summer months bass often suspend around structures and many times they prefer a shiner that's swimming free. Simply hook the shiner through the lips without any added weight and allow to swim freely. If the shiner is fresh it'll usually swim right down to the bottom structure (shiners are bottom-oriented). But they have to be fresh and lively or they won't go to the bottom. Usually one cast is all you get before they weaken and won't go down. Some shiners are too active and won't go down either; they'll swim off instead of settling onto the structure. A little tap on the head with your pliers sometimes slows them down just enough. I use free-swimming shiners when I already know bass are using a structure; it's too slow a method to search for bass with. But once the fish are found, letting a shiner do its thing in an unrestricted, natural manner can be deadly.

Shoreline Dipping

When the water is up and high in the shoreline cover (usually a spring and summer pattern), dipping shiners along the shorelines can be outstanding. I use a #1 or #2 hook with a big popping rod or flipping stick and work the cover adjacent to the deep turn-ins, cuts and draws which connect the shallows to deep water. I poke some split shot into the mouth of the shiner before threading a weedless hook through its lips. The weight slows them down and limits their mobility, and I've found this method tops for dipping shiners through shoreline cover. There are many more days when they'll hit a shiner than they will a jig and pig.

FISHING A JIG AND PIG

Basically, a leadhead jig is an easy lure to fish, but like all aspects of trophy bass angling small details in presentation make a big difference. To start with, jig fishing is an exercise in concentration

Few lures can compare to the versatility of a jig and split tail pork trailer when big bass are holding on outside edges in deep water.

and timing. The jig size, shape, color, hook, skirt, weedguard, and trailer all influence its overall appeal, and certain alterations can transform a standard jig into a big bass enticer.

I prefer stand-up "Arky" style head designs with the hook eye positioned in the front, or on top of the head. When a stand-up style jig is stopped, or when it falls off an object, it will settle in a natural-looking manner and the hook will ride upwards in a perfect hooking position.

I prefer to fish with a light weedguard whenever possible, but in heavy cover I'll use a jig with a weedguard made of more monofilament strands for extra deflection. Mono fiberguards on most store-bought jigs are long and thick, and should be trimmed and thinned out for normal cover. Fiberguards which are too long or thick can cause missed strikes, so it's best to shorten and spread them out.

Many anglers use jigs with large, heavy-guage, flipping-style hooks, but I find large hooks impractical for many structure situations. Extra-large hooks require heavy line and stout tackle to penetrate, and while heavy tackle may be appropriate when fishing thick cover, it can be totally out of place when trying to finesse cautious bass in an area with sparse cover. Thick cover tends to mask

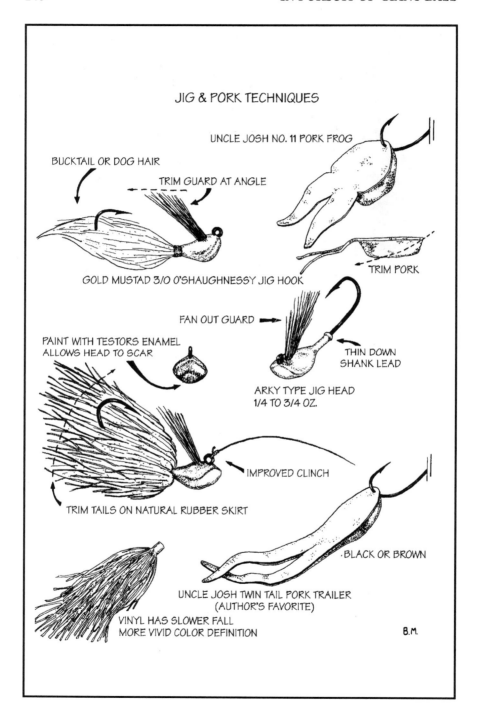

JIG & PORK TECHNIQUES

UNCLE JOSH NO. 11 PORK FROG

BUCKTAIL OR DOG HAIR

TRIM GUARD AT ANGLE

TRIM PORK

GOLD MUSTAD 3/0 O'SHAUGHNESSY JIG HOOK

FAN OUT GUARD

PAINT WITH TESTORS ENAMEL
ALLOWS HEAD TO SCAR

THIN DOWN
SHANK LEAD

ARKY TYPE JIG HEAD
1/4 TO 3/4 OZ.

IMPROVED CLINCH

TRIM TAILS ON NATURAL RUBBER SKIRT

BLACK OR BROWN

UNCLE JOSH TWIN TAIL PORK TRAILER
(AUTHOR'S FAVORITE)

VINYL HAS SLOWER FALL
MORE VIVID COLOR DEFINITION

B.M.

Two of the authors favorite jig and pork combinations; natural rubber skirted jigs with either a modified pork frog or a twin tail eel trailer.

large hooks and heavy line, but in situations where bass can examine a lure closely, a jig with a large hook may lose its appeal. I make my own jigs with a short, stout hook that isn't offensive to bass, yet is capable of landing a 20 pounder. My favorite jig hook is a Mustad #91753 O'Shaghnessy with gold plate in sizes 2/0 and 3/0. I use a 3/0 hook for jigs 1/2 oz. and larger, and a 2/0 hook for 1/4 oz. heads. Sometimes, when bass are extra spooky, I'll use a 1/2 oz. jig with a 2/0 hook. The #91753 O'Shaughnessy is a forged hook that is super strong, and it has a small barb that penetrates easily when using a medium weight line. For some reason I've had far greater success with giant bass using gold hooks rather than standard bronze.

Although jig skirts made from hair, rubber, vinyl, and feathers all catch bass, jig skirts have more big fish appeal when thinned and shortened. Trophy bass don't seem to like skirts that are thick and full. Jigs made with hair, for example, work better when wrapped with sparse amounts of hair, and it's always a good idea to thin out rubber and vinyl skirts too. I like to shorten the skirt so it doesn't cover the pork, or plastic trailer.

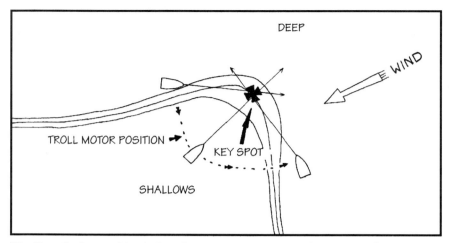

Working the boat with an electric motor gives you the freedom to fish a jig and pig from all angles. I like to fish from the inside of the break throwing slightly out and across a spot, or just off the break, throwing over and across. Pay attention to depth, action, and retrieve angle of every bite. One angle will outfish all others.

Overall weight is probably **THE** most important ingredient in fooling a trophy bass with a jig, and generally speaking, a jig with a slower decent, or falling action, will outproduce a fast-falling jig. When bass want a large bait with a slow drop speed, I've had good results adding a large #11 Uncle Josh pork frog; large pork adds bulk and can slow the drop speed needed to enhance the bite.

Unless you need a heavy jig to penetrate thick cover, my advice would be to always use the lightest jig possible. Even if the cover is fairly thick, I always start out with a 1/4 oz. jig when fishing 15 ft. or less. I might switch to a heavier size if the jig couldn't be manipulated through the cover, but I always favor a slow-falling jig, so I start out as light as possible. Even in deep water, I always think light first. For extra-deep water, say over 50 ft., a 3/4 oz. jig might be the best choice, but I'll still start out with a 1/2 oz. or 5/8 oz. jig because even in deep water the biggest bass often respond better to a slower sink. During a strong active period, when bass might hit a fast-falling jig better, they probably would be active enough to hit a crankbait, and speed trolling a crankbait might be a better choice to cover water faster.

If I were limited to only one jig size, I would pick a 1/2 oz. head. When searching for bass you never know where you'll cast next-off a deep ledge, or toward a shoreline-and even though a 1/2 oz. jig is a little too heavy for most shallow spots, and a little light for extra-deep water, I find a 1/2 oz. jig a nice compromise that is fairly versatile and productive at all depths.

Adding the right pork rind trailer can turn an ordinary jig into a deadly big bass producer. Pork adds color, bulk, slows the fall rate, and is a meaty mouthful bass tend to hold longer. I don't like using long pork rinds because they often wad up on the hook and cause poor hooking. I favor a short, compact pork dressing like an Uncle Josh frog or split-tail eel. When bass are on a good jig bite, I'll rotate between frogs and split-tail eels to see if they have a preference; I'll also rotate different colors. Lately, I've been having more success with split-tail eels which I think is a result of more anglers currently using frogs.

Pork rind has a soft, fluid motion, but pork right from the jar has to be softened in most cases. I like to kneed and squeeze pork baits with my fingers before putting them on the hook. I also trim a little fat off the head, to create a better action and to allow the pork to rotate more freely. Use fabric dye on trimmed areas to subdue the flash of white pork.

Many of my old jigs, with chipped paint and exposed lead, produce better than new jigs. I belive this is a result of the exposed lead making a more unique sound, as the jig scraps over various bottom objects. Jigs painted with vinyl paint, on the other hand, or epoxy, look nice, but rarely sound as good as jigs painted with enamel that chips or skins off easily. I've always used Testors enamel for all my jig heads so I guess this is another reason why making your own jigs is a good idea. A paint which chips off easily can also help you determine bottom content. Besides adding sound, when a jig comes back scraped and beaten, the exposed lead means it has been through a hard bottom area that I might not have felt.

Unlike some lures, jig combo's produce best in low-keyed colors. My all time favorite color is a black or brown jig with either a brown or blue pork trailer. I've also had good success with a brown/orange jig and orange pork in murky water situations. Like all other lures, you have to experiment with color to see what the fish prefer.

Finding the right color is important, but you also must consider the right size. I use the same fishing procedures with jigs as I do with plastic worms, live bait, and any other technique that I'm trying to establish a pattern with-first, I try to find the best color, then I focus on the best size. Be aware of how the fish are responding. If they bump a lure, but don't take it, switching to another color would be the first move. But when you're catching some fish on a certain color, but not a lot of fish, switching to a different size bait in the same color might produce a bass on every cast.

Jigs have better action on a light to medium weight line, and I generally stay with a thin-diameter, low-visibility line. Lately, I've been using Bagley's Silverthread in winter and early spring, when the water color is clear to grey, and it's been working well on big fish. Later in summer, when the water gets more algae content, I'll use green line. In either case, I generally stay with 12 lb. line.

I compliment my jig fishing with a 5 1/2 ft., or 6 ft. Fenwick HMG casting rod in a #6 power, and a Lew's BB1N casting reel, the finest casting reel I've ever owned.

Working a Jig

A jig that is either slowly falling, or slowly crawling across the bottom like a live crayfish with maybe a subtle jump or two, has the most big-fish appeal. I prefer to drag a jig across the bottom making contact with as much bottom structure as I can. Big bass like a crankbait bouncing and deflecting along the bottom, and I believe there's a certain sound and action in fishing a jig that big bass prefer. It has been my experience that jumping a jig too high off the bottom can sometimes spook big bass in pressured lakes. Most of the time big bass responds best to a jig worked slowly with frequent pauses. My favorite retrieve is a slow crawl produced by gently twitching the rod tip. Twitch it forward, stop it dead for a few seconds, then twitch it in a series of short tics, then crawl it forward again-big bass love this action! I try to give the jig a very subtle action without actually moving it too far, keeping it in the prime area as long as possible. When you feel a rock or bush, shake the jig up and over the object and let it fall on a slack line. You might even feed a little line as it sinks, then shake it again right at the base of the cover. Instead of making big movements and pulling the jig quickly through potential cover, slow down and keep the jig dancing in one spot by quivering the rod tip; this action is deadly on any bass within viewing distance.

On many occasions bass hit jigs that are sinking, either sinking toward the bottom after the cast or falling off a piece of cover. But then there are days when bass will only hit a jig if it's worked along the bottom. You must always be alert to the action of your jig when it's bitten. Sometimes the retrieve angle and the way you work the jig across a particular structure can have an impact. I've had spots where I had to cast out into deep water working the jig up and over the edge of the channel lip or the fish wouldn't strike. For some odd reason known only to the fish, they wouldn't strike unless the jig came out of deep water first. If you would approach this spot from any other direction you'd swear it was void of bass, but the right cast produced a bass on every cast. Many people like to work jigs downhill (which is very productive on rock piles where working uphill causes excessive snagging), but you can't assume that fishing downhill is best on all structures. When I fish creek channels, subtle draws and ditches, or flat structures with relatively little cover, I like to cast out, or across the spot, into deeper water and work the jig back up against ledge or side of the structure; sometimes working uphill on this terrain produces a more natural crayfish action. Even in winter, when letting a jig fall from shelf to shelf on steep structures is highly productive, don't discount getting in tight and working uphill.

Although few anglers drift fish a jig, controlled drifting is one of my top methods for covering water at a precise depth. Once I discover the depth bass are using, I'll parallel a structure at the right depth. I let out enough line to achieve a nice 45 degree line angle between rod tip and lure, and use my trolling motor to control the position as I follow the right depth contour. Drift fishing is a great method when searching for bass in deep water, and it may be the only way to effectively keep a jig in a deep-water strike zone with adequate feel on a windy day.

When a big bass bites a jig you'll normally feel a distinct **"POP!"** What you feel after the strike depends on how they intercepted the jig. If the fish is moving toward you the line will go slack, but if the fish is moving away you'll feel the line tense. Big bass have a tendency to hold onto a jig and pig, however, its smart to be alert to the most subtle bite. After I feel a strike, I quickly reel to tighten the line, then I set the hook. The strike should be firm, but not so hard as to break 12 lb. line. Once hooked, a big bass often makes a strong run, so I'll play it on a fairly loose drag in case the hook didn't penetrate well. Be aware that a big bass can shake its head and use the jig as leverage to dislodge the hook. When you see the line rising toward the surface, put your rod tip in the water and try to keep the fish from jumping.

Preference for jigs can change daily, and you should experiment with other techniques if consistency is your goal. After I find a productive spot with a jig, I'll generally try another technique or two to see if something else works better. What I use after first finding fish with a jig depends on the time of the year. At certain times bass may want a jig over everything else, but if I find big bass on a prime structural area with a jig and it's the type of spot I can fish from an anchored position, I'll guarantee that in most every situation I'll catch more bass stitching than by continuing to work the spot with a jig. And just because you found the fish with a jig doesn't mean that a jig, or even a live crayfish, would be the best thing to cast after you anchored. Color would likely be a key. For example, if I had found the fish with a brown/blue jig, chances are good that other bass, and possibly bigger bass, would respond more positively to a slowly stitched brown/blue plastic worm. I would alternate between stitching a live crayfish and a plastic worm in the same color as the jig, but I wouldn't continue casting the jig once I anchored. I don't like using jigs when anchored because they snag easily and I would have to move the boat too often to retrieve them. Some people bust off jigs like they do plastic worms, but I don't believe in throwing away productive lures. Every fish-catching lure has a proven personality; its effectiveness could be in the way it was molded, or maybe from the amount of scuffing on its head, but whatever reason, when I find a lure that catches big bass I try not to lose them, they're too important

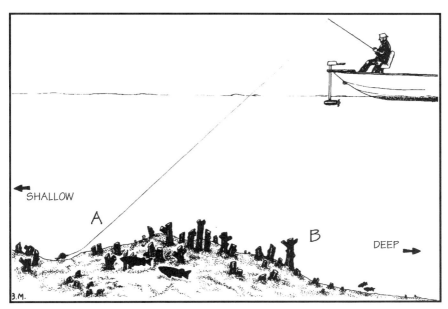

Big bass don't always hold on outside edges. At times, bass relate to inside edges of structures (A) and only move to outside edges (B) when spooked. Baitfish may also relate to inside edges because they're afraid to move along the deep edges where big bass normally lie. Inside edge bass can be spooky. Hold off the spot and make long casts.

to break off. Once I anchor, I usually switch to either a plastic worm or a crayfish because both are expendable and justify being broken off. However, keep in mind that stitching may not be the best approach either. If the fish were active to the point of moving and roaming, it might be possible to intercept more fish by continuing to cover water and work fast with the jig rather than working one spot from a fixed position. The best pattern for that day might be to fish as many spots as possible at the right depth during the peak active period, and jig fishing would be an excellent maneuver at this time. So jigging can have a better potential than stitching given the right situation. You might briefly stitch a spot to see if the bass responded to that method better, then continue to work quickly with the jig. And when the action slows, you can always go back and stitch the key areas slowly and carefully in the hope of extracting a few more bass before the bite is completely over.

A CASE FOR SPINNERBAITS

As we saw in the preceding chapter, a jig is a specialized tool better suited for covering water than working a specific spot from an anchored position. Another lure that is ideally suited for covering water is a spinnerbait. Spinnerbaits are probably the most versatile lure you can use to fish all varieties of largemouth habitat. Spinnerbaits perform well at both medium and slow speeds, in almost any type of cover, and in all depths from shallow shorelines to the deepest winter sanctuaries. Spinnerbaits are only limited by the angler who uses them, and in the hands of an expert "blade man" spinnerbaits become effective year-round bass producers.

Many people limit their use of spinnerbaits to shallow water fishing in spring, but this trend is not due to any particular limitation of the lure itself. Spinnerbaits are combination lures. By mixing and matching lure designs, weights, colors, and blades, you can usually find a spinnerbait that appeals to some bass in just about every situation. Be aware, however, that an effective setup for one situation may not be right for another. For example, a spinnerbait combination that works well for shallow bass may not be suited for deep winter sanctuaries. And a spinnerbait that catches bass from winter sanctuaries may not work the same for deep bass in summer. Each situation may require different lure designs, techniques, or presentations to make spinnerbaits effective. Spinnerbait fishing is an art, and there's a lot more detail to catching lunker bass with spinnerbaits than casting and retrieving the currently most popular models.

Spinnerbaits work best in off-colored water and low-light conditions. Dark water and low light enhance the look of a spinnerbait and make them more appealing. Spinnerbaits are best early and late in the day, or during midday hours with a good cloud cover, an approaching front, or strong wave action which diffuses light penetration. Any condition which stimulates movement and roaming activity is a good time to fish spinnerbaits.

Spinnerbaits have a proven history as effective bass lures in practically every part of the country, but spinnerbaits only play a small role in my system for catching the biggest bass in structured lakes. Spinnerbaits are fun to use but they're not the kind of lure to target giant bass. Spinnerbaits tend to catch nice bass (2 to 3-pounds on the low end, and 10 or 12-pounds on the high end), but from a year-round perspective, spinnerbaits are not a high-percentage big bass bait. Spinnerbaits become high-percentage baits in pre-spawn when some big fish move to shallow, but even then there are usually techniques that offer a higher percentage of success. Spinnerbaits are best when the fish are active and roaming. Periods with high activity are generally short which means spinnerbaits may have limited effectiveness even when bass are shallow. And not all the big fish move shallow in pre- spawn. I normally find a greater number of the bigger fish on deeper structures off the spawning flats during most of the early and late spring period. Stitching these deeper spots from an anchored position is usually the high-percentage technique at this time. You have to constantly keep in mind that this book is about high-percentage big bass fishing. In order to catch big fish consistently, you're going to have to use the lures and techniques that appeal to lunkers most often. Jigs are normally a higher-percentage lure for big bass than spinnerbaits because jigs happen to be bottom-walking lures which are more apt to appeal to a giant bass in more situations. Spinnerbaits are best when bass are active and chasing, but big bass won't chase for long, and they may only chase for a short time of any given day. But spinnerbaits have their place too. It might be a year when conditions are such where even the biggest bass move shallow and are aggressive for longer periods of time. If there's a lot of activity in the shallows, it might be better to cover water with a spinnerbait than to anchor on a deeper structure. You always should follow what the fish want. If you use a certain technique when conditions are not right for that technique, you're wasting your time. When one technique dries up, it's usually a sign to switch to another. Bass might bite better in the shallows in the morning, then stitching deeper structure works better during midday hours, but after 4 p.m.. the deep bite quits and anglers working the shallows begin catching fish again. Big bass fishing is a game of percentages, and you should always follow what those percentages dictate. I'm not saying that big bass can't be caught on spinnerbaits, I only want you to be aware that in most situations in structured lake environments, the biggest fish are normally in positions and active states where other techniques are more likely to appeal to them better. But you have to keep an open mind and be ready, because there will be times when spinnerbaits are deadly!

Spinnerbait Components

For all intents and purposes, a spinnerbait is simply a jig with a blade. Without the blade, a spinnerbait becomes just another modified jig. But sometimes the fish want that blade. Sometimes they'll hit a jig better, but then there are days when they want the vibration and flash of a blade.

There are many variations in the components which make up a spinnerbait, such as blade size, skirt material, and bait color, and all these things are very important because one guy always seems to catch more fish. A successful spinnerbait fisherman knows how to tune the lure, how to work it, and he believes in what he's doing. A confidant spinnerbait man will fish several different combinations of blades, sizes and colors until he figures out how the fish are responding on that particular day. Another fisherman might give up after a few hours and try a different technique, but a good spinnerbait man sticks with it because he knows there is always a way to catch bass on spinnerbaits when conditions are favorable.

It's not important to have a lot of different brands of spinnerbaits, find one brand you like and make your own modifications-change blade sizes, colors, skirts and trailers. I favor a single blade setup for big bass. I like the way they fall, and my timing is geared for a single blade. Using a tandem spinnerbait with giant blades isn't necessary; they might work on active fish but in many situations this action is too much for large bass. A spinnerbait with a single blade is most versatile because you can use it for both deep jigging and horizontal

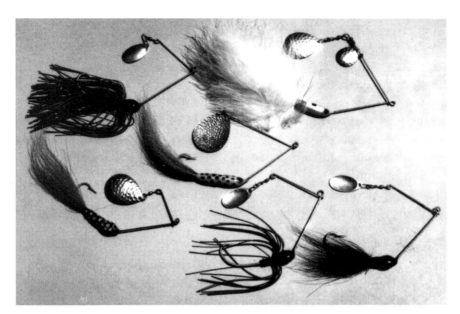

Assortment of Authors Favorite Spinnerbaits - Note the various jig skirts starting clockwise from upper right: white turkey maribou; black bucktail; spider skirt; dog hair and monkey hair; and living rubber. Long, straight tails when big bass key on large baitfish.

retrieves around shallow cover. My all-time favorite model is a simple single spin with one small blade attached to a short wire arm by a tiny swivel. For some reason, big bass love this combination. The only condition I have found where a tandem blade outperforms a single blade is when bass are cruising shoreline brush and logs in shallow murky water. I generally don't use tandem blades because they tend to catch more small to medium fish, and they often require a trailer hook. Trailer hooks are not a good idea and I don't like to use them. You can eliminate the need for a trailer hook by making sure the blade doesn't extend past the curve of the hook.

I make my own spinnerbaits with .045 dia. stainless wire and strong forged Mustad No. 91753 O'Shaughnessy hooks, size 4/0 and in gold. I shorten the wire to where a single Colorado or Indiana blade just ticks the point of the hook as the blade turns. When you use this setup long enough, you'll notice that the blade becomes etched by the hook point. This subtle ticking sound as the rotating blade scrapes the hook point can turn an average spinnerbait into a big bass spinnerbait. The sound, vibration, and the flash caused by the blade, in the right size, all create a spinnerbait with a special appeal. Keep in mind that the harder the fishing and the bigger the bass, the more well-tuned these elements have to be.

Many of my spinnerbaits are tied with animal hair. I believe spinnerbaits most often imitate baitfish or the illusion of a tight school of minnows, and sparsely tied hair enhances this illusion with its life-like action and appeal. I also favor vinyl or rubber skirts for certain conditions, rubber gives a faster action, and vinyl skirts can add vibrant colors unequalled in natural rubber. For the most part though, I like carefully tied bucktail or dog hair dressing on spinner-baits for big bass. Besides it gives the lure a look that is different and not as familiar to as many bass.

My favorite size for fishing a single blade in most situations is a 1/2 oz. spinnerbait. Always use a bait just heavy enough to get the job done. You want a lure that falls slowly in shallow water and faster in deeper water. Fall speed is more critical with big bass because big bass aren't likely to hit something that falls too quickly. A big bass generally reacts better to a slower fall, it may be because a crayfish just kind of floats when it jumps off a rock or bush. Whatever the reason, if a lure doesn't stay within their feeding rhythm it won't be effective. A heavy spinnerbait with large blades has to be fished too fast to be effective under most conditions. But you always experiment to see how the fish react. One of the best shallow water spinnerbaits for large bass, one year, was a 1/8 oz. model with a tiny blade that looked more like a big crappie lure than it did a bass lure, but it caught a lot of big bass, so who's to tell.

Spinnerbaits can work well without adding a trailer, but there are times when a pork dressing pays big dividends. Long trailers can ruin a spinnerbait's action, so I usually favor short pork strips, frogs, and split-tail lizards. Adding a 4 inch pork eel or lizard is supper in winter. Pork adds bulk making a spinnerbait appear bigger and more of a meal to a hungry old bass. It also makes spinnerbaits fall more slowly, however, I think they really like that meaty aroma and taste. Pork also adds color appeal, and the right combination of blade color, skirt color, and pork color can create a very positive effect.

**Spinnerbaits with large blades may promote savage
strikes in spring, but smaller blades catch more giant
bass on pressured waters.**

Blade Size

Big willow blades have become very popular, but I think a lot
of the big-blade success with tandem spinnerbaits is due to the lure
giving the bass a different look. Bass are oriented to differences,

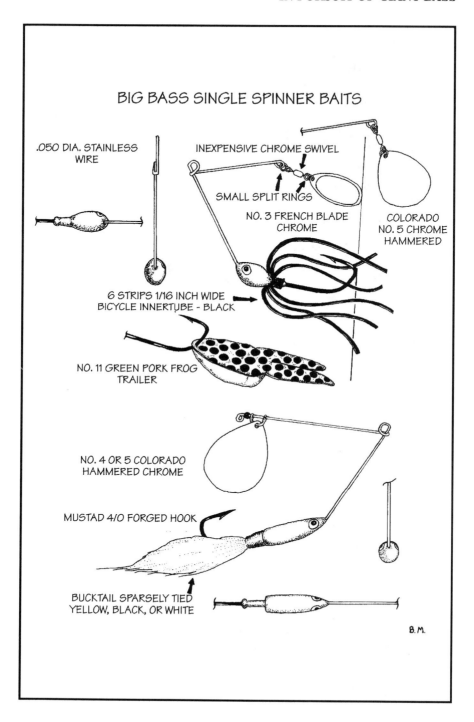

BIG BASS SINGLE SPINNER BAITS

.050 DIA. STAINLESS WIRE

INEXPENSIVE CHROME SWIVEL

SMALL SPLIT RINGS

NO. 3 FRENCH BLADE CHROME

COLORADO NO. 5 CHROME HAMMERED

6 STRIPS 1/16 INCH WIDE BICYCLE INNERTUBE - BLACK

NO. 11 GREEN PORK FROG TRAILER

NO. 4 OR 5 COLORADO HAMMERED CHROME

MUSTAD 4/0 FORGED HOOK

BUCKTAIL SPARSELY TIED YELLOW, BLACK, OR WHITE

B. M.

whether it be a structure or a lure, and a new look often triggers a positive reaction even though it may not have long-term success. Big blades tend to work best during pre-spawn and spawn when big bass are shallow and have a pugnacious nature. But as far as the rest of the year, I've always found that the biggest bass respond better to **SMALLER** blades, and this is especially true on heavily-fished waters. The purpose of the blade is to attract but not to alert. Big bass seem to prefer a blade that produces a little flash like a small shad or bluegill darting around the twigs. The biggest bass normally aren't super aggressive, and it's often more productive if your approach is conservative-keep the blade size down just like the sound of a rattle. Sometimes big bass will favor large baitfish, and that's when big blades will produce other than pre-spawn and spawn, but most of the time it's been my experience to catch far more trophy-size bass on smaller blades; too big a blade seems to disturb them in most situations.

My favorite size in a Colorado, Indiana, or French blade is a #4, #3, and #2. All these are big bass blades. Sometimes a tiny #2 blade will work on lunker bass like nothing else. In a willow leaf blade, I like a #3 or #4. Besides being effective sizes, the nice thing about using a small willow blade is that when you buzz them fast right under the surface (which is a good tactic for aggressive shallow bass in pre-spawn), they won't cause the lure to roll on its side like larger willow blades.

Spinnerbait Colors

Big bass often prefer a spinnerbait of one solid color except for the blade. Examples are: a black head, black skirt or hair, and black trailer; other good producers are all brown, all blue, and all white. Black spinnerbaits work best with a nickel blade. A white spinnerbait can have either nickel or white blades. All brown spinnerbaits should have a gold blade.

Water color often dictates what spinnerbait colors work best. Yellow or white are both good colors in murky or stained water. Intense color sometimes produces better in murky or muddy water, and I've had good results using the vinyl skirts under these conditions. Vinyl has more vivid color than rubber, and a vinyl skirt in black, black/yellow, yellow, chartreuse or white may be just the ticket for dark water bass. In clear water it's better to use minnow colors. Good skirt colors in clear water include: clear sparkle, smoke sparkle, silver sparkle, gold sparkle, and black sparkle. In winter, I find subdued colors like brown, purple, blue and orange can be excellent.

My favorite blade colors are: nickel, gold, pearl, yellow, white, black, brown, chartreuse and blue. Nickel blades can be used with practically any color spinnerbait, but I find that gold works best with a plain yellow, orange or brown skirt. I switch to gold in murky water rather than go to a bigger blade.

In spring I use pork frog trailers in black, brown and green. In summer, white pork strips are good, and in winter, a small pork eel in either black, blue or brown adds a lot to a spinnerbait. In clear water I use a transparent plastic trailer the same color as the skirt.

Color

Here are some proven Big Bass combinations:

BLADE	HEAD	SKIRT	TRAILER
Nickel	Black	Black	Black or Green
Nickel	White	Yellow	Black
Nickel	Black	White	White
Nickel	Yellow	Yellow/Black	Black
Nickel	Black	Yellow/Black	Black
Nickel	Pink	White	White
Black	Black	Orange	Black
Chartreuse	White	Chartreuse	No Trailer
Gold	Yellow	Yellow	White
Nickel	White	Blue	Blue

The problem with any discussion about color is that there is no accurate way to predict the best color. People always want to know definite answers, but the bass in each lake can respond differently. A friend and I once won a big tournament working a yellow/black vinyl skirted spinnerbait in 25 ft. of water off short bluff points in winter. A yellow/black vinyl skirt is a great murky water color, but this lake had crystal clear water and we loaded the boat both days of the tournament. You can never be sure about color. Experiment and find out what they want on that particular day.

Spinnerbait Retrieves

The two most effective spinnerbait actions I've found for big bass are: 1) a slow, steady retrieve all the way back to the boat, and 2) a lift-and-drop retrieve which creates high frequency vibrations on the upward pull and a controlled flutter on the drop. I like the slow, steady retrieve for working shallow cover. I'll work parallel to the cover bringing the spinnerbait tight against the sides or through the cover. I just reel fast enough to keep the blade rotating and the spinnerbait working horizontal to the bottom. As the lure approaches a stump or bush, raise the rod tip and work the spinnerbait up and over the obstacle. When the spinner lurches forward, causing the blade to rotate more intensely creating a higher frequency throb, a strike will most likely occur. After it clears the object, continue slowly reeling or let it flutter to the base of the object, but usually the fish will respond better to a more horizontal type retrieve in shallow water. When using the lift-and-drop retrieve, I'll cast toward the shallows and retrieve the single spin downhill so it can flutter down from ledge to ledge. This is a more difficult retrieve and the lure must be fished by controlling the slack as it falls. Monitor the lure without restricting its fall by following the bait down with the rod tip. Feeling the lure and watching the line as it falls is the secret behind this technique. Watch where the line enters the water for the subtle twitch of a strike. Line watching can be hard on windy days with a choppy surface, so I developed the habit of always beginning my retrieve (after the spinnerbait has sunk to the bottom) with a short, hard hookset. You'd be surprised how many times bass grab the bait on the sink where you can't detect a strike. Single spins are also effective lures for flipping into heavy shallow cover. I like a 3/8 oz. model with either a split-tail eel, lizard or frog trailer. Using a spinnerbait instead of the standard jig and pig adds vibration to the flipping presentation, and this technique can be very effective when bass want that blade.

I always tie directly to spinnerbaits and use 12 lb. or 15 lb. line depending on the cover. A line moving through the water is a lot less visible than a stationary line on the end a plastic worm, but I seldom use 20 lb. test even in the heaviest cover. If you hook a giant bass in heavy cover you're going to have to go in and work it out by hand anyway, and I believe you'll get more bites from big bass on lighter line. In thick cover I'll use a 15 lb. high abrasion line like Maxima or Trilene Big Game.

My spinnerbait tackle includes a medium action 6 ft. graphite casting rod and a Lew's BB1N casting reel. This combination is well suited for both the lift and drop retrieve and the more traditional slow and steady presentation.

When bass strike a spinnerbait, the bite usually feels like a sharp "pop", but you might also feel a gentle tug, or a spongy feeling like you've snagged an old waterlogged sock. By watching the point where the line enters the water, you may see the line jump or move off to one side: this is your cue to set the hook immediately. If the line goes slack while retrieving, a bass has grabbed the lure and is swimming toward you; reel up the slack quickly and strike hard: with practice, it's easy to learn the difference between the slight tick of a branch and the tick from the bite of a big bass. Veteran spinnerbait anglers can detect even the slight skip in blade rhythm caused when a bass rushes to strike but turns away at the last moment.

Although spinnerbaits are not my first choice to pursue giant bass, spinnerbaits are fun to use and are very effective bass baits in general. There is usually some combination of size and color that will produce in almost every situation.

CRANKIN' CRANKBAITS

Crankplugs can be great big bass baits, but they are not necessarily high percentage trophy lures. Crankbaits are most effective during times of peak activity which can mean only a short time on any given day. When bass hit crankbaits the action can be fast and furious (often times, you'll catch nice bass on cast after cast), but from the standpoint of consistency, there could be long dry spells in between moments of success. Inactive and neutral bass generally don't respond well to crankbaits, but I always have a crankbait ready. Stitching a plastic worm or bait through a spot may be the highest percentage technique in most situations, but when the activity lulls and the target is in the right depth it may be the signal to throw a crankbait. Crankbaits can catch active bass in a hurry, and they have an uncanny ability to produce the biggest bass from a spot even when the stitching technique produces more bass. Also, keep in mind that from a seasonal point of view, crankbaits become the highest percentage technique during certain times of the year. In early summer, for example, when the spawn is finished and bass begin to gather on outside structures near deep water, there is generally a two-to-three-week period when casting and trolling crankbaits is the very best technique. Stitching a plastic worm may become a secondary technique at this time. There are times when trolling a crankbait really enhances its big bass appeal, and trolling will be covered in detail in another chapter.

Author caught this 14 lb. 12 oz. monster on a Tennessee Shad Bomber Model A.

Crankbait Basics

All lures are more effective when fine tuned to where they run perfectly straight. When a baitfish swims off to one side in an erratic manner, bass can tell something is wrong and the movement can cause bass to strike. But when a lure runs off to one side it triggers an opposite reaction; suddenly, the lure looks phony. A baitfish out of tune draws attention, but a lure out of tune repels.

Regardless how fast or slow you work a plug, it has to run perfectly straight; it should never go to one side or the other. A plug should never run off center at any speed. If it runs just a little off, big fish won't respond to it, and this is especially true on days when fishing is tough. Some anglers try to make their plugs run sideways so they can reach unfishable areas under piers and trees, but while this trick may catch a few bass, it's been my experience that working parallel to the cover with a plug in perfect tune is much more attractive to the bigger fish. There's a certain vibration a plug makes when it's running absolutely true that the big fish really like. A true-running plug gives off **MAXIMUM** vibrations. It gets its power from working straight to the pressure of the water. It can't go right or left so it goes straight forward causing the lip to bear down and vibrate creating maximum vibration and depth. And when you work a perfectly running plug parallel to cover, its vibration is so attractive, bass will often rush out and grab it. A good angler with a properly adjusted crankbait can often make it produce even when conditions aren't the best for crankbaits. I'll spend a lot of time getting a plug to run just right. If a plug can't be made to run true, you might as well throw it away.

I always use a split ring to attach line to a crankbait. I don't particularly like snaps because the small diameter wire is more traumatic on the knot than a double strand split ring. I use the smallest split ring I can in relationship to the size of the plug. When you tie on a plug, make sure you don't tie the line over the little notch in the split ring. Tie onto the even part of the ring with the groove off to the side. This will help make the plug run straight and keep the line strong.

A Sound for Big Bass

Studies have shown that bass can detect the sound of a crayfish scratching on the bottom from great distances, and that's not hard to believe because my most incredible observation while diving was the silence! The loudest thing was the silence; it was deafening it was so quiet. I could seemingly hear every little movement, and I've only got regular hearing. But something that lives underwater and is in-tune with their world undoubtedly would have little trouble finding crayfish by sound.

I've done a lot of experimenting with sound, and big bass definitely respond better to certain sounds; I don't mean just any bass, but the biggest bass. Some sounds scare big bass, others attract. It's all in the pitch. Bass are used to feeding by sound. The bait which they feed upon all make certain identifiable sounds, and those sounds have specific pitches or pulses. If your lures don't produce a familiar sound, they may repulse rather than attract. Here I'm only describing the habits of big fish because the smaller bass don't seem to care. You can only find what attracts by trial and error. Every lure has a different vibration, and what you put inside them creates a different sound. You can't match the sound of a natural shiner, or the natural sound, a school of shad makes, but I think certain sounds in lures help bass key in on the lure by some association. I think lures with loud, BB type rattles are overdone. Rattle baits seem to be the lure of the 80's and a lot of nice bass have been caught with them, but if enough people use any bait long enough some big fish will be caught, but that doesn't necessarily mean they are good big bass baits. I have found that the most productive lures aren't particularly noisy. The best lures make a deep, rather low, kind of throaty sound; they have a dull throb rather than the high-pitched sound of rattling BB's. The old Water Gator was one of the first sonar baits to have a rattle, but it had a single weight that made a dull, clunking sound and it caught tons of big bass. The Bomber Model A's have a nice, heavy sounding rattle, and although the knock, or clatter, of a single weight chamber may not mimic anything in nature, I find its subdued sound more attractive than anything high-pitched. I've experimented with BB type rattle chambers in plastic worms, and you'd be surprised how many days bass won't hit a worm with a rattle, and it's more days than not! The biggest bass like lures with a low-pitched, subtle sound, and that's true with spinnerbaits, plastic worms, or any other lure. Sound is why I like the old wooden plugs, instead of plastic, when I can get them. Wood plugs make a thud when they bounce off objects instead of the clicking sound produced by plastic plugs. Also the bottom hook scraped the underside of the old plugs and made a deep scraping sound.

At times, fishing a crankbait will upset the natural atmosphere of a spot, and the time it takes for the fish to recover can be influenced by the type of plug. When you fish a spot with a crankbait, you often have to fish the same spot for some time before a bass will strike. You might make ten casts without a bite, but on the eleventh cast you catch a fish and then it's one right after another on every cast. I believe in cases like this the crankbait actually spooked the fish, and then after a time they adjust to, or accept, the presence of the plug as being normal. And I've found that bass recover faster when you use a plug with a dead-sounding rattle.

Another advantage of plugs with a single-weight sound chamber is that the weight causes a slight variation in the lure path as it's being retrieved. The single weight is transferred back and forth from side to side as the plug wiggles, and this movement causes a variation in the wiggle which fish can detect. I believe that slight change in rhythm is one reason why big bass find these plugs appealing. The bigger the weight, and the more dead the sound, the better it is for big fish. A single-weight chamber alters the lure path and the bigger fish will accept these lures more quickly.

Crank Colors

Crankbaits cast work best in murky water, and over the years I've had most success in murky water and low-light conditions with either yellow or orange plugs. With a yellow or orange plug, I like a black coachdog or black rib pattern. Chartreuse and blue is a big fish combination, although chartreuse is not a consistent big bass producer for me in my area. All-white or pearl can also be effective in murky water.

In clear water, I like shad and shiner patterns and silver scale. I like silver with a white belly and either a black, blue or green scale. I don't like green plugs as a rule, but a green back, or the Tennessee Shad pattern, is excellent (Tennessee Shad is a natural pattern with a white undercoat and green scales). All white plugs can be good in clear water, if not too large, as well as a white plug with a blue back, or with a red head. On rare occasions an all brown plug can be good, but not to the point where I would carry a whole box full of brown, crayfish patterns. I really don't like to use plugs that closely resemble real bait. Exact patterns and photo-finishes are my **LEAST** productive crankbaits.

You don't need a lot of different crankbaits to catch big bass. Find one style that is strong, runs true, and catches fish, then buy various sizes in all the best colors. But don't buy different colors in all different baits. Find one style that works well, and buy all the colors in that lure. My favorite crankbaits are made by Bomber, both

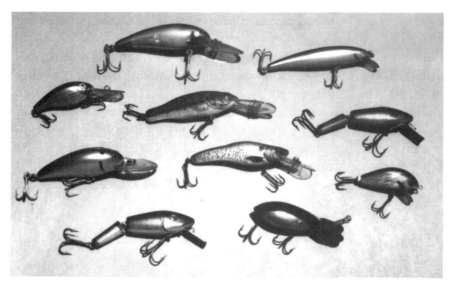

Some of the authors favorite crankbaits for big bass.

the old style and the new Model A's. Someone at the Bomber Company really knows how to design big bass lures.

Keep in mind that the top colors in my area may vary from your lakes. Chartreuse in crank plugs, for example, has never produced well for big bass for me in my area, although chartreuse is considered an excellent color in many parts of the country. Also, keep in mind that Florida-strain bass respond to different colors and different lures than northern bass. After fishing for northern largemouth before the Florida bass were introduced, it is my opinion that northern bass bite a much greater variety of colors. I used to catch northern bass on practically every pattern Bomber made, but the Florida bass are more selective. Florida's like colors that look like minnows such as shiner colors, and lures with grey and green shad scale patterns. But rarely photo-finish colored lures; these are probably the weakest for both species.

PROVEN BIG BASS COLORS IN AUTHOR'S AREA

Tennessee Shad	**Year Round**
Baby Bass	**Post-Spawn**
Green Back-Silver Side	**Spring & Summer**
Black Back-Silver Side	**Spring, Summer & Fall**
Black Back-Gold Side	**Summer**
Christmas Tree	**Year Round**
All Black	**Low-light & Night**
All Brown	**Low-light & Fall**
Pearl	**Winter, Spring & Summer**
Yellow Black Ribs	**Murky Water, Late Winter & Spring**
Orange-Black Ribs	**Winter**
Yellow Coachdog	**Late Winter, Spring & Fall**
White Coachdog	**Winter**
Blue Back-Silver Side	**Fall, Winter & Spring**
Rainbow Trout Pattern	**Winter, Spring & Late Summer**

Silver is an excellent big bass color in clear water, but I didn't add it to my top color listing because I'm not talking about a chrome color. I don't like a shiny chrome lure. A silver Rapala is a great lure, but they have a mute silver color, and I believe the subdued color is why they work so well. I paint chrome plugs with about 15 coats of pearl fingernail polish which mutes the classic chrome finish. You can also sand blast the chrome finish before the pearl coating, and this creates a very effective color. I love adding fingernail polish to my baits. I even paint the blades of spinnerbaits. Instead of having a real bright flash, the painted blades are more subdued which big bass like. I've discovered that adding pearl, blue, and pink polish can make crankbaits much more appealing to big bass. I start by painting a lure with white lacquer. Then I paint the top and sides with dabs of blue and pink. While these are still wet I next paint about 15 coats of pearl over the entire plug and finish with a protective coat of clear epoxy. It's important not to paint the lip where the eye, or line attachment, is. The eye should always be clear of any paint. When bass are hitting white plugs, or plugs with shad patterns, they really go nuts over the same colors toned down with polish. However, like everything else, painting a plug with fingernail polish doesn't mean that it will always out produce store-bought plugs, polish is just a variation, but it can be a deadly variation for bigger bass. Some anglers leave their plugs to bake in the sun which dulls the color, but you can achieve the same results and a better finish by using fingernail polish.

Another thing to keep in mind concerning color is that brighter colors appear larger and more exaggerated underwater than dark colors. Overweight people look slimmer in black and navy, and it's the same with plugs-the brighter the color, the larger the lure will appear underwater. I only mention this because there are times when bass want a bigger, or smaller, plug. One time I found the bass on the bottom at the 16 ft. level, but they would only respond to a small bait. Trouble was that I needed a large # 600 Bomber to reach that level. The fish were hitting shad colors best, but a shad color in the # 600 lure was just too big to get a lot of bites. Henry "Red" DeZeeuw had the answer which was to use an all-black #600 plug with a small patch of white pearl paint on the sides of the plug in the shape of a baitfish. The big lure got to the right depth, and the small pearl shape on the black background gave the illusion of a small baitfish which the fish wanted.

Crankbait size is always a consideration. Every once in a while, for some reason, all of a sudden the fish get on big live baits, big worms, and big plugs. Then for 5 or 6 years the fish bite medium or small size lures better. And it doesn't have anything to do with matching the hatch because when the fish want big plugs the bait may only be an inch long. Size response phenomena is important to be aware of but not to question why. There aren't any set rules concerning size, you just have to be versatile and experiment with different things and be tuned in to what they're hitting so you can take advantage of the situation. At times, small plugs produce better

Henry "Red" DeZeeuw came up with the idea of using nail polish to enhance the color of plugs. By painting a small side of a black, #600 Bomber, DeZeeuw was able to present a small-looking lure in deeper water. It worked great when bass wanted a smaller plug.

in well-fished waters, and you might have to troll a small plug to get it deeper when bass prefer a smaller plug at a depth not obtainable by casting.

Crankbait Retrieves

With the #600 Bomber, the only way to fish them effectively was by trolling. So a few of us designed 7 1/2 ft. spinning rods with big foul-proof guides and used a big, light-saltwater spinning reel to cast them (as it turned out this rod and reel were perfect for stitching too). With my big spinning rig I could cast crankbaits a mile, and the combination helped get a crankbait down and keep it down. The soft, fiberglass tip section was ideal for using a fast-moving bait, and the long length and big reel allow me to crank all day without fatigue.

I always work a crankbait with some type of bottom structure in mind, and I always work them along the bottom. In my opinion, a stop-and-go retrieve is less effective for giant bass. It's much more effective to let the bottom structure and cover slow the plug and make

Garcia Mitchell 306 Spinning reel: Note modern bail but original small handle. This reel covers all methods calling for a substantial spinning reel.

it run erratically. When a plug hits the bottom, or an object, it changes direction and speed, and this change in rhythm often produces the strike. You can fish a crankbait off the bottom and change the rhythm manually with a stop-and-go retrieve, but fishing off the bottom is less effective for big bass. Even when baitfish suspend over a spot, a bass might move up and grab some, but move right back down to their holding area when finished.

Always cast crankbaits horizontal to the bank. Don't throw them in and bring them out. Once you establish the right depth, hold that depth with the trolling motor and work parallel to the bank, throwing slightly in and slightly out to test the areas adjacent to the magic depth. Always use a lure that will run slightly deeper than the depth you want to work. If you have to reel hard all the time to obtain the right depth, then that one speed is the only speed you can use without loosing depth control. But if you use a lure that runs slightly deeper than that depth, you can crank it down to the bottom and then slow it up to create a different action at the same depth. A deeper-running lure simply gives you more control options like action and speed control.

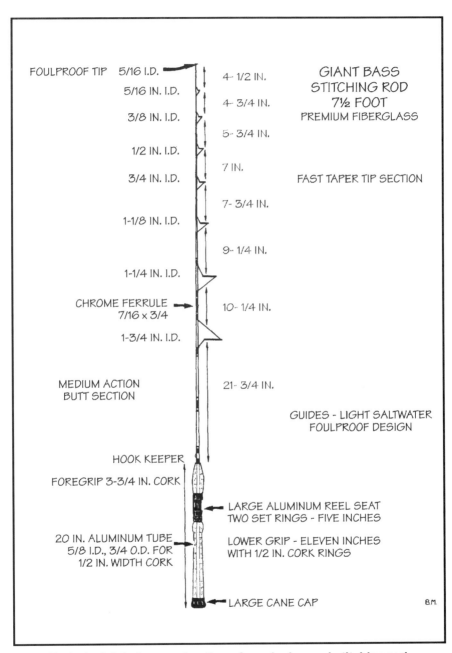

FOULPROOF TIP 5/16 I.D.

5/16 IN. I.D.

3/8 IN. I.D.

1/2 IN. I.D.

3/4 IN. I.D.

1-1/8 IN. I.D.

1-1/4 IN. I.D.

CHROME FERRULE
7/16 x 3/4

1-3/4 IN. I.D.

MEDIUM ACTION
BUTT SECTION

HOOK KEEPER

FOREGRIP 3-3/4 IN. CORK

20 IN. ALUMINUM TUBE
5/8 I.D., 3/4 O.D. FOR
1/2 IN. WIDTH CORK

4- 1/2 IN.

4- 3/4 IN.

5- 3/4 IN.

7 IN.

7- 3/4 IN.

9- 1/4 IN.

10- 1/4 IN.

21- 3/4 IN.

GIANT BASS
STITCHING ROD
7½ FOOT
PREMIUM FIBERGLASS

FAST TAPER TIP SECTION

GUIDES - LIGHT SALTWATER
FOULPROOF DESIGN

LARGE ALUMINUM REEL SEAT
TWO SET RINGS - FIVE INCHES

LOWER GRIP - ELEVEN INCHES
WITH 1/2 IN. CORK RINGS

LARGE CANE CAP

B.M.

Technical data for construction of crank plug and stitching rod.

When I'm fishing during a period of peak activity, the fish may be too pumped up to respond well to slower speeds and finesse presentations. Active bass may be roaming from their holding areas, and in many cases a lure which covers a lot of water like a crankbait will intercept these moving fish. It's common for very active bass to pick up a plastic worm and drop it, or just bump the worm without inhaling it. When this happens, and the depth range is right, I immediately cast a crankbait to the same spot, and the bass will often explode on the lure. You'll generally find active bass responding best to a crankbait retrieved, or trolled, at a high rate of speed. In very warm water the speed necessary to produce a strike might be faster than can be obtained by casting and retrieving alone. Speed trolling takes over at this time, and trolling may be the only way to present a crankbait at the right depth with the right speed.

Burning a crankbait, however, isn't always the best retrieve. In nature, a baitfish frantically swimming off usually means it's being pursued by a predator, and a big bass in neutral mood may lose interest. One of my favorite retrieves when bass are responding this way is to slow down the retrieve slightly just as it comes off an object. It's not a stop and go retrieve, I just pause for a second as it deflects off an object, and then continue cranking normally. I just slow the lure down to where it's barely moving and almost stationary, and that's when I'll usually get bit. Slowing down changes the rhythm and big bass often want a change of rhythm; they think there's something wrong and they nail it. It's the same reaction when a spinnerbait rolls over an object-it slows down slightly, changes rhythm, and a bass grabs it. A change in rhythm is a definite pattern for big bass.

Sometimes the bass can get worn out with crankbaits. You'll catch them like crazy, then suddenly they turn off. Most of the time this is due to an active period ending, but sometimes the fish just quit hitting crankbaits. Sometimes the spot will pick up again after you let it rest for some period of time. By leaving a productive spot you allow those fish time to forget, and when you come back you'll find the fish again responding favorably to the same crankbaits.

SEASONAL PATTERNS

Distinct and Transitional Patterns

When examining seasonal patterns, it's important to approach the various seasons with a different mind set. Instead of separating the seasonal cycle into individual pieces, each seasonal pattern flows evenly from one part of the year to the next without rigid boundaries or barriers. Although each seasonal pattern may have a different personality, in reality they are all connected.

Actually, there are only two **DISTINCT** seasonal patterns-summer and winter. Fall is a transition from summer to winter patterns, and spring is a transition from winter to summer patterns influenced, or interrupted, by the spawning period. The most distinct seasonal patterns for big bass are summer and winter because each of these patterns is influenced by stable oxygen content. In summer, for example, if a thermocline forms at 16 ft., bass are restricted to a zone from the surface down to 16 ft. Although confining, thermocline layers can remain somewhat stable throughout the summer and bass usually settle into fairly predictable patterns. In winter, the oxygen distribution is different, but it is also a period with general, overall stability. After turn-over, sufficient oxygen can be found in the deepest basins and bass are free to use any depth. But once bass settle into a winter pattern, the stability of the winter environment causes the fish to be fairly predictable just like in summer.

Big bass follow the changing oxygen levels throughout the year just like herds of elk and caribou migrate to summer and winter pastures. But following a particular food source normally isn't important to big bass because in a healthy lake there is abundant food sources at all key locations where big bass gather. Just because you don't graph baitfish near a structure doesn't mean that bass aren't feeding on crayfish or some other food source that can't be graphed. And the food source doesn't have to be that close anyway. Who's to say where a big bass might sit during a neutral period? One spot may

Veteran big bass anglers have four things in common: 1) They can read water and quickly evaluate its potential. 2) They have an intimate knowledge of a particular water. 3) They possess a large backlog of previous big fish encounters. 4) They have developed a unique intuition born from experience.

be a great place to feed, but it might not be the kind of place a big bass stays when inactive. You don't sit behind Burger King all day in case you might get hungry. Following a food source can be a small bass trait, but when you're talking about large adult fish, I think oxygen and security are always the first considerations, besides, both bass and bait are generally all vying for the same ideal situations.

Although summer and winter tend to have stable patterns, from a seasonal standpoint there are more inactive periods in summer and winter than in spring and fall. Activity increases in spring and fall because bass are in transition. Environmental factors cause bass to move deeper in fall almost directly opposite to the factors which cause them to move shallow in spring. During fall, for example, the water clarity and temperature is changing, life forms are maturing, and bass are following the oxygen as it sinks deeper into the basin. There are also meteorological influences; weather can be more unstable in spring and fall than any other time of the year, and weather is another reason why patterns are so unpredictable during transitional periods. It is important to fish often and monitor the fish in spring and fall because that's when they move the most. In summer and winter bass relate to particular patterns that usually hold up throughout that period. It is common for big bass to remain at certain depths either suspended in open water or holding on individual holding spots on structure during summer and winter. The only time they move, or change their location, is during active feeding periods. So in this sense, there are two seasonal patterns that are predictable (summer and winter), and two seasonal patterns that are unstable (spring and fall). But the seasonal patterns are all closely related. The spots themselves remain somewhat the same all the time. A summer stratification might move a fish shallower, and they might move deeper after turn-over, but the spots remain the same; a good spot that offers big bass the security of a deep-water escape route, and has abundant and varied food sources will be a good spot during all seasonal periods. The depth the fish hold at is the only thing that really changes.

Seasonal Peaks

Every region of the country has it's own timetable of good big bass fishing. In southern California, my best months are: February, March, July, October, and December. In the upper Midwest around the Great Lakes region, the best big bass months are: April, June, July, September, and November. The best months coincide with seasonal periods of peak activity such as pre-spawn, early summer, early fall, etc. A seasonal peak for big bass is a period when numbers of lunker fish gather into areas where they are highly vulnerable to anglers. Obviously, it pays to be fishing often when seasonal peaks are taking place, and with experience you can become aware of the best months to fish in your area. But don't get locked into good and bad seasonal periods, because you can often turn every month into a good big bass period when you're patient with what you're doing!

Sometimes bass fishing can be universal where good or bad fishing trends tend to be the same all across the country. July, for example, tends to be a good month for big bass wherever you fish. General conditions can also last for years; some lakes seem to go dead for years and everyone thinks they're fished out, but then they rebound with phenomenal big bass fishing, yet nobody can explain why. So in this sense, the conditions that influence good and bad fishing can be much broader than what you perceive as important local conditions like barometric pressure and moon phases. Maybe it stems from how the earth sits on its axis, or how far the earth is from the sun at any given time, and how all this affects weather systems and universal conditions. I only mention this to make you aware that the scope of bass fishing is much broader than what you might currently believe. That fishing has its ups and downs is one of the few constants in big bass fishing.

PRELUDE TO PRE-SPAWN

Why is it that some spawning areas produce lunker bass year after year, while other shallow areas which have similar habitat and bottom content produce few big bass? What makes a shallow area a consistent big bass producer are the deeper structural elements associated with it. When the shallow zones of a lake are basically composed of softer, nondesirable muck and silt-covered bottom, any area with gravel, marl or clay would attract spawning bass no matter how they were associated with other structural features in the lake. But in a lake filled with clay and gravel banks, the structural combinations which link shallow zones with deep water habitat become the key. Big bass may travel great distances from winter sanctuaries to spawning locations in lakes with limited shallow habitat, but in a typical structured lake, certain spawning areas become consistent big bass producers because of the deep water structures associated with them. The best spawning areas have the bottom composition big bass need, and they have a good track (channeling or deeper depression) which big bass follow from winter sanctuaries to pre-spawn areas, and from pre-spawn areas into eventual spawning sites. The biggest bass always select the key spots, and without the proper set of characteristics, a shallow area will only be a marginal big bass producer at best.

I believe bass often return to their place of origin to spawn when at all possible, especially if it is an ideal spawning site. Like salmon or sea bass or any other creature that instinctively comes back to spawn, I think bass have a migratory route imprinted in their genetic program that they get from birth. The developing fry live in a certain area that becomes their home, and that area is all they know as a youngster. When they become large enough and first move from the spawning area, all their experiences become recorded. And when bass

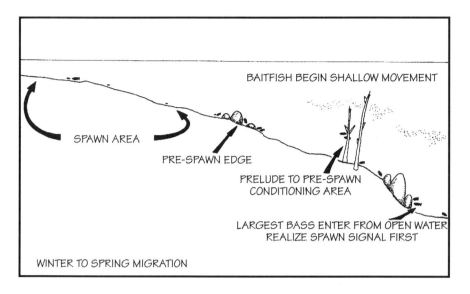

become adults, all their entrances and exits (tracks) to and from the shallows are mapped out in their gyroscope. It's like when you first learned how to fish, the spots where you first started catching bass and putting this sport together are the places you always compare new spots to because they're constantly on your mind. I think bass use a similar mechanism to return to the same spawning sites year after year. Of course this is only my theory and nobody but the fish knows for sure, but I think this visualization is important because, although it may not be biologically correct, this vision of how bass move from winter sanctuaries to eventual spawning sites can help you track these big fish and put yourself in a good position to catch some.

Prelude Spots

When bass move out from deep winter sanctuaries, they move to early pre-spawn areas. I call these locations "prelude spots," and they are the farthest, most remote, outlying structural areas associated with eventual spawning sites. Prelude spots are contact points where bass begin their journey shallower. Many people associate vertical banks near spawning grounds with early pre-spawn movements, but vertical banks may not attract big bass activity. When I'm talking about the earliest pre-spawn movement, I'm describing fish that are first starting to move from winter sanctuaries. In southern California the top pre-spawn month is generally March, but the first spawning movement to outside prelude areas takes place in late January or early February. Some people might call this winter fishing but I don't. The prelude spots are different locations than winter sanctuaries. The first spots pre-spawn bass move to, are the most remote outlying structural features like rock piles and ledges that are connected with eventual spawning areas. Bass remain in these early spots for some time as if climatizing or adjusting to what they eventually will have to do. They have remained in winter sanctuaries for several months, and even though spawning urges are starting to take over and direct them, the big females seem reluctant to leave the comfort and security of deep water. I have my best activity at this time of year on structures anywhere from 35 ft. to 45 ft. deep. This is in relationship to lakes where winter sanctuary depths might be 50 ft. or 60 ft. deep. Many anglers miss the abundance of these prelude areas because the focus of their early spring fishing is the shallows. Oftentimes, when the first movement of bass reaches the shallows, the bigger females are still at prelude depths or pre-spawn edges and the shallow anglers never contact them. Early pre-spawn can be a great time to catch trophy bass, but you've got to fish the right areas.

One important feature of a good prelude spot is a deeper channel. The first contact spot and eventual spawning sites are connected in some way by a channel or some type of depression in the lake bottom. Big bass use these depressions as migration routes or highways as they move to and from spawning areas. Even in highland reservoirs where channels may be much deeper than the depth bass are holding, bass may suspend over the channels but they still relate to the channel in the same way. Even a slight depression only a few feet deeper than the rest of the bottom can make all the difference whether a big bass will use a spot or not. It has been my experience that a channel or deeper depression near a spawning area is the key element that will draw big fish to that particular location. And the importance of this depression is a factor in the productivity of all the structures con-nected with the spawning location at all depths. Winter sanctuaries are often associated with the same channels that lead bass up to spawning areas. Once spawning instincts begin to take over, the

Prelude lunkers are hard to catch but it can be done. This 16-pounder was caught stitching a crayfish at 38 ft. on the deep edge of a break with standing timber.

larger females begin to vacate winter sanctuaries and move up from a channel into a prelude area. After spending a few days on these remote, early pre-spawn structures, they move shallower into pre-spawn locations adjacent to ledges and drop-offs. Pre-spawn spots would have rocks, stickups or whatever type of cover that is dominant on that particular lake. During certain moon phases and monthly active periods, bass leave pre-spawn spots and move into spawning areas. The spawning process is over in a day, a half day, or even a few hours, and when they come off the spawning flats, bass move back onto pre-spawn structures which now serve as post-spawn spots. The entire spawning process is a movement from one location to another, and all these elements have to be fairly close together. Big bass won't travel too far from the channel to a prelude spot, and they

Prelude to pre-spawn is a deep water situation. The angler depicted here is actually anchored near the pre-spawn spot and is working deeper on the prelude area. Note the severe anchor and line angles. Maximum depth could be 65 ft. You work the spot on a more vertical axis. The key prelude spot has hard bottom, broken timber and very cautious bass. Prelude is probably the toughest time of the year to catch giant bass. Fish very slowly with a lift and drop retrieve.

won't move to a pre-spawn structure up shallower if the spot is far from the prelude area. There has to be a close correlation between structural elements or the bigger bass won't use them. Trophy fish hang near the edges of deep water until it's time to actually move in to spawn, and the biggest bass tend to spawn on the edges of the flats near deeper water.

Another important characteristic of a good prelude spot is wood. The foundation of the spot may be the channel, but standing timber, stumps, brush, or even a few stickups can definitely make a prelude spot more attractive to big bass. I've seen bluegill rubbing against wood in shallow water, and it's possible that bass do the same thing in deep water. Some people believe bass rub on wood to dislodge egg sacks, but maybe the swelling in their bellies causes their skin to itch the way excessive weight gain and capillary expansion in humans causes our skin to itch; and maybe they have an urge to scratch similar to the way cows rub up against a fence post? Maybe they get parasites from spending the winter in a fairly confined area? Whatever the reason, a deeper channel and wood cover are key elements that make a prelude spot appeal to big bass. Even in older lakes where the wood has rotted away, big bass will have already established the route they travel and will use the same route even though most of the wood is gone. This is another reason why I believe bass instinctively return to key spawning areas year after year. Even when bass suspend off the bottom they still may relate to wood. I've graphed bass suspending 30 ft. off the bottom, but they were still over trees.

If timber wasn't natural to the lake, then a prelude spot would need rocks or weeds or whatever is the next most powerful drawing agent in that lake. The attraction of wood to early pre-spawn bass may not be biological fact, but the **VISION** is compatible with any type of lake or reservoir environment. In one lake a deep timberline is the key, but in another lake the key element might be pockets of weeds growing on the edge of a deep flat. You have to use your imagination and adapt to what you have, but the principle remains the same.

Psychological Changes

There is more to the prelude period than a locational change from winter to early pre-spawn habitat, there is also a change in mood. Big bass are now becoming more positive and attack oriented. Egg sacks are developing rapidly, and the fish are influenced by the growth. They're not browsing for mid pre-spawn areas yet, but they're getting more active than a pure winter state. Bass may only bite one day a week in the dead of winter, but the appetites of bass at prelude locations increase. The shallower prelude and pre-spawn areas have a different habitat and a different quality of water. The hard bottom areas which they relate to have a richer mineral and nutrient base than was available in deeper winter sanctuaries, and bass are able to extract a wider variety of vitamins and minerals to develop their eggs. Their diet is changing too. Bass begin feeding more on crayfish. Whether crayfish have any special nutrients bass need for egg production is hard to tell, maybe they **APPEAR** to switch from baitfish to crayfish simply because crayfish are a more readily available food source in the areas they move to. But all these different things are happening as the fish move from winter sanctuaries to shallow prelude and pre-spawn areas, and it has to do with the cycle that the bass are going through. Big bass are reacting to both physical and metaphysical changes, and they are easier to catch than in winter because they're more aggressive and their interest in feeding is intensified.

Early Pre-Spawn Activity

Early pre-spawn activity starts long before most anglers realize. Many people feel that late winter/early spring is a poor time to catch lunkers because the activity in the shallows doesn't really heat up until late pre-spawn. But this only reflects how people fish. Early pre-spawn is an excellent time to capture a trophy if you work the right areas in deep water, even though you may have to brave some inclement weather.

Serious trophy anglers spend time monitoring early pre-spawn locations before the actual pre-spawn movement begins. You don't have to monitor these spots all winter but I recommend going out once a week, or at least once every two weeks, to monitor the prelude areas and get an insight as to what's happening. Graph these spots, and maybe fish them a little, to keep in touch when bass begin to show up.

When I fish during late winter, I monitor the prelude spots and watch for signs of what the shallow fishermen are doing. For example, when I'm doing well by trolling plugs in deep winter sanctuaries with leadcore line, most of the anglers who typically fish the shallows have little or no success. But there'll be a time in early spring when some fish begin showing in the shallows and these anglers start catching. That tells me the first movement from winter to spring has begun. The first fish to show in the shallows are generally small males, but the bigger females may already be positioning on outlying prelude spots. The appearance of action in the shallows signals the end of deep-trolling and the beginning of anchoring and casting the early prelude and deep pre-spawn structures. You might still be able to catch fish trolling, but as word spreads that fishing is getting better, there will be more boats to contend with making accurate trolling passes more difficult. In this respect it might be more efficient to anchor and cast specific areas.

Prelude areas generally produce for a week or two, then there's a lull. The timing on different lakes can be a little different, but in my area the lull generally takes place from about February 8 until February 14; this represents a dead period where you can't hardly get a bite on any prelude elements. What's happening is the bass are suspending and moving to mid pre-spawn areas. The best way to catch bass during the lull is to troll because suspended bass are more vulnerable to an open water technique which covers water quickly; anchoring specific structures is generally a poor technique at this time. Once the fish move to mid pre-spawn spots, anchoring once again becomes the most productive method.

PRE-SPAWN TO POST-SPAWN

When it's time for female bass to leave prelude structures, they move toward the spawning areas via the next key structural elements which are the pre-spawn spots. Pre-spawn spots are areas just off or outside the spawning locations which connect the spawning flats with deep water; they are classic structures big bass use to move to and from holding areas. Pre-spawn spots vary depending on the lake type, but all good pre-spawn spots have certain features in common such as: hard bottom content, cover, close access to deeper water and a connection with a channel or some type of depression that leads from the deepest water right into the shallows. In the lakes I fish, rock piles and high spots at the correct depth tend to be the best pre-spawn locations. A classic big bass spot would be a long reef that comes out into the lake and drops off into the main lake basin or a deep water channel; it has flats on the shallow end for spawning with numerous dips and high spots at various depths all the way into deep water. An isolated rock pile that doesn't have spawning habitat nearby or is too deep won't attract giant bass; the spot has to have a close connection between spawning areas and deep water.

The key to finding the best pre-spawn locations is depth. It has been my experience that the best pre-spawn depth for the bigger fish is between 25 ft. and 35 ft. deep. But each lake has its own personality and the right pre-spawn depth is something each angler must establish for himself. The right depth can at times be difficult to determine because pre-spawn bass are often in a traveling mode and can be difficult to graph. Sometimes the only way to find the right depth is by relating past experiences on a particular lake or by piecing together a depth pattern by actually catching fish. Traveling around in large groups is a typical pre-spawn characteristic in some lakes. Big females often travel together and when you encounter an active group

A 15 lb. 14 oz. pre-spawn female taken from an undercut edge on an old roadbed.

the fishing can be wild! I once witnessed a pack of giant bass roaming through an area where one guy caught a 10-pounder, another boat landed an 11-pounder, and then another big bass was lost on a jump about 50 feet away. Sometimes you can detect the movement of the pack by observing the action, and you can plot their movement and intercept them further off the spot. Because pre-spawn bass move so much, the best way to determine the right depth is simply by fishing often and experimenting. Start by locating the best-looking outlying areas and associated structures on a good topo map, and fish each one until a pattern develops.

Pre-Spawn Strategy

Giant bass are poor spawners in pressured lakes. Sloppy lure presentations, electric motors, rod tips and anchors scraping aluminum boats, and even the activity of lots of other bass in an area can prevent the biggest bass from spawning in traditional settings. I've often noticed that trophy bass spawn in marginal areas for the sake of remaining near the security of deep water and structural elements. In many cases, they spawn on flat areas near pre-spawn structures out in open water. These spots are seldom associated with spawning but they are often the very best big bass spawning sites in the whole lake. But even in the best situations, leaving the security of deep water to spawn makes big bass nervous and skittish; they rarely relax enough to complete the spawning cycle, and in many cases simply go through the motions. Trophy bass like to hold on the outer pre-spawn areas overlooking the spawning flats. When everything looks right, they may move in quickly, but if something spooks them back out they'll only drop part of their eggs. You may catch one of these partially-spawned females during post-spawn and think they haven't spawned yet, but in truth they have already. If the activity is too upsetting, a big bass may not spawn at all. Big females frequently reabsorb their eggs rather than going against their instincts and moving shallow. When you catch bass with eggs in summer, they aren't producing eggs for the following year, those fish are in the process of reabsorbing eggs from an aborted spawn. Sometimes the fish can't reabsorb their eggs and they crystalize into hard golden nugget shapes. The older the bass and the larger and wider their egg sacks, the greater the likelihood crystalized nuggets will form. After several aborted spawns, crystalization of the unabsorbed eggs may cause the fish to die. The prime spawners are female bass in the 3-to-5-pound class; they're still young enough not to get spooked out by everything, and they have that reckless feeling of security that allows them to perform much better in shallow water than giant bass. Even small males are

This diagram shows an ideal big bass spawning situation. The angler is anchored up shallow and casting to a rocky spine on the outer edge of a spawning flat. Pre-spawn females relate mostly to the outer edge features and make movements periodically on the flat. The angler can reach both spots with an easy cast. But what makes this spot an ideal big bass spot are the features that connect the shallows with the deeper wintering areas. Note the prelude trees in the background. Spots like this produce giant bass every spring, year after year, because they have the right combination of elements giant bass want.

Spots like this can be ideal spring locations. The deep edge of the point could be a great pre-spawn spot. It has a quick access to deep water, an old channel, and good current flow. Big bass could spawn shallower on the bar itself, which has a firm bottom content with scattered cobblestones. Areas like this could be a year-round big bass location.

more relaxed with smaller females in the area. I once caught a 15-pound female with a 1/2 pound bass in its belly, so a giant bass roaming through a nesting area has to make the males somewhat nervous. Some giant bass may fail to spawn simply because there were no males aggressive enough to approach them.

During most of the spring season my big bass strategy is to focus on the primary pre-spawn structures and catch bass before and after they spawn. I'm only after the biggest bass and I believe fishing pre-spawn spots exclusively produces the most trophy bass in the long run. All lunker females don't spawn at the same time. There will be females in all stages of spawning activity throughout the entire spawning season. While some females are on beds, others will be at pre-spawn spots, and other fish will already have dropped their eggs and be at post-spawn areas all at the same time. Pre-spawn structures are actually the same places where post-spawn bass retreat to. I'll frequently catch some bass bursting with roe, and others that are thin, worn-out and empty of eggs from the same spot. Spawned-out

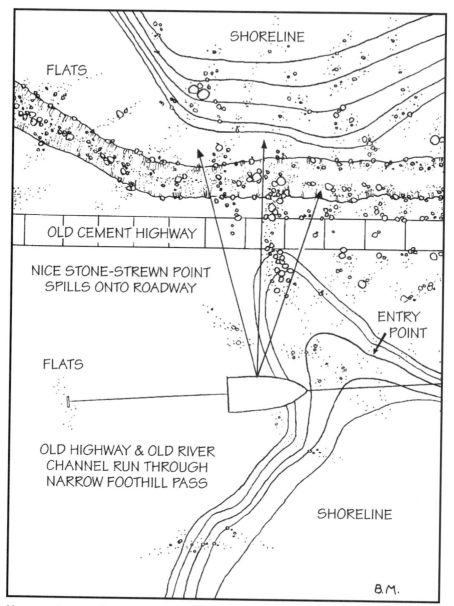

SHORELINE

FLATS

OLD CEMENT HIGHWAY

NICE STONE-STREWN POINT
SPILLS ONTO ROADWAY

ENTRY
POINT

FLATS

OLD HIGHWAY & OLD RIVER
CHANNEL RUN THROUGH
NARROW FOOTHILL PASS

SHORELINE

B.M.

Narrow places where shorelines come close together can be big bass areas. Narrowing creates more current and confines bait. Big bass lay in key spots because they're sure bait will come through there from time to time.

females generally don't stay in these areas as long as pre-spawn fish, but enough will be making short stays to make it worth fishing prime pre-spawn sites right through the post-spawn. Also, it's important to know that females often move in and out of the spawning grounds with different males or the same male over and over again. Each time she leaves the spawning area, she moves back to the pre-spawn structure and holds there until she goes in again. Because there is so much big fish activity on the primary pre-spawn structures, students of trophy fishing need never bother bedding females. Nesting bass aren't interested in feeding and their reactions to lures and live bait is erratic. Often times, you have to antagonize them for some time before provoking a strike. Personally, I find no sport in this kind of fishing. Even if a nesting bass is released, studies suggest that fighting may wear them down to a point where nesting, or guarding the nest and fry, suffers. Fishing pre-spawn spots, however, is a different story. Big females at pre-spawn locations generally take a bait with great intensity and they are less likely to drop or reject an offering once they decide to eat. And quickly releasing bass caught from deep water does not interrupt their natural spawning cycle and causes little stress other than possibly making them more cautious. There are certain ethics a bass fisherman has to live by, and I don't believe in fishing for nesting bass. Besides, big bass are far easier to catch in pre-spawn locations anyway. When bass first start nesting in the shallows, there should be enough big ones on pre-spawn spots to keep an angler busy without invading spawning areas. You can stay on the easier-to-catch females throughout the entire spawning period simply by concentrating on pre-spawn locations exclusively. Be aware, however, that even though the outside structures are where the bigger fish will be most of the time, they may slide by you and move to the inside of a point during pre-spawn. So, at times, thinking deep exclusively will backfire on you, and you have to be aware of that. I often watch what the shallow anglers are doing and let them check this situation for me.

Timing on pre-spawn spots is critical. You have to be there when the big fish show up, and they usually aren't there for too long. The three days before and after the full moon period is a peak time to intercept trophy bass. If you can put yourself on a known big bass spot on the front side of a weather change during this lunar period you stand a great chance of catching the biggest bass that swim in any body of water. An incoming storm system coupled with a peak moon phase put trophy-class bass in a positive attack mood and activity can be frantic. I normally fish to find out the time of day they're hitting best, then I'll plan the following trip to coincide with a 3/4 rising moon or an incoming frontal system or both. Then it becomes a matter of timing; I'll anchor the spot and be in the right position when the big fish move in. Bass movements in spring, however, can be unpredictable and patterns can change hourly. A positive moon phase will enhance activity, but it doesn't **DICTATE** activity.

During pre-spawn it is better to position your boat as far as possible from the spot you intend to fish and make long casts. Though bass may strike with reckless abandon at this time, the bigger fish may still be cautious and nervous about moving shallow. Seemingly innocent noises like waves slapping the side of a boat, the purr of an electric motor, or a rod tip tapping the side of an aluminum boat may alarm big bass. If a female feels that things are not right about the route leading into the nesting area, she may turn back and move into open water. For best results, hold on the perimeters of pre-spawn areas with an electric motor, or better yet, by anchoring and present your lures or live bait with as little splash as possible. The pressure from splashing lures and the presence of a boat may keep over-cautious lunkers from moving into a spot, and at times better results can be had by stopping fishing and letting the spot rest. Plastic worms and live crayfish are top baits at this time of year, although jig and pig or spinnerbaits often nail the largest bass.

Let's say you hit everything right and caught three bass over 10-pounds apiece. You feel terrific about your catch, but you might not have realized that an 18-pounder (the fish of a lifetime) was watching the whole episode from a safe distance away. Perhaps the activity of catching other fish kept her from the productive area. But whatever the reason, events like this take place more often than realized. For this reason, I always make several casts just off the prime area and several more far off of it. It's important to make these casts during the most active period when you're actually having good

This rock pile on the outer edge of a spawning flat is the structural link connecting the flat to deeper areas. With abundant cover and a quick access to deeper open water, it is the type of spot big bass gravitate to in pre-spawn. The subliminal sand and gravel areas may also serve as spawning sites for cautious females that are reluctant to move shallow.

fishing on the prime area. I know it's hard to cast away from the prime spot, but checking out the entire area within the limits of my casting range has produced some of my biggest bass.

In summary, I'd like to say that the spring is a most curious time of the year. It is the one time when trophy bass make mistakes. Sexual reproduction influences their normal instincts of caution and security, and like a buck in rut, big bass are less likely to pay attention to things which threaten their survival. It's easy for them to get caught up in the activity in the shallows as well. Crayfish which had been hibernating all winter are emerging from the mud, and schools of baitfish are moving shallower. There's also a lot of aggression and fear at this time. Panfish come in to raid bass nests and pick off fry, and bass, in turn, feed on the panfish. The smaller males are active, and it's easy for the bigger females to get caught up in their activity. All these things can make trophy bass easier to catch than any other time of year. The closer they are to the actual spawn and the stronger their

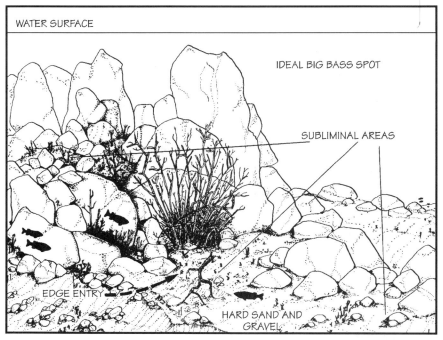

WATER SURFACE

IDEAL BIG BASS SPOT

SUBLIMINAL AREAS

EDGE ENTRY

HARD SAND AND GRAVEL

This is a break down of spot in photo on previous page, when water covers the main rock structure. Note how big bass are depicted as gravitating toward small isolated brush and small entry edge. Sand and gravel between small stones offer an ideal spawning composition, plus the fast deep water access guarantees large numbers of big fish will visit this spot during the pre-spawn period.

spawning urges become, the less they will be spooked by boats or heavy line. Even when a boat spooks them away from a spot, they'll only move down the bank a little and come right back as soon as you move. So in this sense, springtime is not a true test of angling ability. They do things they'd never do at other times of the year, and they become vulnerable to a point where they can be taken with techniques that normally only produce smaller bass. Trophy bass are also easier to land at this time because they're still sluggish from the cold-water winter period. In another month or so when the water temperature moves higher, they become fireballs and will rip your tackle to pieces.

How to Pattern Pre-Spawn Spots

One of the most important factors in spring success is to fish one lake often and learn the timing on specific pre-spawn spots. Spring fishing has its ups and downs and the tendency is to move to a new lake when fishing is bad, but the worst thing you can do is leave a lake after putting in weeks of effort. Even experts can get worn down and lose their concentration when fishing is slow, but if you leave you'll never reap the rewards when fishing improves. Maybe fishing is bad because the lake is getting more and more pressure as the weather improves, and the increase in pressure limits your freedom because there are so many more anglers in different areas? But there's always ways to make bad situations better. You may notice that most of the less dedicated anglers leave the lake after 3 p.m., and after the fish have a chance to settle down you can often move into these vacated areas and have good fishing for the rest of the afternoon. Timing is everything in spring fishing; you have to be at the right locations when the big fish move in. Dedicated anglers who have been checking and monitoring during the slow periods will know all the spots with the best potential, and these are the fishermen who make the most impressive big bass catches when the fishing gets good. Learning the right spots and fishing those spots when the big fish show up is the key to pre-spawn success. If you hop from lake to lake, the likelihood of being in the right spot when the big fish move in is dramatically reduced. Success comes to those who stick with one or two lakes and keep with it right through the dead periods.

Many anglers won't fish a pre-spawn structure unless they first meter fish, but you can't always meter bass on structure at this time of year because the fish often move so much. Some spots that yield tons of bass **NEVER** meter a single fish! Fishing only after you meter bass is really an inconsistent way to catch big bass anyway. Some anglers travel around to various spots hoping to meter fish at the time they visit those spots, but you'd still have to find fish in the right active mode where you can move in and catch them right after metering. At times this strategy will work in spring because the closer you get to the actual spawning cycle the less likely the fish will be disturbed by the presence of a boat. But the best way to take full advantage of a good pre-spawn spot is to get on them early in the day, anchor in the right casting position, and patiently wait for the fish to move in. When I check a new spot and meter fish, I sometimes won't fish it until the following day or the next time I go fishing. I'll anchor on the spot in early morning **BEFORE** the fish show up, and then work on them as they come into the structure. Generally, if you fish a spot right after metering fish, the movement and disturbance of the boat will spook the largest bass. But if you anchor before the fish show up and create a natural atmosphere, then you're likely to catch a giant bass and possibly a number of lunker fish.

Always keep in mind that just because you don't meter fish on a structure at the moment you happen to check it doesn't mean that bass aren't using the spot or that they won't move into that spot later in the day. Even if bass were on a spot when you happened to come by they might move off into deeper water or under a ledge where a graph would show no visible signs of life on structure. If you motor across a shallow flat where you can see bass, you'll notice that the fish move away as the boat approaches; move faster and the fish swim faster; slow down and they slow down. That's how bass sometimes react when your boat moves back and forth over a structure as you graph it; the fish just keep moving away from the boat and the graph's cone angle. I've always found that when you're after big bass it's a better strategy to first find a potential spot, then come back at another time and anchor it by using shoreline sightings instead of endlessly metering and moving across the spot over and over.

During pre-spawn I generally fish one proven spot from morning to noon and then spend the rest of the day monitoring other potential areas. From the information I gained fishing and metering that afternoon, I'll select the best new structure and fish it the following day from morning until noon, and then go back to my original proven spot and work it from noon until dark. So even though I'm only fishing two spots all day, I have varied my time on the proven pre-spawn spot and worked in a potential new spot. When I'm working a two-spot system like this, I'll still try to devote the last hour of the day for checking new spots. When a spot starts producing in late afternoon, it's usually a signal that the spot will start producing

Many anglers wouldn't consider this a big bass spawning area, but compound spots like this have great potential. These spots appeal to the big bass with cautious natures. The bigger females key on the draw, and they can use the rock point on the right for pre-spawn and post-spawn activities, and they could spawn on the flats to the right of the point or left of the draw. Sometimes bass spawn in the draw itself.

bass all day long. By fishing one lake often and learning productive spots from preceding years, I'll keep checking all these productive spots and when I happen to catch a big fish off one in late afternoon, that's my signal to get on that spot early the following day and patiently fish it all day or a majority of that day. If you hop from lake to lake, it's unlikely that you'll ever discover the timing that's so critical in making a good spot produce.

The spawning season, as a general rule, can make a disciplined structure fisherman crazy. Spring can be a difficult time to catch big bass even though everyone believes the contrary. Big bass are probably more unpredictable at this time than any other seasonal period. You can study a topo map and select four spots with identical structural make-up and bottom composition, but if you pick the wrong one of the four (which is very easy to do) you might catch nothing while fishermen on another spot load up.

Ideal Spawning Bank
**Extended flat with hard bottom content consisting of decomposed granite,
hard sand over clay, and shells. Scattered stones, roots and stumps enhance
the spot, but the key big bass feature is the deep water access off the side.**

Suppose you had a good pre-spawn spot that you had monitored all winter. When you started contacting bass on this spot in early spring, the spot only yielded 3 and 4-pounders. But then you write it off and one of your buddies fishes it two days later and catches a 12-pounder, this kind of stuff can drive you nuts. These fish can be so unpredictable in spring there's absolutely no way to calculate accurately where they're going to be next and when they're going to show up. Sometimes you never do catch on to what the fish are doing until after the spawning is over when the bass calm down and get on more predictable patterns in late spring and early summer. Sometimes you have to wait until the peak activity in the shallows is over before a good outside structure technique begins producing bass that are moving back and forth into the shallows for a second and third time; some of these pre-spawn spots didn't produce early, it just took more time for them to get hot. Maybe the late fish you're catching are just behind the rest because their eggs didn't ripen as fast? So spring can be a guessing game, but I can say that the guys who fish the most are more likely to be in-tune with these movements when they occur.

Working Through the Pre-Spawn Lull

Right before the action of the best pre-spawn fishing there is usually a lull or interruption of normal pre-spawn activity that lasts for about a week. For some reason, bass seem to come up from deep water, look around and then go back deep. It's like a groundhog that comes up in early spring to check conditions and then goes back down for a while. It's like front-runners check shallow conditions and then everyone gets the message and they all come up. Before the lull you might find a lot of 4, 5, and 6-pound bass on key pre-spawn structures, then the spots become somewhat void of quality bass for a while, but when fishing improves you're likely to catch 10-pounders off the same spot. It's weird but this scenario seems to happen every spring. It could be that so many fish are roaming and checking potential spawning areas in early spring you only contact a few on pre-spawn spots, but when more fish discover the prime areas they appear to show up en masse. There are certain pre-spawn spots where the bigger fish move in before the bulk of the bass population, but there are other types of spots where the biggest bass show up just after the lull. You might contact some nice bass on an outer edge spot, and then the spot goes dead for several days, and when you're just about to give up on it you catch an 11-pounder; and from that point on you catch a big bass every time you fish it and sometimes more than one giant fish per day.

In the height of pre-spawn, big bass will use the outer perimeters and edges of structures at the proper depth, and they'll be relating to the bottom. Females are searching for ideal bottom compositions to lay their eggs and they'll be looking for beds that are already made. They'll move through an area observing clean spots and what type of conditions prevail that particular year. I like to stitch plastic worms and crayfish on pre-spawn structures because females generally relate to the bottom. But during the pre-spawn lull, females often pull off key spots and suspend near the edges where they aren't in a good position to be caught by stitching. Anglers who troll or work the perimeters of these spots with free-swimming shiners often have the best results because they are keying on fish that are not bottom-related. So in this sense, the pre-spawn lull is not a true lull in activity -bass can still be caught-rather it is a lull for fishermen who continue to fish bottom structure methods like stitching. During the lull you might have 20% of all bass caught on plastic worms and crayfish, 70% on shiners and trolled plugs, and 10% on all other methods. But these percentages change once bass move back on structure; plastic worms and crayfish would then account for 70% of all fish caught. You have to be versatile at this time; anytime the fish get off what you're using, it's time to make a switch.

High Water

Bass relating to thick shoreline cover is normally a spring pattern. Some larger fish may move into thick cover during high water periods in winter, but the best movement into shoreline cover typically takes place after periods of high water caused by early spring run-off. If the movement into shoreline cover is a strong trend, then you could expect some big fish to be up shallow even on a structured lake.

A shoreline cover pattern is usually a size pattern. When you find small bass up in the brush it's likely that there will be lots of small bass-but not big bass. But if you catch a 7-pounder tucked under a flooded tree, there's a good chance that more big fish will be in the area. Big fish patterns are harder to judge than small fish patterns because you aren't talking about as many fish, and when a big bass moves into the brush it will be a loner in respect to its territory. You might fish down a bank 25-or-30-yards and catch another big fish, but that fish would have its own territory too. When bass use a structural element they often share the most desirable area, but on a flooded bank pattern they tend to be more territorial; they'll have their own little niche and you'll seldom find two or three big ones bunched up together.

If you caught a big bass up on top of a deep water structure, you would work progressively farther out trying to find more bass which might be deeper on the spot, but on a flooded bank pattern the bigger fish tend to hold shallower. It's not in the nature of this pattern to have big fish shallow and big fish deeper at the same time.

Certain areas along a flooded shoreline always attract the better fish. Deeper spots along the bank, and the relationship of a bank to a drop-off, are often the keys to making a flooded shoreline draw big bass. A little shelf in the brush which drops into deeper water would make an ideal big bass spot. Access to deeper water is always a key in big bass location in structured lakes regardless if you're fishing shallow or deep. They may not use it but big bass always like to be near deep water access points. Moving far back into flooded timber away from deep water is more of a small bass pattern. Many times you'll find an old creek channel which is close to a flooded shoreline -that's the shoreline to concentrate on big fish. A shoreline which drops straight into the channel generally won't attract many lunkers, but the flatter spots formed where the channel swings away from a shoreline is an ideal big fish spot. Bank fishing is just like deep structure fishing, there are only certain spots that trophy bass gravitate to. Get a good contour map and circle all the spots on a flooded shoreline where the deep water swings in and where it swings out.

Heavy cover is not a finesse situation. There never should be any consideration about how to get the fish out. You set the hook and just keep pulling until the fish breaks free of the brush and comes out of the hole you dropped your lure into. I use a long casting outfit and a strong abrasion-resistant line like Maxima or Trilene Big Game in 15 to 25 lb. test. Keep the line fresh and retie often as any nick will weaken the line. Moving the boat with a trolling motor and dropping a bait into holes in the cover is a standard flooded shoreline technique, but some areas can be fished better by walking the shoreline. About 95% of the time when the fish are in thick cover, they'll hit your lure on the sink. A good technique is to let your lure free-fall in an open spot, shake it a few times, then drop it into another spot. You can use a 7 1/2 ft. rod and lower the lure from spot to spot just like a crappie fisherman.

My two favorite lures for working heavy shoreline cover are plastic worms and a jig and pig. I use plastic worms pegged with a slip sinker or on the back of a bucktail or maribou jig. I'll use a 1/2 oz. weight if I want the worm to fall fast to the base of the brush, but I generally use just enough weight to make it fall through the type of cover I'm working. A slow fall is generally much more attractive to bigger fish. I use the same worm colors that work for big bass on deep structures in that lake. If the water is off-colored in the shallows and has been off-colored for some time, I don't believe gaudy colors will make them bite better. I want to find the worm color the bass prefer and it has nothing to do with how well they can see it. I would experiment to find the hot color for that lake and fish it in shallow water as well as deep structure. Use the same strategy when fishing a jig and pig. I try to find the hot color for big fish on that lake and I stick with that color at all depths.

High water in spring, however, does not guarantee good shallow water fishing. High water may put the ideal level for big fish in areas not conducive to good fishing. In a high water situation, the ideal level where big bass come up during pre-spawn may put them in spots that are covered by grass due to the water level flooding and inundating the former shoreline. In this case, bass are using areas with grass and brush which limits effective presentation; you can't even work a plastic worm through it without getting fouled on every cast. At normal pool, however, the ideal pre-spawn depths would coincide with prime structures which have hard clean bottom content, but rising water can put the fish on new spots so covered with growth that they hinder effective presentation. You might still catch a few big bass during high water but not the numbers you would have if the water level was at normal pool or lower than normal.

The way to combat high water conditions that make prime structures unfishable is to change your focus from the larger structures off spawning flats to short points. Short points don't weed over like longer flatter structures that have ample area for vegetation to grow. Short points become key spots because even though they tend to harbor fewer big bass, you can fish them without becoming continually fouled, so in the long run you catch more big fish.

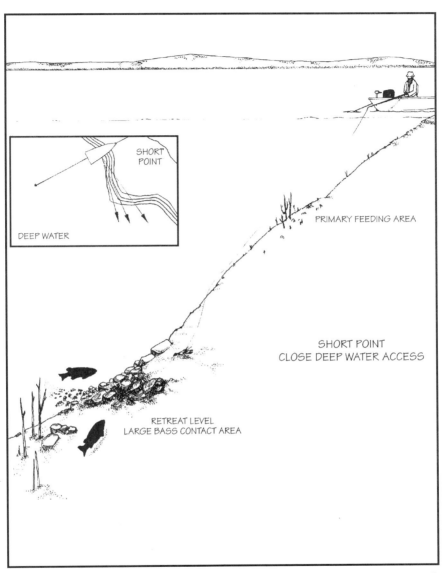

Short points never produce lots of bass but they are excellent spots to catch giant bass especially during high water conditions. Few people fish these spots and that's one reason why giant bass like them. Anchor in tight and to the side, and cast out and over the point.

For a short point to be productive during pre-spawn it needs some type of hard bottom like clay mixed with cobblestones or chunk rock, and it needs to be close to a deep water channel with a fast drop into the channel. Points composed of solid rock are generally **NOT** big bass producers; females need some areas with softer material to fan out their spawning beds. Bass spawn on the flat sections on top of short points but they come in from the deep side and then move to the flat areas. When you understand this fact, you can approach the point from a different angle than most other anglers who traditionally work around the perimeter of the point and cast in. Get in close to the bank and fish up and across the point retrieving your bait off and into deeper water. By anchoring in working over and down, you're in perfect position to intercept bass at whatever depth they happen to approach the spot from deep water.

Muddy Water

Heavy spring rains can create a sudden influx of muddy water that may have a negative influence on fishing. Muddy water is a claustrophobic condition which often causes bass to sit tight. Pre-spawn bass tend to roam and use the expanse of their environment, but when the water suddenly turns to chocolate, the cubic feet of water surrounding the rock or bush they hold next to now becomes their whole world. In pressured lakes, big bass become very cautious because every noise and unseen thing they can't verify at a distance is blown out of proportion, and anything unusual puts them on the offensive. In many cases they absolutely refuse to chase after or move to pursue a bait. It's like being in a room when someone shuts off the light. Initially you become confused, but once you maneuver around the room and slowly discover where everything is, it then becomes easier in the dark. I think that's how bass react when their world suddenly becomes dark. Initially, a sudden influx of muddy water shuts off a good bite, but after time the fish adapt to the condition and begin to resume their normal patterns. During the first few days of a muddy condition, bass appear psychologically tied to a spot because they aren't sure what's going on and they don't want to venture out into the unknown, especially in a lake that's pressured and full of disturbing sounds. (But they still can hear vibrations and will bite if you can work your bait close enough.) I view the negative influence of muddy water as a temporary condition. It can hurt fishing over-night but once the fish adjust to it they often respond in the same way as when the water is clearer.

When stitching pre-spawn areas that are suddenly affected by muddy water, I like to use plastic worms in colors that contrast with the water. I like black, black/chartreuse, and orange/brown. I've always had more success with highly visible plastics under these conditions than with live crayfish. But I'll only use these colors for the first few days of muddy water. Big largemouth are creatures that adapt very fast and very well to any environmental change. If the water remains muddy for over a week or more, the bigger fish often begin responding better to the same color preferences that they did when the water had a normal color. Live crayfish may begin working better too.

Post-Spawn

Big bass are pretty well worn out after spawning. They've exerted a lot of effort and it seems like they just go and hide for a while. When any creature is not active and feeding, they hide, and it's been my experience that big bass seek sheltered places away from direct sunlight after spawning. When they suspend, they hold at a level just below direct light penetration, and they also like to hold near bluffs, piers and pilings, and any type of cover that offers shade and security. I think this behavior is the result of being exposed in shallow water for such a long time. Moving shallow is something completely against the nature of a big bass in a structured lake, and during post-spawn they seem to want to revert back to some type of seclusion. I think this behavior is one reason why post-spawn fishing is so tough.

It's not that the fish are in a real negative mood, I think it's tough because the fish are in very negative places to fish. Seclusion and absence of light is the key to their location. Look for quiet places where there's a lot of shade and seclusion such as the dark sides of

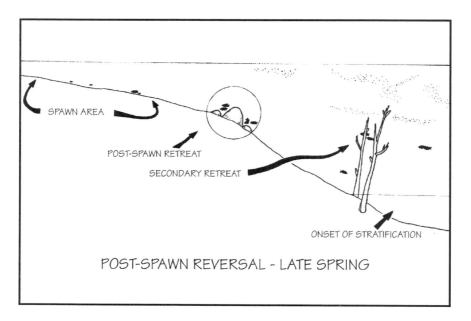

SPAWN AREA

POST-SPAWN RETREAT

SECONDARY RETREAT

ONSET OF STRATIFICATION

POST-SPAWN REVERSAL - LATE SPRING

deep water structures, bluff banks, piers and pilings, and the edges of heavy cover. I don't know why this phenomenon occurs but this pattern seems to repeat itself every post-spawn.

Rather than a big change in location, I believe another reason why big bass fishing is tough during post-spawn is that the fish simply lose interest in feeding. Females are trying to rejuvenate. There are severe changes going on throughout their bodies and they don't follow strict feeding cycles while these changes are taking place. Consequently, feeding cycles are going to be very sporadic and consistent patterns will be hard to establish.

Post-spawn bass really aren't as difficult to catch as many fishermen believe. You're always fishing for the catchable fish, and when you find a pattern that works it changes the way you feel about these fish. Most people determine what the fish are doing by their own success. But just because you can't catch bass in a certain area doesn't mean they're not there. And just because more people don't have great success during post-spawn doesn't mean that these fish can't be caught. Naturally a guy is going to use his favorite pattern whether it's trolling, casting, pitching worms, or whatever, and he'll judge the bass community by how and where he catches them. But an angler who is truly versatile and can fish so many more places with a variety of techniques will have a much better perspective on things. Big bass can be caught in post-spawn, but it may require a switch to a different technique or a different location than what you're used to fishing. It's also important to remember that individual fish are moving in and out of the spawning areas at different times. It's always possible to hit a certain batch of fish that have already gone through the down cycle and are players again; these are the catchable fish that we want to target in post-spawn.

There is one distinct pattern I've found that produces well during post-spawn. This is a shallow pattern that hinges around the spawning areas. After most largemouth finish spawning there is still a lot of activity in the shallows. Male bass will be guarding the nests and fry, while bluegill and related panfish will feed and spawn in the same general vicinity where largemouth spawned. This excitement attracts some big bass into the shallows. While it's true the majority of big fish may move out into deeper zones after spawning, some continue to hang around spawning areas. They have been using these areas for some time, and they still have tendencies of association with these locations. Big bass don't like to chase roaming schools of bait, and some lunker fish prefer to pick off a vulnerable bedding bluegill or a small male bass instead. If there is an abundance of bait in the shallows, big fish often travel from the outside edges to maraud through the shallows. They don't want to go back into shallow water particularly if fishing pressure is still intense, but some fish will travel to feed if that's where the bait is. But they still seek security; rather than move way up into the shallows, the bigger fish might hold on a gravel drop at the edge of a shallow weedbed.

When panfish finish spawning and the activity in the shallows begins to subside, the shallow bass pattern breaks down as the fish move out into deeper water and relate to their normal pattern of working edge spots on outside structures. When they leave the shallows some big bass settle back into the pre-spawn areas which now become post-spawn spots. They don't move back into the early pre-spawn areas in deep water because the lake is warming and stratifying and the deeper zones can no longer support them. Baitfish also feel this thermocline squeeze and the bass will hold at the same levels that support the bait. But there isn't a great migration for most fish; I think the biggest bass stay in the same general areas throughout the entire year. Big bass are individual creatures that aren't being dictated to by anything but natural instincts; big bass simply wander at will. After the spawning cycle is complete their original natural instincts begin taking over, and post-spawn fish start relating to edges associated with drop-offs like they normally do. Moving in and out of key structures is a normal big bass pattern throughout the year. The biggest fish have areas that are conducive to good feeding and they stick with them. Where they go and what they do when not feeding is anyone's guess, but when they feed they normally pick a good area and come into that area all the time. Bass are very simple creatures, and they stick with a good situation until something turns them off of it. Humans are always looking for something better, but bass don't have that kind of intelligence. If you find a good pre-spawn spot, then chances are good it will also be a good post-spawn spot; structural areas that attract are prime areas and big bass don't like to leave them.

My favorite pattern for contacting big fish during the post-spawn is to anchor on the pre-spawn areas. Post-spawn fish may not stay on these spots as long as the pre-spawn activity, but if you have the patience to wait them out you might get a bite or two, and it could be a monster bass! I prefer to stitch pre-spawn spots right through the post-spawn, but as the water warms and the season blends into early summer, speed trolling these outside edge spots with plugs becomes a very important technique as well.

EARLY SUMMER-SPEED UP THE PACE

The early summer period-from late May through early July in many areas-is a time of the year when bait is very abundant and bass feed often and heavily. The whole lake environment is alive and flourishing-weedbeds are thick and green and reaching maximum depth, baitfish hatches are complete, and insects and larva are everywhere. Warming water temperatures and abundant prey create an ideal situation for big bass angling. Lunker fish are recovering from post-spawn behavior with feeding on their mind, and the warming water speeds up their metabolism which demands that they eat more and more often. Many people imagine that when food is abundant, bass are harder to catch because they are full, but in reality nature works just the opposite. More food means more feeding, and a **BETTER** chance of catching bass. Early summer bass are as big and fat as any time of the year. And they're aggressive! Fish the right spot at the right time and you might catch a jumbo largemouth on every cast or every trolling pass.

Location

By early summer the majority of lunker bass have pulled out of the shallows and relocated around the perimeters of main lake basins and deep water channels. This movement of bass also parallels the movements of larger baitfish. Big bluegill, crappie, shad, shiners and lake minnows are moving toward deeper areas too, and the larger bass have a tendency to stop feeding heavily on crayfish (like they did all spring) and change to baitfish forage.

The same structures that attracted females in pre-spawn now serve as primarily early summer spots as well. It's amazing how consistent good big bass structure is. When a structure has the right combination of elements it may attract bass from pre-spawn right through summer, and in some cases throughout fall and winter as well.

There are two types of patterns that develop in conjunction with these structures: (1) bass holding on the outside perimeters, and (2) bass suspending over deep water in association with these outside perimeters. Some females suspend in tree tops off prelude areas if the tops are not too deep or too far from primarily early summer structures. However, not all suspended bass remain suspended, and not all structure bass remain on structure. Bass moving back and forth from structured areas to suspended areas is the general pattern for early summer. The depth they hold on structure and the depth they suspend at is usually related.

Bass in early summer tend to relate to the shallow sections of structures. During pre-spawn, bass used deeper structure areas because they were coming up from deep water, but in early summer bass are moving out from relatively shallow water and they tend to move to shallower structure sections first rather than making dramatic locational shifts into deep water. For example, during pre-spawn the heaviest concentration of bass might be at 25 ft. with a maximum depth of 30 ft., but in early summer depths from 15 ft. to 20 ft. would likely draw most bass on the same structure. And bass suspending off these structures would hold more-or-less at the same depths. In conjunction with this psychological tendency of bass to use shallow sections of structure, warming water temperatures can cause a lake to begin stratifying which forces water with adequate oxygen content toward the surface into shallower lake zones. Some bass might drop deeper right after spawning, but these fish move shallower as the thermocline rises. These factors, plus the tendency for bait schools to use shallow zones at this time, cause the majority of big bass to relate to shallow sections of outside structures in early summer. However, this pattern is not reliable in all lakes. Some lakes have characteristics which put bass shallow, but other lakes, such as lakes with artificial aeration systems or fresh-flowing tributaries, may not stratify above 40 ft. all summer, and bass can be found quite deep in early summer. Structural configuration and mass also play a part in the depths which bass use. If a structure has only one major breakline

Summer trolling can be an excellent way to find large bass when they are on the move out on large flats next to channel edges.

or drop-off edge with nothing but a straight fast-breaking drop below that edge, the majority of bass using that structure will use levels at the breakline depth, or shallower, even when adequate oxygen is found below that level. But if a structure has multiple ledges, rises and drops at various depths from the shallow limits of the structural mass into the deepest connecting basins, bass may relate to key features at any depth above the thermocline. The depths bass use in early summer can be different with each lake, and it's up to each angler to discover this depth for himself.

Presentation -Crank it Up!

Warming water temperatures and abundant prey shift bass into high gear. Now fully recovered from post-spawn, bass feed aggressively and may even chase after fast-moving baits and lures. Their aggressive nature and the fact that they are changing from bottom-hugging forage to open-water forage makes bass highly vulnerable to crankbaits. Although crankbaits are low-percentage big bass lures most of the time (because bass tend to respond best to crankbaits only

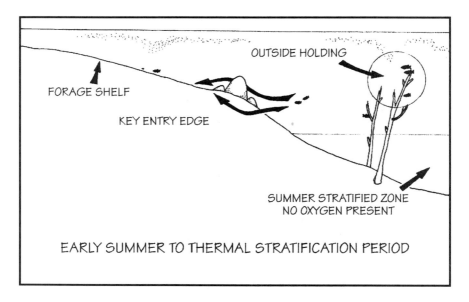

OUTSIDE HOLDING

FORAGE SHELF

KEY ENTRY EDGE

SUMMER STRATIFIED ZONE
NO OXYGEN PRESENT

EARLY SUMMER TO THERMAL STRATIFICATION PERIOD

during short periods of heightened activity), crankbaits can produce almost all the time in early summer because early summer is such an active time for bass. Early summer is one time of year when crankbaits actually can become **THE** high-percentage big bass bait and other techniques become secondary or alternate techniques.

Although casting crankbaits is an excellent way to fish specific areas, trolling crankbaits has applications far beyond the capacity of casting. While some anglers look down at trolling as if trolling is simply dragging a lure behind a boat, precise spot structure trolling is one of the most difficult presentations to master. It takes practice, an eye for perspective and an ability to coordinate to make a lure trailing far behind the boat hit exactly the right spot at the right depth and speed. Modern anglers have been conditioned against trolling for bass because of tournament practices and the trend toward large, heavy boats that are ill-suited for accurate trolling. But I have yet to meet a man who didn't thoroughly enjoy or wasn't fascinated by trolling once they were introduced to the proper equipment and shown how effective the technique can be. Trolling is one of the best ways to gain knowledge and work out a lake; trolling a lake gives you an opportunity to see the lake in the grand picture. Trolling is an exceptional way to check large expansive structures with numerous points, turns and high spots that would be tedious and time-consuming to fish by casting alone. When you work a spot by casting a crankbait the lure is only in productive water for about 1/3 of the retrieve, but when you troll a crankbait unless the lure becomes snagged or fouled it remains in the productive zone 100% of the time! It might take a caster an hour to cover a big structure, whereas the same structure could be efficiently trolled in one third of that time. Trolling is effective in lake areas where wind and waves are too strong to work with a trolling motor or from an anchored position, and is an ideal way to fish when bass are on individual patterns-one fish here and one fish there-throughout a structure. Trolling can trigger fish by creating speeds and actions not obtainable by casting alone, yet it is not uncommon to find situations where bass will only hit a trolled plug. When you cast to the same spot with the same lure, you don't catch a thing, but when you resume trolling again you hook one on every pass-only experienced trollers are aware of this! Trolling can be the only way to present a plug in deeper water below the depth achieved by casting, and it is just as effective on an outside weedline on a glacial lake in Wisconsin, a subtle hard-bottom breakline on a shallow lake in Florida, or the edge of a timber-lined creek channel in Texas. Once the majority of fish leave the shallows and begin grouping on outside structures, trolling and casting crankbaits can be the best way to locate and catch them.

My trolling tackle for most crankbaits consists of either a Garcia 5000 or Lew's BB1N casting reel on a 7-1/2 ft. graphite or fiberglass rod in medium-light action. A trolling reel needs to hold at least 200 yds. of 10 or 12-pound line for most situations. I select a color to match conditions, in clear water I use clear or grey Ande or Maxima, and for muddy water or when fishing around wood, I like brown Royal Bonnyl II.

My favorite crankbait for both trolling and casting is a Bomber Model A which has a functional style and a proven big bass wiggle which is lacking in many other crankbaits. Model A's have a dead-sounding solid rattle which lunker bass seem to like, and they feature a moulded lip that never breaks. I've had the best success on giant Florida largemouth using shad colors like Tennessee Shad, Silver Shad and Blue Shad. Yellow or chartreuse plugs work well on

Heavy weedbeds bordering the main lake drop-off is a common feature in many natural lakes. In clear water lakes, bass typically feed around weed edges and take cover in the weed roots when inactive. In lakes with dark water color, however, big bass often roam feeding shelves outside the outer weedlines. Some of the prime feeding areas are nothing more than flat cover-free hard-bottom areas on the lip of a drop-off.

northern-strain largemouth in off-colored water, but for some reason they seldom work for me on Florida bass. But you always have to keep an open mind concerning color; every lake has pet colors in certain lure types that are more effective.

Whichever crankbait style you decide to use, I recommend buying all the available sizes in the best colors. Don't buy different colors in ten different crankbaits. Find a crankbait that works for you and buy all the sizes in the best colors. The best crankbait fishermen are generally those who have used one or two types of crankbaits so long they become masters of efficiency, and they make these crankbaits produce even in situations where crankbaits are low- percentage lures. Of course, when the fish get on a good crankbait bite, these anglers win tournaments and bring in bass the size of which few anglers ever see.

Each crankbait must be tuned to run perfectly straight at very fast speeds, and you must also determine the exact running depth of each lure. To find how deep a plug runs, select a flat section on a lake and drop marker buoys at various depths such as 5 ft., 10 ft., 15 ft., etc. Pick a crankbait that is supposed to run close to the marker depth and then troll the plug by the marker with enough line until it contacts the bottom. Length of line, line size and trolling speed all determine depth. Until you become familiar with how each lure runs, it might be best to record your findings in a small notebook for easy reference. Some companies make line counters that attach to the rod, or you can color-code your line every ten yards.

I like to start by trolling into the wind whenever possible as this allows for greater boat control, and when a big fish is hooked you can drift back toward the fish creating a better fighting angle. Always select a lure which has a maximum running depth as the same depth you want to fish; this avoids excessive snagging caused by a lure running too deep and plowing along the bottom. I usually begin trolling with at least 30 yds. of line as this length gives the fish time to calm down from the boat disturbance before the lure reaches the spot. Bass may tolerate boat noise in lakes with plenty of water skiers and boat traffic, but I've seen many times when I had to put a lure 50 yds. or more behind the boat before a fish would strike. Short lines offer more control, but if you're not catching fish it might be a signal

Speed trolling bags another lunker.

to experiment with more length. Careful manipulation of line length is the secret of keeping your lure at the correct depth regardless of speed.

I generally start with a slow-to-medium speed when trolling a structure for the first time. This is an ideal speed for metering a spot, and I can meter and check if fish are responding to slower speeds at

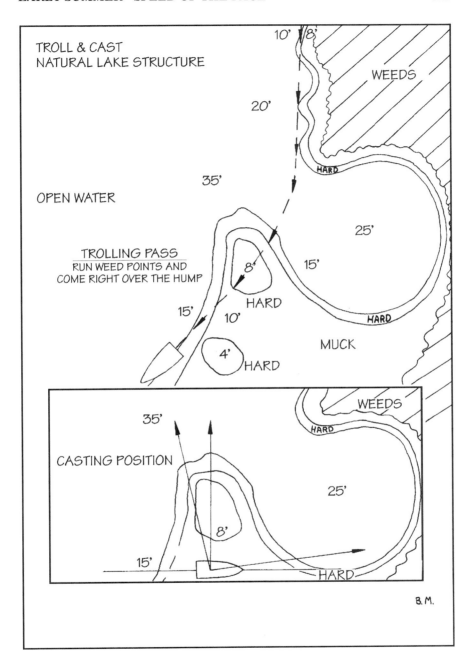

TROLL & CAST
NATURAL LAKE STRUCTURE

WEEDS

10' 8'

20'

HARD

35'

OPEN WATER

25'

TROLLING PASS
RUN WEED POINTS AND
COME RIGHT OVER THE HUMP

8'

15'

HARD

15'

10'

HARD

HARD

4' HARD

MUCK

WEEDS

HARD

CASTING POSITION

35'

25'

8'

15'

HARD

B. M.

the same time. Once I've made a few passes at slow speeds and get a general idea of how the structure is shaped, then I'll be more able to anticipate the points, twists and turns where I can keep contact with the structure at faster speeds. I never consider a spot checked for bass unless it has been thoroughly fished with a variety of speeds and actions. Oftentimes, you won't catch a single fish until you determine the exact speed and action they want. Big bass aren't always the big, lazy, energy-conserving creatures they're made out to be. At times they will only take a speed that is much faster than obtainable by casting. When you're trolling faster than you think a fish could catch it, sometimes you have to troll even faster. But a very fast speed is only one triggering option. Sometimes bass require that a lure bumps the bottom or deflects and ricochets off cover. At other times they only want a lure that is free-swimming inches off the bottom or the edges of cover. Sometimes the fish demand that the lure is moving so slowly it hardly wiggles. When I first started to troll, I used to think the only way to catch big bass was to keep my lure working along the bottom, but as my control became better, I learned that working a lure slightly off the bottom or slightly over the cover and only bumping the bottom or touching the cover on occasion is usually a more productive big bass tactic. Because I now work around the cover, I can troll with lighter line, and I believe the combination of lighter line, a lure with the right shape, color and sound, and the right speed and action, is the key to successful trolling.

Another very effective lure for trolling is Buck Perry's original Spoonplug. Unlike floating-diving plugs which run at different depths according to speed, Spoonplugs are designed to hold specific depth regardless of speed fluctuation. Length of line and not speed determines depth. For example, a 100 series Spoonplug runs approximately 11 ft. with 20 yds. of line and 13 ft. with 30 yds. of line. And it will hold these depths whether you troll extra-slow or so fast the rod almost pulls from your hand. Because Spoonplugs have such precise depth control, they are ideal for fishing tight situations. Running an irregular edge of a weedline or timberline can be difficult if an extra-long line is required to make a floating plug reach the right depth, but you can use a larger-size Spoonplug on a short line (15-to-20 yds.) and hug every contour. Instead of just trolling the tips

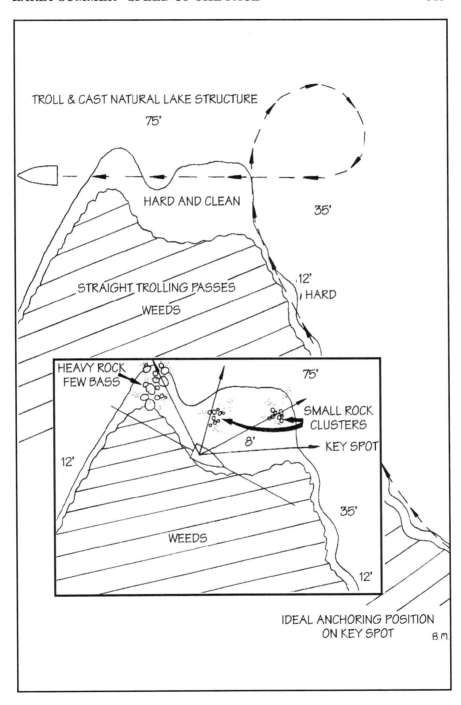

TROLL & CAST NATURAL LAKE STRUCTURE
75'

HARD AND CLEAN

35'

STRAIGHT TROLLING PASSES
WEEDS

12'
HARD

HEAVY ROCK
FEW BASS

75'

SMALL ROCK
CLUSTERS

8'

KEY SPOT

12'

35'

WEEDS

12'

IDEAL ANCHORING POSITION
ON KEY SPOT

B.m.

of points, an experienced spoonplugger can hit the tips and also reach far inside the cuts and turns. He can also tickle the deep edges of heavy weedbeds and make his lure touch the tips of heavy brush cover without becoming continually fouled. Because Spoonplugs tend to snag easily, heavy tackle is needed to rip them free from obstructions. Perry recommends a short stiff-action 4-1/2 ft. or 5 ft. rod and heavy no-bo trolling line. Spoonplugs work best in off-colored water in areas above 20 ft. deep.

Regardless of what you troll, accuracy is essential. When bass are holding by bushes in shallow water, at times they might move out from the brush and take a lure, but generally the closer your lure passes by the brush the more fish you'll catch. The same holds true when trolling deep-water structure. If you want to catch big bass you'll have to make your lure hit exactly at the right spot with a speed and action the fish want. If your lure is too far off to the side or too far up on top of a structure, it might be out of the range of most big bass. You always want your lure to travel along the outside edge of structure or in close proximity to the edge. The ability to control the lure and put that lure right on the money, even though it may be 50 yds. behind the boat, is what makes a good spot troller. A good troller attacks deep structure with the same precision an expert shallow fisherman would work visible cover. He'll analyze the structure and use shoreline sightings to line up trolling passes, and he'll use marker buoys to pinpoint hard-to-run points and inside turns. He'll stick with trolling until the fish get active and moving (he may fish for hours without a bite and then catch a limit of lunker bass in minutes). With each trolling pass his accuracy improves, and by the end of the day his lure is working the edges of deep structure with the same precision of a lure bumping the edges of a boat dock. This is how a good spot troller makes trolling work. You can't get the same results by trolling in a haphazard manner or using a large boat with a steering wheel. Trolling is a science and one of the hardest presentation skills to master. But the rewards are worth the effort, for at times trolling will catch giant bass like no other technique.

When you catch a bass by trolling, going back and forth and working the spot by casting is often the best way to extract the most fish from that spot provided it's shallow enough to be effectively worked by casting. Trolling may prove to be the only way to catch those fish, and you might have to stay with trolling, but I always troll with the idea of setting up a casting position. You always try to make the best method you know work the best it can. For example, if you're really good with a jig and pig, jig fishing is the way you want to try to catch bass because that's what you're best at, so you constantly try to put fish into a position best suited for you. You may use another technique like trolling to hunt for bass, but you're only hunting so you can establish a position where you can nail them with your best technique. I would stitch all the time if I could, because I know it is an exceptional big bass technique in most situations, consequently whenever I catch a big bass by trolling, my first inclination is to find the spot where the fish came from and work it by stitching. But there are times when you can actually over-finesse them. I adopted stitching to pull big bass off heavily-fished spots, but finesse fishing isn't always the answer, that's why standard techniques work so well at times. There is an intermediate period in early summer when bass prefer speed better than finesse. They may only bump a slow-moving worm and blow it back out. But cast to that same fish with a faster presentation and it might explode on the bait. When I go back and cast to a spot in early summer, my primary lures are a crankbait, a slide- sinker plastic worm and a jig and pig. At times, the fish will only hit a crankbait fished with the same action and speed that the fish struck on the trolling pass. But sometimes you can get more out of a spot with a worm or jig. I may still stitch the spot but I'll use a fast stitch with a 1/8 oz. slide sinker above the worm. I'll keep the worm right along the bottom and work it through the spot at a fairly fast pace. With a jig, I'll work in more hops and erratic movements that I normally would. Speed is often a critical factor in early summer, and it must be worked into each presentation.

When you're catching bass but they suddenly quit biting, it means the fish have changed from what they were doing. They've either begun feeding on a different type of prey or they've moved off the spot. Any change in fish behavior is my signal to change tactics. If I had been catching one bass after another on a plastic worm and the action suddenly came to a halt, that's my signal to switch to a crankbait. If the crankbait starts producing it means either the fish in

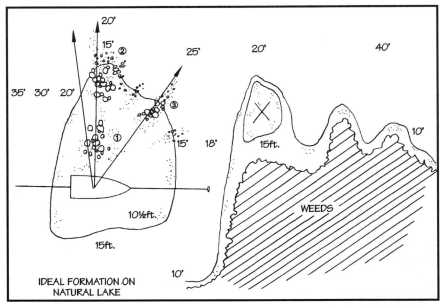

Outside structural features bordering deep water are often the key big bass location in early summer. This spot is a small hump outside the weedline on a natural lake in southern Wisconsin. Big bass show up on this spot in mid-June and the pattern may hold through early August. Element (2) is a small finger projection with scattered rocks, it is the most consistent bass location on the hump for bass of all sizes. Element (3) is a small rock pile on an outside corner that only attracts big bass from 4-to-6-pounds. More bass relate to the outside edge under most conditions, but during peak active periods some big bass move up to the top of the structure on the small rock flat (1).

general have changed or you're now appealing to fish with a different personality. Sometimes a school of bluegill or shad moves into the area and their presence triggers a change in feeding response. I think the fish change just like a new program was punched into their computer, and once it's punched in the fish get activated in a different direction. Bait, weather conditions and a host of other factors could cause fish to change patterns. But then there are other fish with distinctly different personalities. In other words, the fish that hit a crankbait might be "plug fish" that are more prone to hit baitfish type presentations. These bass are seldom triggered by plastic worms because worms don't represent the right kind of action that triggers a response from them. I always work a crankbait even when fishing is red-hot with a slower technique, because experience has taught me that the biggest bass on a spot may not respond to the same technique as the bass population in general. But, for whatever reason this happens, rotating between fast and slow presentations is the best way to extract as many bites from a spot as possible.

The patterns I've described in this chapter may only last for three weeks or less, but they can be some of the most productive big bass patterns of the entire year. Early summer is not a popular time to catch trophy bass for many anglers because the fish have changed from what most anglers are doing. Shallow water is the focus of most angling efforts in spring, and this is also true of early summer even though the majority of big fish are now relating to structures far from shorelines. The secret to making early summer produce is flexibility and presentation. You have to be flexible and do what the fish require. As the water gets warmer, you have to incorporate more speed into your presentation even in deep water. You can't be fishing with a trolling motor when the fish demand that you speed-troll a crankbait; you're destined to have only sporadic success if you do. But if you use spot trolling as your number one presentation with the idea of trolling to find the right spot and to set up a casting position, then all the bases are covered and early summer will quickly become one of your favorite times to catch trophy bass.

SUMMER SUSPENSION

Contrary to popular belief big bass don't stop biting during the hottest parts of summer. Hot weather can drain the concentration and effort of the hardiest fishermen, but bass don't care about temperature, they continue to feed and pursue prey in relationship to prime active periods and good moon phases just like they do at all times of the year. Bass are perfectly adaptable to hot weather and warm water conditions; it's the fishermen who get put off by extreme weather.

The interesting thing about summer, from an angling point of view, is that there are always large bass that relate to structural elements just like they do in the fall, however, there are individual big bass that spend the summer traveling in open water. So, a big bass angler has two options: (1) He can cast and troll primary structures, or (2) he can work for bass suspending out in open water. Structure bass tend to be the most reliable pattern, but working on suspended fish can be very rewarding especially in mid-to-late summer.

How Thermoclines Influence Position

Various conditions cause bass to hold at certain levels throughout the year, but summer stratification is perhaps the most noticeable. A thermocline is a layer of water where the temperature gradient is cooler than the warmer layer above and warmer than the layer below. But the temperature differences themselves are not the reason why thermoclines influence the levels fish use. Thermoclines also indicate a change in oxygen content-greater oxygen is found in the warmer water above a thermocline, and less oxygen is present in the cooler water below a thermocline-and it is the change in oxygen content which ultimately limits where bass can be.

Two lunker largemouths taken on black plastic worms in 18 ft. off a summer outside structure. Big bass often visit large boulder piles periodically throughout the day during this time of the year.

As surface layers continue to heat up in summer, lake stratification becomes more of an influence in shallower depths. By mid-summer, the lakes in my area can stratify between 16 ft. and 32 ft., although lakes with artificial aeration systems may stratify between 21 ft. and 50 ft. By late summer, the thermocline may be shallower in all lakes regardless of artificial aeration. You can usually find the thermocline depth simply by graphing deep, open water. A powerful unit may show a thermocline as a hazy layer, but if they don't show the thermocline itself, the stratification layer can still be detected by observing the abundance of life above a certain depth and the noticeable absence of life below that depth. Thermo stratification can also be found by checking various depths with a temperature probe until you find a layer of water where the temperature changes rapidly. Once

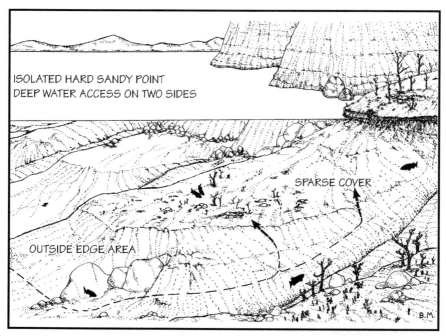

ISOLATED HARD SANDY POINT
DEEP WATER ACCESS ON TWO SIDES

SPARSE COVER

OUTSIDE EDGE AREA

This hard sandy point on the windward side of the lake is the dominant structural feature on an otherwise steep shoreline. The outside edge area has no fish in the morning, but by late afternoon strong winds have dropped the thermocline from 15 ft. deep to 26 ft. deep and bass begin showing up on the outside edge.

you find a thermocline depth, you can eliminate all of the unfishable water just by reviewing a topo-map and focusing on only the areas above the thermocline.

Prime structures located far from shore in and around the main lake basins will continue to be the key spots throughout summer for big bass which relate to structure, but levels of stratified water can restrict which parts of these structures bass use. Big bass like to use the outer perimeters of prime structures, and they prefer to hold on key spots on the outer edges where a stratification zone intersects the structure. Wherever a thermocline intersects a structure the bigger bass usually will be near the **BASE** and just above the thermo layer. Big bass prefer the cooler temperatures at the base of the thermocline, but they can't go any deeper because of the lack of sufficient oxygen below; they will seek cooler water with adequate oxygen to support them. When they become active, or go into a feeding mode, big bass often move to a shallower part of the structure where the water is warmer and more oxygenated. You might find big bass anywhere on a structure, but a good rule of thumb in summer is to fish where a thermocline intersects a structure because that's where the largest bass spend the majority of the day.

Although it is typical behavior for structure related bass to use the area where a thermocline intersects a structure, bass which suspend off structure also tend to relate to the thermocline depth. During peak active periods, suspended bass move toward structure to feed, and then they move back out into open water when feeding activity is over. Peak active periods also stimulate neutral bass, that were holding on remote structural features at the base of the thermo layer, to move shallower on the structure, and the peak feeding spot may have a combination of bass from suspended positions and structured positions bunching together at this time. This is the moment an angler in the right position can make a phenomenal catch.

Sometimes you can actually follow bass as they move in and out from a prime structure. Bass come into a spot at the same depth they were suspending at, and when they are very active, they may move up shallower on the structure. Buck Perry came to the conclusion that bass migrated up and down structures in schools because that's how he caught them. Sometimes he caught bass up shallow, and then he caught some more deeper as they moved out. If you anchor deep and cast shallow, sometimes you'll catch bass from shallow sections of a structure and keep catching them as they move back down until you're catching them right underneath the boat. But very seldom can you cast behind the boat into even deeper water and continue catching them. What happened is that you anchored at the dispersal area where bass either leave the structure to go back out and suspend, or where they disperse to their individual neutral holding spots on isolated pieces of cover. In summer, the dispersal depth is usually associated with a thermocline. Casting deeper won't produce because you're working deeper than the fish can go. Bass do migrate, but only during periods of peak activity. Most of the time they either suspend or hold in non-active positions.

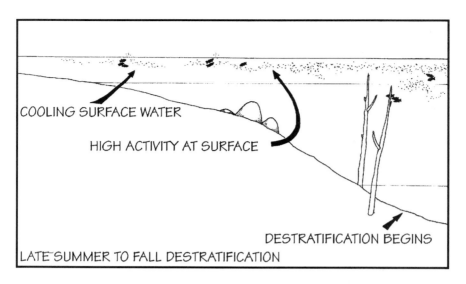

COOLING SURFACE WATER

HIGH ACTIVITY AT SURFACE

DESTRATIFICATION BEGINS

LATE SUMMER TO FALL DESTRATIFICATION

When you think about the thermocline and its relationship to big bass fishing, it's important to understand that although a thermocline represents an oxygen barrier, thermoclines are not immovable objects. Try to picture a thermocline like a sheet of cellophane that is flexible and can bend. A thermocline can bend down on a windward shoreline, and it can raise up on the lee side. And changes in thermocline depth can change hourly: During a day with strong winds, a thermocline may lower as oxygenated water is mixed into deeper layers; but at night, when the winds die down, the thermocline rises back up. So a thermocline is not something that is steady all the time.

But the whole principle behind the way bass react to a thermocline is this-the closer the thermocline gets toward the surface, the more **STRESSFUL** the condition is to bass. A thermocline close to the surface, in effect, creates a low water condition. Bass will react the same way in low water because they have less area to use; it actually makes a lake smaller because anything below the thermocline is dead water as far as the fish are concerned. So the bass react in the same way as a stressful, low water condition. Instead of having deeper water as their security blanket, bass which are squeezed into a limited area now use **OPEN WATER** as their first security. A fast access to open water is why big bass use the outer edges of prime structures. They can move right in from open water, and they have a fast exit right back out.

Schooling Activity

Some lakes produce better than others in summer, and it seems like the hotter the weather gets the better the bass fishing is on these lakes. Good summer fishing tends to coincide with abundant forage, and lakes with healthy populations of shad, shiners, and panfish usually have good hot weather bass fishing. There's no mystery about where to find big bass in summer; if you don't have an abundance of prey, then you're fishing the wrong part of the lake.

By mid-July, prey spawn have hatched, and the fry have grown to a good size. Shad and shiners now become primary bass forage in many waters, but shad and shiners have distinct behavior differences. In the lakes I fish, shiners tend to be bottom structure oriented, and they relate to little draws, humps, and various forms of cover. The only time they'll come up to the surface is during feeding sprees. Shad, on the other hand, tend to run shallow in summer relating to open water and following surface currents and wind direction. Some people think wind generated currents blow shad to windy sides of a lake, but in truth, shad follow wind currents because the wind causes natural aeration and a cooling of the surface water. There can be millions of shad in huge, flat schools out in the middle of a lake just following the ripples of the water and wind direction. Sometimes bass will use large shad schools for shade much the same way saltwater bonita hide under floating mats of seaweed on a sunny day. As long as the bass don't torment the shad, the schools won't disperse and the bait pays little attention to them.

With huge schools of baitfish roaming open water areas it's no wonder bass follow bait, but big bass seldom follow bait schools like smaller bass. It's more typical for big fish to hold on key structural features rather than chase forage in open water. An occasional lunker bass or two might join the smaller bass in a feeding binge, but generally speaking, big bass that relate to structure only intercept bait schools when the bait passes by their holding areas. When bait schools move across a prime big bass structure, big bass come out of their holding positions and converge on the bait. The mechanics of how this works is in perfect harmony. Shad and shiners become active during the same periods big bass do, and they often gravitate to structured areas at these times because healthy and vibrant structural features also offers food sources for the baitfish. So everything falls into place. Baitfish schools move to more outlying structures during certain times of the day, and it so happens that these movements coincide with the same active periods which stimulate bass. Big bass wait until the bait shows up. Bait moving into a prime big bass feeding area at the right time is another example of nature's perfect balance. Nature made baitfish for other fish to eat, that's why nature made them without spines and programed them to show up at prime feeding areas during prime feeding times for bass. Why would lunker bass expend unnecessary energy following shad around when they know where the shad will be at a certain time? Coyotes roam their whole lives and they're as skinny as a rail, but it's not in the nature of a giant bass to be a roamer. Experience and repetition cause instinctive behaviors in adult bass which allow them to predict what baitfish will do. They learn to sit and wait because they know where and when the bait schools come by. Smaller bass follow bait because they haven't had time to learn these tricks. However, you don't want to get too scientific about how you approach bass in summer, or any other season, because there are no absolutes in big bass fishing. What I'm explaining are only general tendencies and they can be deviated from very easily. It's like saying that you always walk to work the same way every day. But every once-in-a-while you probably walk a different way just for a change of pace or to stop at a store. It's the same with big bass. They might hold around certain structures most of the time, but then there might be times when they get sidetracked because they chased a shad school three hundred yards from the prime structure. But there are bass that always come back; these fish always retain a certain pattern of behavior even though there may be slight variations or deviations in their patterns.

Throughout the summer months my basic technique for fishing prime structural areas is stitching. My one-two punch for this period is small plastic worms and live shiners. Plastics are probably the most consistent approach, but when bass are in positions or attitudes where they don't respond well to worms, shiners can be magic. Shiners are abundant and easily caught in summer, and I like to catch 40-or-50 medium shiners before I anchor a key area. I may fish with a crayfish if plastic worms and shiners aren't working, but crayfish generally won't become a hot bait again until early fall. Extra detail tends to catch more bass in summer. I generally fish a smaller plastic worm with a smaller hook and a lighter split shot, and I'll work uphill so my line is camouflaged along the bottom. I won't consider a structure checked until I cast out past the structure and work for bass which may be suspending off the sides. Suspended bass may bite a plastic worm on the sink, but if you're getting bites but no fish, it might prove better to use shiners, either casting them or drifting along the outer perimeters of the structure. If structure techniques fail to produce, I'll check to see if bass are laying off the edges of the outer perimeters, and from there I'll move off into open water.

Open Water Lunkers

Although structure related bass can be the highest-percentage pattern throughout much of the summer period, I believe there is a percentage of the bigger fish that **NEVER** use structural elements. Some bass are so turned off by fishing pressure that they seldom frequent areas where they would even come into contact with an artificial lure. The only chance of these fish getting caught is when they come in to spawn, but these are the large females that tend to spawn much earlier or later than the bass population in general. If lunker bass can secure abundant food, and good oxygen in open water, there's really no reason to use bottom structure. In early summer more bass relate to structure than use open water, but by mid-to-late summer, more and more big bass leave structural elements and suspend in areas unrelated to any bottom structure; this is when open water bass fishing is at its best.

Open water has always been a "black hole" of angling knowledge. Open water is the ultimate protection for some of the biggest bass, and they can navigate wide expanses of open water with pinpoint accuracy. If a diver swam out into the middle of a lake

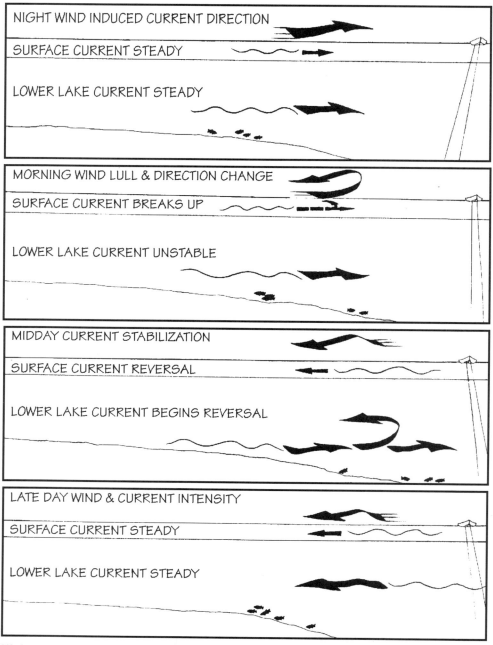

NIGHT WIND INDUCED CURRENT DIRECTION

SURFACE CURRENT STEADY

LOWER LAKE CURRENT STEADY

MORNING WIND LULL & DIRECTION CHANGE

SURFACE CURRENT BREAKS UP

LOWER LAKE CURRENT UNSTABLE

MIDDAY CURRENT STABILIZATION

SURFACE CURRENT REVERSAL

LOWER LAKE CURRENT BEGINS REVERSAL

LATE DAY WIND & CURRENT INTENSITY

SURFACE CURRENT STEADY

LOWER LAKE CURRENT STEADY

Night winds set up the currents and baitfish paths, and the daytime wind from a different direction may take hours to change that current.

underwater and turned around three times, he wouldn't be able to swim back to his starting location without the aid of a compass. But tracking studies have shown that bass can swim several miles right down the center of a lake over open water to the exact site of capture. Bass are completely comfortable and adaptable to open water, and they seem to have some sort of gyroscope mechanism in their brain that tells them where they are at all times.

Generally speaking, bass that use open water parts of a lake roam throughout areas far from any structural element, but they still prefer certain areas. Fishermen may think there is no rhyme or reason to open water location, but there are patterns within patterns even in open water. To a fish with the exceptional eyesight of bass, open water is all different. When you analyze open water from the perspective of currents, water colors, and light refraction, like bass do, then open water becomes complex and varied. One of the best places to find open water bass is in conjunction with current breaklines. Wind and wave action create currents in many parts of a lake, and baitfish use these currents as highways to travel to different areas and to escape from predators. Big bass know how baitfish move, and they lay off the perimeters of these current routes and bushwhack prey as the bait schools move by. Current flow and mixtures of various water colors actually conceal bass in open water, and bass use this concealment to feed effectively near the baitfish paths. Bass are object oriented, even in open water, and they seek out anything they can relate to such as water color breaklines, current breaklines (currents of different speeds working in a similar or opposite direction), water density breaklines, buoy lines, and even each other for lack of something else. The biggest bass in open water are often solo, or with another one or two bass of equal size, but certain areas can be a sanctuary, or gathering place, for bass of all sizes. Extensive searching and fishing is the best way to discover these key open water areas.

Have you ever fished a spot where the water pulls your line against the direction of the wind? These are reverse currents caused by prevailing winds which were blowing from a different direction than the wind direction you presently experience. Observing present wind conditions only may fool you into believing that the currents are running a certain way when in reality they may be working in another direction. It's important to know which way currents are running because sometimes bass will only strike a plug worked with or against the current. Night winds set up the currents and baitfish paths, and a daytime wind from a different direction may take hours to change the currents. Sometimes night influenced currents won't change until after 11 or 12 o'clock, and this is one reason why some spots produce better in late morning. I like to wake up with a lake in the summer to see how nature is operating. I want to see which part of the lake comes alive first, how the fish are reacting, and which way the wind has been blowing throughout the night. By getting on a lake early I'm able to observe many important details which help my fishing for the rest of the day.

Long-Line Trolling

Late summer is the time to troll in open water. Once the summer is in full swing and a majority of the fish have moved out into open water, long-line trolling with little plugs on light line becomes the high-percentage pattern. Trolling might not be a high-percentage technique for numbers of small bass, but trolling can give you the greatest chance at catching lunker bass that are suspended.

Summer trolling differs from winter trolling in that it is not a deliberate type of presentation focused on specific areas. Winter bass hold in certain deep sanctuaries that are more definable as to their boundaries. Summer bass, on the other hand, move around more as they pursue roaming schools of baitfish, consequently, summer trolling is based on covering wide areas of water searching for groups of bass that can be widely separated from one day to the next.

Because thermoclines restrict bass to fairly shallow zones in summer, it is more effective to troll with long lengths of line which gives bass time to recover from the disturbance of your boat before the lure reaches them. If the water is clear and the fish are extra spooky and sensitive about boat pressure, oftentimes, you won't get a bite unless you troll with at least 100 feet of line. Because big bass in shallower zones can be very spooky, whenever you're fishing an area without cover, a good rule of thumb is to always use the lightest line you can handle. For me, 10 lb. test line is ideal for open water trolling.

Light line simply gets more strikes, and it has nothing to do with water clarity. Big bass are often just as line shy in dark water as they are in crystal clear water. When you skin dive in a murky lake the water looks very dark from the surface, but when you look at your hand inches in front of your face at 30 ft., you can see every hair! That's the kind of vision bass have. Even when you're trolling fast, a big bass can easily swim next to your plug for a second or two and examine it, and if something looks wrong it won't strike. Of course murky water, faster speeds, and reaction impulses can make line diameter less critical, but when you're fishing for the biggest bass you always have to take into consideration how cautious and analytical those fish can be. My experiences have proven to me that lighter line tricks more lunker bass even in murky water.

The same lures that produced in early summer generally work in the summer period as well, although I'll troll with medium size lures that won't dive much deeper than 12 ft. with 100 to 150 feet. of line; it's always more effective to troll slightly above suspended bass than below them. My favorite open water lures are medium Bomber Model A's, and jointed Mirrolures in the Panfishmaster and Bassmaster sizes. I like the shad patterns in the Bomber and the silver/black back or silver/green back in Mirrolures. Shad, shiners, and panfish all emit different vibrations, and I have found that certain plugs are more effective when bass key on a certain types of baitfish. For this reason, it's always a good idea to experiment with different plug actions and body styles when one particular style isn't working. Plug size is probably the least important factor, although there are times when bass may bite a small plug or a large plug better.

Trolling the current paths and subsequent baitfish paths is often the key pattern to finding open water bass, but generally speaking, you'll have to fish large areas to determine if bass are present. The only way to accurately find productive spots is to troll up and down the current runs from different directions. Trolling direction is critical because many times big bass only hit a lure presented or worked through a spot in a certain way or angle. By trolling a current path, or current breakline, you'll discover that there are both currents and dead spots and transitions between the two. The key spots are usually the transition areas, but how your lure works through those areas is

Another "teen fish" falls to a stitched plastic worm in summer.

ultimately what determines if it appeals to bass or not. When a plug comes into a current, or out from a current, the plugs action and motion is altered causing it to cut in or jerk out from its true trolling path. A current influenced plug often appeals to big bass because it imitates the way natural bait look as they come through the same current. The only way to discover the right triggering action is to troll the current paths from two or three different directions and observe the results.

Sometimes making a turn can be an important triggering action. One year San Vicente Lake stratified quickly, and by July there was a total stratification at 16 ft. I found a spot out in the middle of the lake, almost 200 yards from the nearest shoreline feature, that consistently held big bass. The first day I caught two 8-pounders, and a 13 lb. 6 oz. trophy. And the following weeks I bagged several bass in the 6 and 7-pound class. But the only way I could get the fish to bite was to make a turn at the right spot. I had the spot triangulated with landmarks and when my lure reached the right spot I would begin my turn. Half way through the turn the line would jump out of the water and straighten out as I hooked another big bass. There's nothing haphazard about fishing open water for lunker bass. The lure has to be right on the money and presented with an action, speed, and color the fish want. And it takes great skill to make it all happen 150 feet behind the boat.

Long-line trolling and deep water trolling with leadcore line are two aspects in the sport of big bass fishing that fishermen have only scratched the surface. There's probably more opportunity in open water fishing than any other direction in bass fishing. As far as technique is concerned, being able to catch bass out in open water away from structural features is completely uncharted territory; it's a different part of bass fishing where few anglers have gone before. The time is right for the new bass fishing pioneers to become leaders in this field.

THE FALL TRANSITION

Fall is a transitional period linking the stable patterns of summer and winter, and the first cool nights of late summer indicate that the fall transition is about to take place. Fall is a time of change-nights get cooler, days get cooler and shorter, there is an increase in winds, crosswinds, and frontal systems, and the water is cooling down; it's almost a complete reversal of the warming trends which helped stimulate activity in spring.

As surface water cools it becomes heavier and begins to sink. Increased wind and wave action causes the heavier water to sink faster and forces water with more oxygen into deeper zones. Stratification still may be a factor in fall, but by mid-fall thermoclines generally begin breaking down. For example, if a lake had complete stratification at 22 ft. in late summer, the majority of bass may still hold at 22 ft. in fall, but at some point you'll begin marking stragglers down at 30 ft. Oxygen content may be higher at 22 ft. and shallower, but enough oxygen filters below the thermocline to begin supporting life in deeper water. Water temperatures may not have changed enough to have a dramatic impact on the deeper bass, but bait schools are getting more active and moving deeper, and I think the deeper bass sense that the whole environment is beginning to change.

As the water continues to cool, bass revert back to the same patterns of behavior they followed in the cooler waters of early spring. One of the most obvious changes is that most big bass become very structure oriented again. Good structure is always important in every calendar period in a structured lake, but fall is one of the best times to fish structure because a lot of big bass that were suspending in open water in late summer now move back on structural elements, and you have greater numbers of lunker bass relating to outside perimeters once again. If you fished the key structures all summer, you'll notice a renewed interest in certain spots at some point in fall. A structure that had been producing a few 2-pounders and an occasional 4-pounder in late summer, may now yield abundant 3 and 4-pound fish and an occasional 6 or 7-pounder; on a good active period the spot may produce a lake-record class bass. Bass may still suspend in fall, but the suspension is generally related to key structural elements. If a key structure in fall has deeper breaks and edges, bass may stay with the structure as they progressively move deeper in late fall and winter.

I have a friend who lives on Bull Shoals Lake, Arkansas, and every October he experiences good shallow water fishing in the back ends of creek arms and coves. The best action lasts for about two weeks, and he catches lots of bass, and a few in the 5-to-7-pound range, by working shoreline logs and bushes with crankbaits. In southern California we have a similar pattern in September on San Vicente Lake where bass can be readily caught on surface lures off windy banks and lee coves. But even though the surface bite produces an occasional bass over 10-pounds, this shallow pattern is actually a small bass pattern. At the same time numbers of smaller bass are biting in the shallows, the real action with big bass is taking place on structural elements off main lake basins and deep creek channels. One of my best fall spots is a long point with a break at 25 ft. that drops off in three directions into 60 ft. It isn't a popular spot because it gets a lot of wind coming right down the lake, but if you can take the boat bobbing up and down all day, and the waves splashing over the side, you can catch bass all day long off this spot in fall. The fish come in flurries-you might sit for an hour without a bite, and then get a nice fish on every cast for fifteen minutes before they quit again; and this can go on all day! A big bass angler must always keep in mind that big bass patterns and small bass patterns are usually widely separated. At the same time the bigger fish are working key structures off main lake basins and deep creek channels, the smaller bass are biting well in the shallows, and it always seems like whenever I'm catching larger bass in deep water, many other fishermen I notice are fishing shallow and throwing toward the bank. This is another example of why the novice big bass angler must change his focus from small bass to big bass.

Another similarity between fall and early spring is the types of lures and live baits bass respond to best. Crayfish took a back seat to plastic worms and shiners in summer, but as the water gets colder live crayfish often become **THE** big bass bait in many lakes just like they did during pre-spawn. On lakes where bass are prone to hit them, live crayfish can outproduce any other technique, and they often trigger the biggest bass. All the bait is bigger in fall, and bass are programed to larger forage. Bass also expect bait to be pretty beat up and tough looking after withstanding the rigors of a long, hot summer. Those big, red, crusty crayfish, that you were reluctant to use all year, are the kinds of crayfish bass are looking for in fall.

Plastic worms are another outstanding fall bait. Crayfish and plastic worms may both produce in the same lake, but then there are lakes where you can trigger more bass with the size and color options only plastics can give you. Fall is a good time to start using bigger plastic worms-7, 9, 12 and even 16 inches long. You can still catch big bass on 4-inch and 6-inch worms, especially right after a strong feeding period, but everything is bigger in fall and it seems like larger worms create more interest. I like to use black worms in early fall because many bass are still feeding on baitfish, and black worms have a proven association with a shad or shiner bite. But as you move toward mid-fall and late-fall, worm colors like brown, green, purple, and rootbeer tend to work better, and these colors normally produce best when bass are feeding more heavily on crayfish. Every lake has a hot color, but always keep in mind that the hot color for the majority of bass may not be the hot color for the biggest bass. On the other hand, a larger worm in the hot color may be all that's needed to trigger the biggest bass on a spot; when everyone is catching 3 and 4-pounders on 7-inch purple worms, it might be the time to throw a 9-inch purple worm, or a big, old, crusty crayfish. But you'll never know what the big fish want unless you experiment in the right areas, and not fishing the prime deep water structures is probably the biggest mistake most anglers make in fall.

Air temperature is another correlation between the best times to fish in fall and spring. I have no idea what air temperature means to bass, but it seems to have a lot to do with how they bite. Everything seems to click at a certain air temperature, but this may only be a

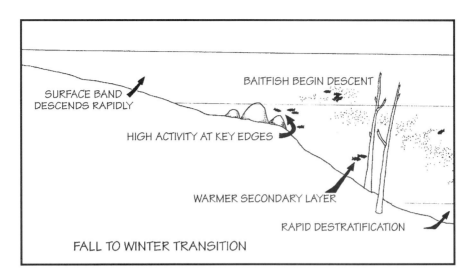

SURFACE BAND
DESCENDS RAPIDLY

BAITFISH BEGIN DESCENT

HIGH ACTIVITY AT KEY EDGES

WARMER SECONDARY LAYER

RAPID DESTRATIFICATION

FALL TO WINTER TRANSITION

symptom of other less obvious things that are taking place. The main thing is to realize that big bass are bunching up on outside structural elements, and as the days get shorter more bass feed during the daylight hours. Try to fish as often as possible. Establish daily feeding periods, and try to fish on a falling barometric pressure or peak moon phase, so you can be at the right spot when they're most active and really ambush them.

Strong winds are a factor you have to learn to contend with in fall. Wind-induced underwater currents are something to watch for in fall as they can stimulate excellent big bass bites. I fished this one spot where the daytime wind was at my back blowing into the spot, but there was an underwater current pulling my line to the right; since the wind had blown all night from the left, there was a constant left-to-right current for most of the day. Most of the fish I caught during this period were small. By late afternoon the wind would shift and blow from the left just like it did all night, and the combination of wind and current really moved water over the spot and helped stimulate the fish. I was fishing a little trough that came out from the bank, and I was using a 9-inch plastic worm with a fairly large slide sinker. I would cast to the left and let the current tumble the worm right through the spot. I couldn't get bit before the wind shifted from the left, but once it did I caught two 9's and one 10-pounder when the current was at its strongest.

This 13 lb. 6 oz. largemouth was taken off a rock pile at 15 ft. on a 6-inch brown plastic worm during the fall transition period.

I often use trolling in the fall to combat excessive winds and to check structures quickly for activity. Productive trolling doesn't come to an end after summer; as the fish get tighter to structure, it only means that you have to troll closer to the prime structures. And trolling is always a great way to locate fish and set up a casting position. One fall I found a rock pile on an outside channel bend that had a fast break right into a deep channel; you couldn't ask for a better-looking spot. I was trolling a small Rapala on lead core line (a method I'll cover in the Winter section) and just looking for a concentration of bass. As my lure passed over the rock pile, and I caught a 5-pound bass on two successive trolling passes. Figuring there might be a nice concentration of fish, I anchored at 45 ft. and cast back to the outer edge of the pile at 22 ft. There was a frontal system moving in and the fish were active, and it only took eight minutes after I let the spot quiet down for the fish to start hitting. The first bass weighted 5 1/2 lbs., then I caught two 6's, and another 5-pounder. Ten minutes later I caught three bass in the 4-pound class, and then the bite was over. If you fish one lake regularly it's often best to anchor on a proven spot and just wait the fish out, but when you need to check a lot of spots, trolling can be ideal, and trolling is a great way to fish main lake spots when the wind is blowing hard.

The fall transition can be a difficult time to fish because transition periods are always the hardest time of the year to locate bass when you haven't been fishing one lake regularly. But once you find the pattern in the transition, all of a sudden it's like jumping on a merry-go-round. In other words, jumping on, or finding the right spot, is the hardest thing. But once you're on the merry-go-round, or know what the fish are doing and how to catch them, you can follow these fish all the way into the winter period. That's why it's so important to fish one lake often even when you're not catching bass, because by fishing often you'll be guaranteed of being out there when things begin to happen. Jumping on to a pattern at the right time and at the right place is the toughest thing about fishing in a transition period, but once you find the pattern you'll have great fishing throughout the entire fall period.

WINTER
SANCTUARIES

The factors that determine big bass location in winter are the same factors that determine location in every seasonal period. Big bass follow the best food sources, the best oxygen and the best structure. Food, security and comfort are their only concern–it directs them to the best locations to function successfully in every seasonal period.

After a lake turns over and adequate oxygen penetrates the deepest basins, all life forms are free to use any depth. As fall turns into winter, cooler surface waters sink deep and often push the warmest water available into deeper zones. Baitfish often follow these warmer bands of water, and bass, of course, follow the bait. Besides relating to food sources, winter bass seek depths where they feel secure and relaxed. Clear water, an absence of cover and heavy fishing pressure are factors which cause bass to move deeper. A colder than normal winter will also drive them deeper. During an average winter in southern California, the majority of bass typically relate to depths between 35 ft. and 55 ft., but during an extremely cold winter more fish may be found at 60 ft. or deeper. But not all bass go deep, a certain percentage of "shallow feeders" tend to remain about 20 ft. to 25 ft. deep all winter. These shallow bass, however, often include the trophy-class fish big bass anglers hunt for. Deep water is the home of the biggest bass in most structured lakes in winter-the majority of bait schools are there and deep water offers them comfort, security and a stable environment. The elements that make a good winter spot are the same elements that make a good pre-spawn spot-only deeper. Key winter bass locations have structural features with hard bottom and quick access to deeper water. Key spots also have favorable oxygen content and a good feeding shelf

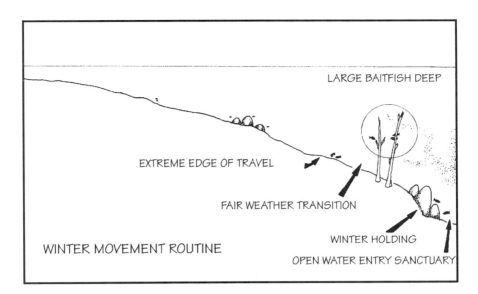

LARGE BAITFISH DEEP

EXTREME EDGE OF TRAVEL

FAIR WEATHER TRANSITION

WINTER HOLDING

WINTER MOVEMENT ROUTINE

OPEN WATER ENTRY SANCTUARY

temperature. Baitfish and other prey find these areas more suitable too. The only difference between winter spots and pre-spawn spots in shallower water is that there are fewer ideal spots for bass to choose from at sanctuary depths. As you go deeper in any lake environment there are generally fewer prime structures. The structures that make up the shallow rim of natural lakes and reservoirs tend to be large and expansive. Wide flats, long bars and expansive reefs comprise shallow lake zones. But as bass move deeper in winter to the base of these structures and beyond, suitable habitat becomes scarce. Instead of having ten possible structures to choose from at 25 ft., at 55 ft. bass may only have one or two spots with prime habitat. A prime spot near the bottom of a basin or creek channel may be nothing more than an isolated rock pile, a small stand of timber on a channel edge, an old road bed with undercut banks, or maybe an old bridge foundation. However, even though sanctuary structures may not have the size or stature of shallower structures, key spots in deep water have the same attractive ingredients of prime spots at all depths. The only difference is that the whole mechanism is revolving at 55 ft. instead of at 25 ft. Baitfish roam deep spots and bass wait for the baitfish to make a wrong move just like they do on any structure. It's the same process because big bass orient to certain spots for the same reasons at all depths.

People tend to be reluctant about fishing deep water, but fishing at extreme depths can actually be easier than fishing shallow once proper techniques are mastered. Big bass don't just sit stone cold in winter; they don't hibernate and come out in spring. Winter bass carry on with their activities like they always do. Nature made bass coldblooded so they can adapt to any temperature. A 14-pound bass doesn't get skinny in winter, it eats all winter to maintain its body weight. A giant bass in winter doesn't look any different than it does in spring. It might have a few more ounces of eggs in spring, but big bass are real "butterballs" in winter because they eat all winter long. They may digest food at a slower rate but they always feed enough to stay fat and healthy in a balanced lake environment.

The problem with fishing in winter is that bass feed less often. There tends to be long periods of dormancy between short periods of active feeding. In summer it's just the opposite-bass feed often because their increased metabolism demands it. But in winter there may only be one short active period every 24 hours, or only one feeding period over the course of a couple of days. In the dead of winter, big bass might only feed two days each week, and the activity on a spot might last less than an hour. Bass are harder to catch in winter because their window of vulnerability is cut way down. Your chances of being in the right place at the right time on the right day of the week is like playing the lottery. That's why anglers who fish often in winter consistently make better catches than casual anglers who only fish once or twice a month. It's far easier for casual anglers to catch bass in summer because bass are digesting food at such a fast rate the casual angler is more liable to hit an active feeding period on practically any day they fish. But there's a fine line in winter; you have to fish often to be on the lake when an active period takes place.

On the plus side, bass can be easier to catch in winter because they often become more relaxed in extreme depths and less sensitive to presentation flaws. All things being equal, I would rather fish for lunker bass at 40 ft. than at 20 ft. because deep bass have a greater tolerance to fishing pressures, and I find that you can actually goad them into biting easier than shallow bass once you discover what triggers them. And when they do bite, winter bass strike with the same ferocity as they do in warmer water. Less light makes everything appear softer in deep water and your presentation becomes less critical, however, anything unusual can still put bass off their feed. You still can't use heavy line or make a lot of noise if you want to fool the biggest bass. I prefer to fish deep because deep bass are not as affected by local weather and surface conditions, and I find that deep bass are "players" that can be triggered into biting once you push the right buttons.

It's tough to catch big bass in winter so it's important to pursue the most active and catchable fish. Deep environments are more stable and less affected by day-to-day weather changes. Storms, rain, snow and cold snaps don't bother deep bass nearly as much as it does fishermen. Stronger influences like barometric pressures and moon phases still have an overall influence on bass at extreme depths. However, stability is the strong factor. Extended periods of nice warm weather with a stable lake level generates the most consistent activity in winter. A few nice sunny days after a long period of overcast seems to bring bass out from under rocks and cover. And an approaching frontal system on the tail end of a nice period can trigger a big bass feeding frenzy. But the trick is timing, just like all seasonal periods.

Fishing Vertically

The intriguing thing about fishing winter sanctuaries is that productive spots often show no signs of life electronically. Graphing a spot can be inconclusive because inactive bass often hold in crevices and under ledges and things making them impossible to graph. In this situation you have to use your instinct and ability to select the right area, and you have to check each spot by fishing it. This is the time to anchor and cast.

My casting technique for winter sanctuaries is to anchor off the spot and cast across it just like I would anchor and fish a spot in shallower water. The only time I would hover directly over a spot with a trolling motor and fish straight up and down is when fishing with a spoon. But I have found that yo-yoing a spoon up and down on bottom structure is not a particularly attractive technique for trophy bass in pressured waters. I've had better luck with spoons when bass are suspended or when bass are busting baitfish on the surface.

I like to anchor off the deep side of a structure and work downhill. Jiggling a lure or live bait down a ledge, just barely moving it inches at a time, is far more appealing to winter bass than working uphill and jumping your presentation over ledges and bottom objects. Anchoring on the deep side and working downhill is the reason why I use 150 ft. of anchor ropes on each end in winter. For example, if the spot I'm trying to fish is at 40 ft., I may have to anchor my boat in 80 ft., or deeper, in order to bring my presentation downhill through the right spot at the right angle; that's when you need extra rope. Big bass can be disturbed by a boat presence even at extreme depth, and you often have to let the spot quiet down and relax before the fish will bite just like fishing any other depth.

Casting to deep structures tends to be a game of line angles. You have to be conscious of the angle of your line, the bow of the line, and how much area down there you're actually working. The actual draw on a steep spot (area covered) will be much less than on a shallow structure because of the severe line angle. In other words, you don't pull a lure directly across a spot at 55 ft.; it's more like you dangle the lure on a string. Instead of pulling across the spot, you only bump the structure momentarily on a somewhat vertical line. For this reason, fishing a key outer edge feature on a deep structure can be a very difficult presentation. While you're learning the angles and limits of your presentation skills, it might be best to mark the target structure with a buoy for reference. But the great thing about fishing extra-deep is that the fish often react positively if you just get the right presentation in the ballpark.

When casting vertically you want to work slowly and pause frequently. If your lure comes over a high spot or a piece of cover, and you don't let it settle back to the bottom, it will pendulum off the spot and away from the productive zone. I always work a bait inches at a time and then pause to let it settle back to the bottom. I repeat this cadence over and over until I establish some kind of dimensional pattern of the spot. And that goes for whatever I happen to be using.

Many anglers make the mistake of using heavier weights when fishing deep water. What you really need to do is go heavier in the mental aspect of fishing. Stay with the same presentation combinations that triggered the bigger fish at shallower depths, but concentrate more on what's going on down below. Deep fishing is a mental game, and that's why good deep water anglers are few and far between. There's only about a dozen fishermen in my area who are good at deep casting and deep trolling, and these guys have the lakes all to themselves in winter. Most anglers stick with heavy spoons and heavy sinkers because they haven't learned how to fish deep water properly. You have to respect the temperament of giant bass even in very deep water and use what triggers them best. You have to use what **THEY** want, not what you want.

I use a variety of baits to cast winter sanctuaries and each has its own triggering characteristics. The plastic worm is a great sanctuary lure. Plastics can work in the coldest water, and there's no truth to the idea that bass quit biting plastic worms because colder water makes them too stiff. Big bass often prefer long worms in winter, and I've caught most big bass on 7, 9, and 11-inch worms. My deep worm approach is to use a 3/16 oz. slide sinker and shake the worm with a subtle shaking motion. Shaking a long worm creates a subtle action cold water bass like. I use the same 6 ft. casting outfit that I fish a jig and pig with. Purple, lavender, black, brown, and sometimes bright green or rootbeer work good at sanctuary depths. Whatever color that caught big bass at other times of the year should also produce in winter on the same lake. However, sometimes winter bass respond to a blanched version of the same color better.

Heddon Sonics and Sonars are two of my favorite cold water baits. These lures can be worked down a bluff or crawled over deep edges of flats. When you apply line tension they practically fish a bluff bank by themselves. Let them sink straight down with pressure, and they arch and swim back to the boat practically on their own. For flat bottom terrain without much cover, crawling these lures slowly on the bottom can be excellent. I like to crawl them across a flat and let them swim off the deep edge-both these lures have tremendous appeal coming off a spot. Other good lures in this category include

Sonar-type lures are great for fishing deep edges with sparse cover.

the Silver Buddy and the old Water Gator. The Water Gator has a dead, thunking solid rattle and really works well on big bass. Sonars and Silver Buddys fish better on a single-strand wire snap.

A jig and pig can be a great winter bait, although some lakes are better jig lakes than others. A jig and pig is one lure where I like the 1/2 and 3/4 oz. sizes. Because of the way I use a jig, lighter jigs don't produce the same effect. If sounds and disturbances can impart negative reactions, it follows that they can also stimulate and promote positive responses. In shallower zones, crankbaits can be effective tools for producing positive reactions. When bass ignore a plastic worm, changing to a nice big jig and lizard combination may also draw a blank, but when you start fishing the worm again there are times when bass will bite on the first cast! The intrusion of the jig caused a mood change. Even though the jig was ignored and the bass wouldn't investigate the activity, vibrations stimulated a positive mood swing and they often strike the first thing that comes close. Mood swings can be triggered by lots of different things, and when fishing deep, other stimuli like size, action, and color become important mood triggers. I often use a heavy 3/4 oz. jig with a big Uncle Josh pork eel as a deep water antagonizer. Bass may be lethargically holding by a rock or bush, but when my big jig comes bouncing and crashing through, the commotion usually moves them from where they are holding. Once they move, it automatically changes their mood one way or another. The disturbance may turn them off to where they won't feed, or it may irritate them into taking a swipe at the next lure that crawls by.

Heavy jigs are also good depth finders. When I get into a new spot I always throw a jig first to get a clear picture of what's below. Heavy jigs have good feel and they help me determine where the hard bottom is, how the drops break, and if snags are present. You can learn so much with a jig, it can even tell you where the bass are by causing them to strike. When bass will bite a jig, of course, I'll stay with the jig, but if a change in tactics is needed the fact that the jig causes bass to change position and mood may make them more susceptible to other presentations. And the jig has already pinpointed where I need to fish slower presentations like plastic worms or bait. That big bass can be antagonized into a more active mood is an important concept when fishing winter sanctuaries.

As a backup presentation to a jig and pig, or when artificials fail to work in general, I'll stitch a sanctuary structure with live crayfish or nightcrawlers. For structures below 35 ft. I may use a larger #4 split shot, otherwise my stitching rig is the same. The only thing that changes in winter is the size of the bait bass prefer. As you go from mid-fall into winter, the live bait preference gets smaller. By mid-winter small green crayfish and small nightcrawlers are the preferred size. And this is at the same time when big bass might bite a long plastic worm or a big jig and pig or a large shiner. Why this happens is anyone's guess. It's just another example of the peculiar selectivity of big bass. The important thing is just to be aware that selectivity like this does take place.

Twin-Spin Creepers

Twin-Spin Creepers are western versions of twin-spin spinnerbaits like the old Shannon Twin-spin which featured two spinner blades separated by double wire arms. The western version has a longer wire primary shaft and a sparsely tied tail made from

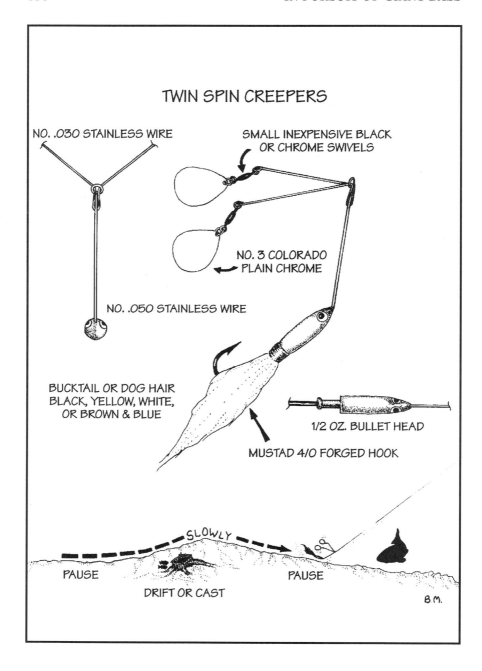

TWIN SPIN CREEPERS

NO. .030 STAINLESS WIRE

SMALL INEXPENSIVE BLACK
OR CHROME SWIVELS

NO. 3 COLORADO
PLAIN CHROME

NO. .050 STAINLESS WIRE

BUCKTAIL OR DOG HAIR
BLACK, YELLOW, WHITE,
OR BROWN & BLUE

1/2 OZ. BULLET HEAD

MUSTAD 4/0 FORGED HOOK

SLOWLY

PAUSE

PAUSE

DRIFT OR CAST

B M.

Twin spin creepers are a spinoff of the famous old type twin spinner, but the western version is by far the more effective lure.

different types of hair. The name creeper originated from the fact that these types of spinnerbaits work best at very slow retrieves. They have continuous action and the double wire arms cause the lure to kick and move erratically. At a slow, dead stop retrieve, a creeper travels along the bottom on one side and when it contacts an object it flips over on its other side. By using small blades which rotate easily, at least one blade is always turning even when the lure is on its side. Although creepers can be effective at any time of year, they're ideally suited for winter sanctuaries where slower speeds and more subtle actions often work best.

Slow Crawling

Creepers are lures designed to work best around bottom cover, and hangups are common; this is definitely not a light line technique. A stout 6 ft. casting rod, a fast-retrieve casting reel, and 14 lb., abrasion-resistant line is a good combination for fishing creepers. The best all-purpose size is a 1/2 oz. creeper, although a 3/4 oz. lure is better suited for deep sanctuary depths. Having a wide range of colors isn't necessary-black, yellow, brown, blue or white are best. My favorite color combination is a straight black body with small or medium chrome blades. Creepers can be more effective with a black or brown 4-inch pork eel attached to the hook. However, always keep spinnerbait trailers short. You want bass to hit the spinnerbait not the trailer. If you're continually getting short strikes, move to a different area where the bass are bigger. Adding a trailer hook is basically for small bass. With double blades on wire arms, hair dressing, and a pork trailer, creepers are a sizeable bait, but big bass love them. When bass are on creepers they don't peck-usually they take the whole lure, wire arms and all. They often mash the lure so hard you need pliers to re-shape the whole thing. The wire probably equates as the sharp spines of a bluegill.

Creepers can be fished by casting or drifting parallel to prime structural features. Slowing the pace is the secret to fishing them, and creepers dragged along channel edges and deep breaks can catch monster bass in winter. The most effective big bass technique with a single blade spinnerbait is to just reel it back slowly like a crankbait and let it tick the tops of bottom cover. But when you fish a creeper the presentation is more comparable to the subtle pulls like you would work a plastic worm. The bait will still helicopter as it comes off objects, but big bass are generally more apt to hit this lure with its subtle action. Lifting and dropping in exaggerated movements is geared more toward smaller bass.

Casting with a creeper is a good way to fish a spot from an anchored boat or work down a bluff bank. Let the lure reach bottom and rest for a few seconds, then point the rod tip at the creeper and slowly turn the reel handle. After retrieving a few feet, pause and let the lure lie motionless. Repeat this cadence-slow reel and pause, slow reel and pause-over the entire structure. Pay attention to any bottom feature that causes the lure to flutter down. Big bass follow this type of lure and often strike when it comes over something and flutters down.

Drifting and using a trolling motor to position the boat is a great way to cover ground and to find bass in deep water with a creeper. Use the wind and trolling motor to drag the lure along the bottom at a 45 degree angle behind the boat. Shake it through rocks and bottom cover as you move along. Work slowly over every little drop and crevice. A bass bite can feel like a heavier feeling, an absence of feeling (the line goes slack), or you'll feel a "pop" like a jig and pig bite. Set the hook hard and set it a second time to compensate for excessive line stretch in deep water. If the lure gets hung up, it will usually come free by maneuvering over the spot with the trolling motor. If it can't be worked free and you feel the spot has a good potential, break it off. Pounding the lure retriever on the bottom will kill the spot for any remaining big fish.

Deepwater Trolling With Leadcore Line

In my opinion, trolling with leadcore line is the most underrated big bass technique in America today. Deep trolling is the best method I have ever found for taking large bass under hard-to-fish winter conditions. It has been so successful at catching big bass in winter, I wouldn't be surprised if leadcore trolling produced the next world record. The potential of deep trolling is unlimited, although few anglers are even aware of the technique.

This nice stringer was caught at 40 ft. on custom painted magnum Rapalas.

Deep trolling works mainly because you're presenting a lure to the fish that imitates the natural baitfish that sanctuary bass feed on. Crayfish which are generally a mainstay diet of big bass year round don't usually go to extreme depths in winter. This is not to say they don't because some do go quite deep, there just isn't a large population down at fifty feet since many of them are hibernating in shallower water. Consequently, when bass move into winter sanctuaries their primary food source is shad or shiners. To pursue bass at 55 ft. with live crayfish works well but is very time consuming. Bass bite crayfish at that depth often out of instinct but they are not their normal forage at this time. On the other hand, trolling a large deep running plug on leadcore line presents a lure that imitates a food source they

**A Lowrance X16 graph and a 350A LCD are
the heart of author's deep tracking system.**

are in tune with during this period. Deep trolling also gives the fish
a different excitement; properly done, it presents a lone disoriented
bait fish that is scared to death.

Leadcore trolling is most effective when bass are deeper than 30
ft. For some reason, leadcore trolling rarely produces above this
depth. Bass above 30 ft. deep are more prone to strike a plug trolled
with long lengths of monofilament. Because you only use shorter
lengths of leadcore when fishing shallow, I think the fish get turned
off by the presence of the boat. But leadcore really comes into its own
in extra- deep water when vertical casting methods become slow and
tedious. An expert troller can keep his lure in the prime feeding area
all day long without interruption and wait for the bass to get active.
It's no wonder this technique is so effective.

I always meter as I troll to see how bass are holding. About 90%
of the bass you'll catch trolling are suspended off structure. However,
they usually suspend in association with some structural element. It
would be rare to find trophy bass suspended out in open water with
no structural connection. The connection may be hard to interpret but

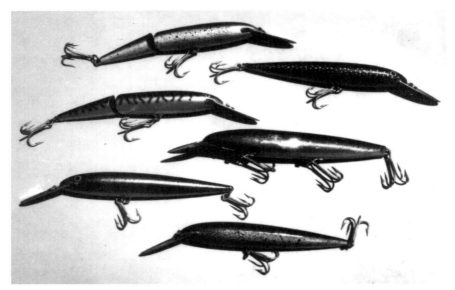

Selection of author's deep trolling plugs. Note custom jointed CD-18 Rapalas.

there's almost always a connection if you can pinpoint it. On closer inspection after catching a bass, you might discover a submerged tree, a small rock cluster, or something in the near vicinity. During a nice sunny period, bass often move up and suspend 8-to-10 ft. off structure. The winter sun is often warmest after 2 p.m., and this is the best time to troll. When bass suspend off structure they can be easily graphed, and once I find suspended fish that's my signal to concentrate on that prime area. When bass can't be graphed, it might prove better to work spots by casting.

Over the years I've experimented with many types of plugs but Rapalas are my favorite for leadcore trolling. Rapalas have the look and action that imitate the bait that sanctuary bass feed upon. I use the original floater in both straight and jointed styles when fishing for suspended bass, and the model CD-18, which is a beefy sinking-diving saltwater plug for fishing specific areas on structure. Thin Rapalas normally work fine but there are times when big bass really go for those big saltwater plugs. I usually start with the smaller Rapalas like the #9 in late fall and early winter, and by late winter I find the bigger #18's produce better. My favorite factory colors are:

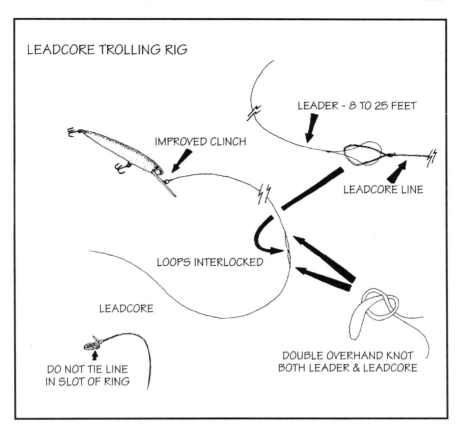

silver/black, silver/blue, gold/black, and green mackerel. Lure size, action and color preferences can change daily and must be experimented with. Sometimes you can enhance a plug by painting them to more closely match specific winter forage. I've painted plugs that look like rainbow trout, shad, shiners and even things that don't exist. But instead of painting exact copies of natural bait, I simply highlight certain outstanding features. When I paint a plug to look like a trout, for example, I paint patches of red and orange on the sides of the head, and blue and green on the back. And I use bright colors to make it more visible at extreme depths. I finish it off with natural brown or black spots. The plug doesn't look exactly like a rainbow trout but there are times when big bass go nuts over this caricature effect in deep water.

California Big Bass angler Allan Nordlund has developed deep leadcore line trolling into a science. Many of the most successful techniques for this method of taking trophy bass have been originated by this innovative angler.

I like to use smaller plugs to establish a color preference and then use a larger plug in that color to fish for giant bass. Smaller plugs generally attract more activity from smaller bass and you can keep switching colors with the smaller plugs until you find which color they respond to best. The same color that small bass like usually will appeal to bigger bass at the same depth. But you can't really experiment with the larger plugs because you might only get one bite all day, and the bigger fish may only bite for a short time during a prime daily active period. Small bass, on the other hand, may bite at any time of the day and it is much easier to establish a color trend with these fish.

For trolling leadcore line I use a 7-1/2 ft. fast-tapering fiberglass rod; it's firm enough to set the hook, yet flexible enough to keep from ripping out the hooks during a hard fight. I use a Garcia Ambassador 7000 when fishing with one hundred yards of leadcore, and a Penn 309 when 200 yards is needed. You don't need a continuous length of leadcore. Tying two hundred yard spools of leadcore together with a blood knot is fine. Besides, the knot acts as a nice spool index to

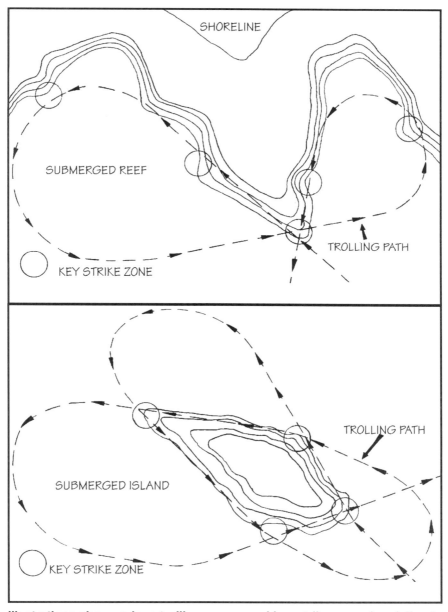

Illustrations show various trolling passes and key strike zones in relation to overall structural formations. Focus on how far your lure is behind the boat and stay on an absolutely straight course until your lure clears the productive area. When your lure is over the key target and forty feet deep, your boat might be over the main lake basin 120 yds. away.

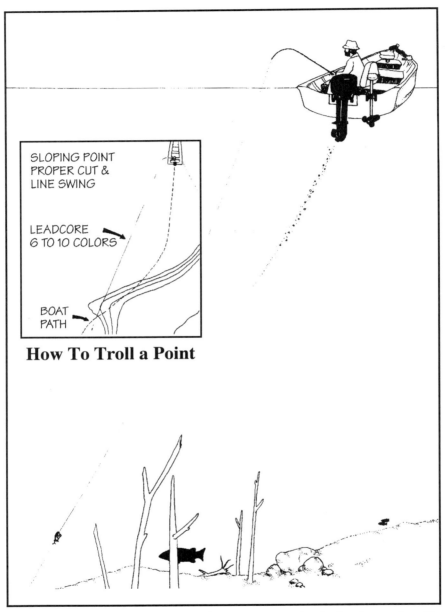

How To Troll a Point

Deep winter leadcore trolling is the best way to catch a lunker bass when it's holding in very deep water, just off a ledge that can't be fished effectively by other methods.

let you know when 100 yds. of line is off the reel. Pick any high-quality leadcore you like, but make sure it's of high quality. Some people favor 27 lb. test leadcore but I generally stick with 18 lb. leadcore in all situations.

I separate my plug and the leadcore with a monofilament leader in either 12 lb. or 14 lb. test. I like Bagley's Silverthread for leaders because it has a small diameter and the color is practically invisible. Connecting leader to leadcore requires a special series of knots. Some knots strangle leadcore and it will break under the strain. Tying a perfect loop knot on both leader and leadcore, and then joining the two loops together makes the strongest and safest connection I know.

Allan Nordlund is one of the best deep water trollers in southern California, and he was one of the first to popularize trolling with leadcore for bass. Al and I have become good friends and we spend hours swapping ideas. Al uses 30 ft. leaders in either 15 lb. or 20 lb. test; he believes the longer leader gives bass a chance to relax after the intrusion of the leadcore, and he doesn't believe heavier line is a factor in extra-deep water. Personally, I favor lighter leaders because I believe that the biggest bass can still be somewhat line-shy at depth. But both leader techniques work. On some days lighter leaders outfish heavier leaders, but it can work the other way too. Nordlund's heavier leaders allow him to recover lures better from bottom cover which gives him the advantage when bass are holding tight. Lighter leaders are more effective when bass are suspending off structures and over heavy cover. So pick a leader that's best suited to the situation you're fishing.

Leadcore is color-coded-each color represents 10 yds. For each color of leadcore you let out, the line trolls approximately 5 ft. deep per color. With leadcore it's best to figure the trolling depth of the line first and compensate for the lure from there. For example, if you want the line to troll at 70 ft., then let out about fourteen colors but be well advised that over ten colors is very hard to handle and turns are to be done with extreme caution. At fourteen colors you have 140 yds. of line out so you must really speed up on the turns to avoid snagging bottom cover.

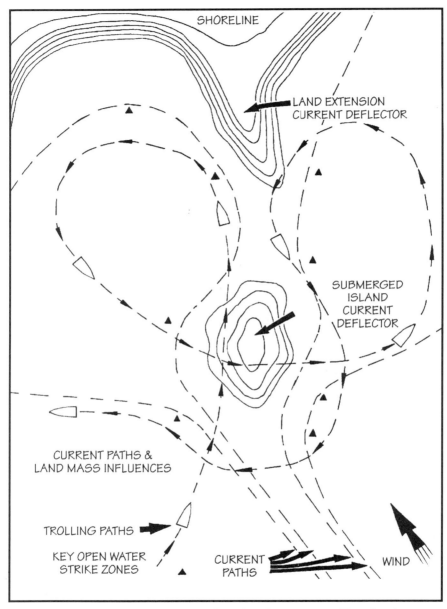

Illustration shows how wind sets up directional currents and how land masses can redirect these currents and also bait, to create open water foraging areas for big bass.

Once the line reaches the appropriate depth, adjusting the line, leader length and boat speed will make your lure run at precise depths. The leadcore should slide over the bottom terrain, but the lure should only touch bottom on occasion. With a 25 ft. leader, a floating Rapala runs about 12 ft. off the bottom on a normal trolling speed (1.7 to 2 mph.) which is just fast enough to give the lure a nice smooth wiggle. An increase in speed makes it track closer to the bottom. Use the boat speed to make the lure run at different depths depending on how the fish are positioned. When you meter bass suspending off the bottom, slow down and let the plug run further off the bottom. Besides lure position, use the boat speed to check the mood of the fish. Although slower speeds normally work best, especially in winter, bass will often strike a plug trolled at a pretty good clip down deep. It's always worth it to vary the boat speed until that magic speed is found.

Rapalas have pretty sharp hooks right out of the box, so they will snag frequently if allowed to plow along the bottom. I have found that by fishing my lure just over potential snags, but giving the fish the right size, speed and color they want, triggers fish in most situations.

Always troll with the rod pointed out over the side of the boat and perpendicular to the boat; this is a good position to feel the lure and to handle a strike. Adjust to a firm drag but just loose enough to give when a big bass strikes the lure. Some giant bass strike so hard they'll pull several yards of line off the reel even though they're 90 yards away. Watch your rod tip for any unusual vibrations. If the plug is running erratically, it probably is fouled on itself or has collected some debris. In either case it must be reeled in and corrected. Leadcore is not easy to handle and you must keep tension on the line at all times. If a kink develops, gently work it out instead of pulling it tight.

Generally, there are two types of strikes. Either you'll see the rod tip bounce a few times and bend over, or the line will slacken and straighten out momentarily before arching over. When you see a strike, leave the motor in the forward position and drop the speed to idle. The forward movement of the boat helps set the hook and takes the stretch out of the long line.

Deepwater trolling is the best method to catch bass in the trophy class during the dead of winter. Depth must be constantly monitored.

One of the problems with fishing Rapalas is that they will hang up when too close to the bottom. When I feel my lure making contact with bottom structure, I raise my rod high overhead. This pulls the lure slightly off the bottom so it won't dig in too hard and snag. If the lure does become snagged, slowly motor back to the spot and don't pull on the rod until your boat is slightly behind where the lure became snagged. Sometimes a few rod shakes will pop it free. If not, use a heavy lure retriever. In a strong wind you may need to anchor the boat over the spot; the retriever won't work if the wind keeps blowing away from the lure. To use a lure retiever properly, you must drop the retriever carefully. It must drop fast, but it must not hit the lure hard. You will be able to tell that it is near the lure when you feel it pass the knot. When you make contact with the lure, it may be necessary to shake the rope from side to side to engage the chains. Tap the lure up and down and from side to side until you catch the lure in the chains. Be patient, it usually will be saved eventually, so stay with it!

When trolling long lengths of leadcore it's better to make straight trolling passes with only minimal or slight turns. After the lure has been trolled well past the target, stop the boat, reel in the lure, and start back in a new direction. Reeling in and starting again is much

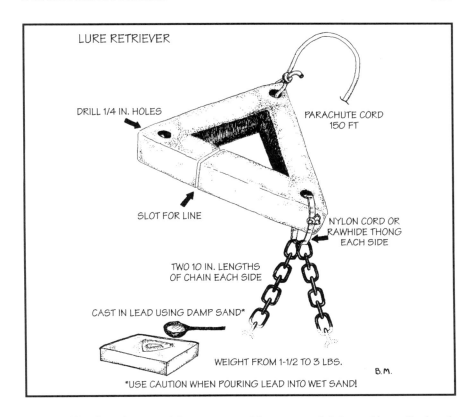

LURE RETRIEVER

DRILL 1/4 IN. HOLES

PARACHUTE CORD
150 FT

SLOT FOR LINE

NYLON CORD OR
RAWHIDE THONG
EACH SIDE

TWO 10 IN. LENGTHS
OF CHAIN EACH SIDE

CAST IN LEAD USING DAMP SAND*

WEIGHT FROM 1-1/2 TO 3 LBS.

B.M.

*USE CAUTION WHEN POURING LEAD INTO WET SAND!

more effective than making extra-wide turns with long line. Go back and forth over a spot with a series of trolling passes similar to the way you would plow a field.

One trick I've learned to enhance the appeal of my lure is to work the rod in a jerking motion while trolling. Every thirty seconds or so, give a good pull on the rod. This causes the Rapala to swing 3-to-4 feet in a different direction followed by a suspension of the lure as it momentarily floats up. This lure action may entice bass that were following, or laying off a spot, to come up and grab it. Also, when I reel in my plug I sweep the rod forward from time to time and then let the lure rest. This stopping and starting can trigger a following bass.

The best trolling pass is often one where the lure approaches the fish from behind them. When a lure comes from behind, it gets much closer to the fish before they become aware of it, and they're more

The most important piece of equipment you can have when leadcore trolling is a good lure retriever. If you're constantly worried about loosing that expensive lure, you won't use it right.

apt to spontaneously react to the plug. If they have time to examine the lure as it comes straight toward them, the lure may not cause the same reaction. You want the lure to come out of nowhere, and you want to make the fish swirl to take it. Most of the time I picture bass either facing toward structure or sideways to structure. So if your lure is working up on a structure, it will be approaching the fish on that side of the structure from behind. When the lure comes up and over the spot and down the other side, then the lure will be hitting the fish head-on on the other side. But these fish might also strike spontaneously because the plug was shielded by the structure and they didn't see it coming. So you trigger a strike both ways. I like to work a spot from 3 or 4 different directions until I either hit a fish, or find a trolling pass that will work the spot effectively without constant snagging. Be particularly alert when your plug comes off a structure and begins tracking over open water. Suspended bass are often triggered by a lure coming off structure.

Proficient trollers chart and track and keep a mental logbook on every area and every fish. When they catch a big bass, they mentally examine where and how it was caught. How much line was out? What was the exact position of the boat and speed of the lure when the bass struck? Did the fish come off a high spot, off the side or down the slope? Was the lure coming into the structure or off the structure? They go through this mental process in order to duplicate their success. The more they can instantly recall, the easier it will be to catch more bass.

But winter fishing is a combination of trolling and casting. If I catch a bass or two off a certain structure, I'll go back and check it casting. Even though it's tough to cast really deep bass, if I can get them to hit a live crayfish or plastic worm I might get a bass on every cast. Trolling can be inefficient when the fish are tightly grouped. It takes time to let out long lines and troll a lure through the right spot, and you might only catch one bass for every 2 or 3 trolling passes. When bass are grouped tightly on structure it can be more efficient to cast to them if they are susceptible to a casting presentation. Successful winter fishermen use a combination of several techniques, but trolling a Rapala can be a high-percentage technique for big bass especially when nothing else will turn a fish.

EPILOGUE

There has always been a fascination and mystery surrounding giant bass. In these chapters I have tried to unlock the mystery and provide reasonable answers to some of the complex questions involving these magnificent creatures. Successful big bass fishing will always be a product of understanding nature and learning how these fish fit in or react to their environment; it will never be totally based on a secret lure or one technique. Hard work, self-discipline, and a proven fishing system is the most consistent game plan. But as our knowledge increases, so must our caring if the sport we love is to survive. Although big bass are often viewed as resourceful and crafty because they can be so difficult to catch, there are times when they are particularly vulnerable to well-trained anglers, and all of us who thrill over catching a trophy are responsible for their future. Big bass are a fragile resource that deserves special consideration.

After devoting most of my life to understanding giant bass and experimenting with countless lures and fishing methods, I believe the system presented in this book to be the soundest information available for catching big bass in pressured lakes. If time on the water grants one the privilege to teach, I guess I qualify, but I realize that as a single angling mind I have only scratched the surface, and future anglers will expand our present knowledge and pioneer new ideas. It is my hope that you will find the same joy and satisfaction as I have in your pursuit of big bass. I hope that you have read this material with an open mind and are able to adapt it into a fishing system that works for you. If only one piece of knowledge points you in a new direction that brings your fishing new dimension and success, then I have accomplished what I set out to do.

Good Luck and Good Fishing,

Bill Murphy

REFERENCE GUIDE

Ande Line
West Germany
United States
Distribution

Bagley's
Box 110 Winterhaven,
Florida, 33880

Berkley and Co
OutdoorTechnolo-
gies Group
One Berkley Dr.
Spirit Lake, Iowa
51360

Bomber Baits
P.O.Box 1058
Gainesville, TX 76240

Browning
Dept. F90
Morgan, Utah 84050

Burke Lures
P.O. Box 72
Traverse City
Michigan 49684

Creme Lure Co.
P.O. Box 87
Tyler, Texas, 75710

Delong Worm Co.
23600 Van Dyke
Warren, MI 48089

Fenwick
5242 Argosy
Huntington Beach,
CA 92649

Garcia Corp.
329 Alfred Ave.
Teaneck, NJ 07666

Gregor Boats
3564 N. Hazel Ave.
Fresno, CA 93711

Hilts Molds
1461 E. Lake Mead
Henderson, NV 89015

Humminbird
#3 Humminbird Lane
Eufaula, AL 36027

James Heddon's
Sons
Dowagiac, Michigan
P.O. Box 167
Fort Smith, Ark 72902

Johnson Outboards
200 Seahorse Dr.
Waukegon, IL 60085

L&S Bait Co.
1500 East Bay Drive
Largo, Florida, 33540

Lowrance Electron-
ics
12000 E. Skelly
Tulsa, OK 74128

Lunker City
Fishing Specialties
P.O. Box 1807
Meridian, CT 06450
203-237-3474

Mann's Bait Co.
P.O. Box 604
Eufaula, AL 36027

Maxima
5 Chrysler St.
Irvine, CA 92718

Minn Kota
1531 Madison Ave.
Mankato, MN 56001

Motor Guide
Brunswick Corp.
P.O. Box 270
Tulsa, OK 74101

Normark Corp.
1710 E. 78th St.
Minneapolis, MN
55423

O. Mustad & Son,
Inc.
247-253 Grant Ave.
P.O. Box 838
Auburn, NY 13021

Plano
431 E. South
Plano, ILL 60545

Penn Reels
3028 West Hunting
Park Ave. PA, 19131

Rebel
P.O. Box 1452
Fort Smith, Ark 72902

Uncle Josh Bait Co.
Fort Atkinson, WI
53538

Wright & McGill Co.
Eagle Claw Dept. A
Box 16011
Denver, CO 80216